THE UNIVERSAL LANGUAGE DISC:
A Reference Manual

By Bill J. Bonnstetter
and Judy I. Suiter

"You can get everything you want in life by helping others get what they want!"
-Zig Ziglar

Tenth Printing
www.ttidisc.com

ISBN 0-9707531-1-X

ABOUT THE AUTHORS

Bill J. Bonnstetter

Bill Bonnstetter, with a master's degree in business, is President and Chief Executive Officer of Target Training International, Ltd., in Scottsdale, Arizona. TTI was formed in 1984 and now markets products in over 50 countries. A leader in human resource development, he has conducted more research on DISC than anyone else in the industry. Bill is the author of 30 software programs and various training programs designed to tap the unlimited potential of the human mind: Building High Performing Teams, Energizing the Organization, Dynamic Communication, Sales Strategy Index, and the TriMetrix™ System. Bill is a Certified Professional Consultant to Management and is listed in *Who's Who* worldwide.

Bill's passion for research and his desire to help others continue on a daily basis. He received a patent on a software program that integrates values and behavior, each producing a report. In 1999 he wrote the book, *If I Knew Then What I Know Now,* which was published by Forbes. Bill J. Bonnstetter is a much sought-after speaker at conferences and organizations throughout the world.

Judy I. Suiter

Judy Suiter is founder and President of Competitive Edge, Inc., in Peachtree City, Georgia, and holds a Bachelor of Science Degree in Industrial and Personnel Psychology from Middle Tennessee State University. She has over fifteen years of marketing and sales experience and over 350 hours of advanced education and training in organizational development and advanced managerial sciences. Ms. Suiter has designed and conducted training programs for over 35,000 people in all types of industries.

TABLE OF CONTENTS

INTRODUCTION

FROM THE AUTHORS

The authors have asked the following questions of seminar participants all over the United States. Please answer them based on your personal experience.

1. **Have you ever been mismanaged?**
   Yes or No

2. **When you were mismanaged, did you take time to discuss it with the person who mismanaged you?**
   Yes or No

Of all seminar participants, 95% said they were mismanaged but did not dialogue with the person who was mismanaging them.

3. **Have you ever left a store vowing NEVER to return?**
   Yes or No

4. **Was it because of the way you were treated?**
   Yes or No

Again, 95% of seminar participants said YES, they have left a store vowing never to return, and it was because of the way they were treated.

5. **Have you ever met a salesperson you did NOT like?**
   Yes or No

6. **Did you buy from that salesperson?**
   Yes or No

Most seminar participants said they have met a salesperson they did NOT like and did NOT buy their product. Some said they only bought the product because they couldn't get it anywhere else.

INTRODUCTION

What were your answers? Did you agree with the seminar participants? Based on over 60 years of experience in the corporate world, we have found the following statements to be true:

1. **You do not sell a product—you influence people!**

2. **People buy from people they like. Therefore if they don't like you, they won't buy from you. Period!**

3. **If employees don't like you, they won't work hard for you!**

4. **You meet and interact with people on a daily basis. Every interaction will either increase or decrease your credibility with that person.**

5. **The way others respond to you is a direct reflection of how you are treating them.**

If your desire is maximum effectiveness in your people interactions, this book is for you. You must learn the universal observable language of behavior, DISC. This book is a reference manual to help you in learning the DISC language. Providing you with all you need to know, it is the most comprehensive, complete book about DISC on the market today.

Research indicates that safety in most cases can be directly related to the D-S relationship.

Every day we live in a laboratory where we have the unique opportunity to learn about people. By developing a strong command of the DISC language, you will:

1. **Know your behavioral style.**

2. **Recognize the behavioral style of others.**

3. **Adapt and blend your style for greater, more effective communication and relationships!**

INTRODUCTION

The DISC language was used to write this book. Many people were surveyed and asked what causes them to read or not read a book. Here are some responses of what people said they wanted in a reference manual:

1. **Easy to read. Quick, brief bullets.**
2. **Fun stories about life.**
3. **Logical presentation of the facts.**
4. **Easy reference.**
5. **Solid data support of conclusions.**
6. **Visually appealing.**
7. **Question and answer section.**

The DISC language, although not always known as DISC, has been in existence since people began watching people. By learning the language and opening your "behavioral eyes," you will take a quantum leap in the effectiveness of your interpersonal communications as you interact daily with people. Our wish, as authors, is for you to learn this unique language and use it to bring out the best in those around you, creating win/win situations. All the best to each of you as you study!

Bill J. Bonnstetter
Judy Suiter

INTRODUCTION

TARGET TRAINING INTERNATIONAL, LTD.: About TTI

"If a picture is worth a thousand words, then a demonstration could be worth a thousand pictures, and Target Training International will demonstrate to you the power of their behavioral assessments."
–Bill J. Bonnstetter

Mission and Purpose Statement

TTI Performance Systems is a research based, professional problem solving resource, which specializes in the resolution of issues related to performance improvement. The company is comprised of individuals who are dedicated to a set of beliefs and values, which reflect a dedication to improving the quality of life in the workplace. It is our mission to show businesses and organizations how they can develop effective strategies for gaining and maintaining more self-control and direction over their organizational destinies.

Further, it is our ever-present intention to provide services that are appropriate, practical, usable, affordable, and above all, supportive of the user's rights and dignities in their application.

TTI's services are specifically designed to help people acquire the knowledge, skills, and wisdom, which will enable them to be more productive and self-directed in their personal and professional lives.

It is our hope that a relationship with TTI will equip our clients with a better understanding on how to effectively manage constantly changing, social, cultural, and economic well-being.

TTI, by its nature, is a constant source of new ideas.

TTI is a value-added, market-driven organization, and, like its clients, depends on market acceptance for its continued survival and growth.

TTI is dedicated to the principle of value-driven, decision-making management. The following are the beliefs and values, which represent and manifest our belief in this philosophy.

INTRODUCTION

TARGET TRAINING INTERNATIONAL, LTD.: About TTI

Value-Based Goals

We believe in self-defined, self-directed, personal and professional lifestyles. We support this belief with on-going research and development into knowledge and training systems that will enable people to acquire the skills which will enhance the best use of their potentials. We practice what we teach—that succeeding is a way of life.

We believe in health as an attitude.
We support this belief with an organizational lifestyle that fosters health for the members of TTI. We strive to be realistic in matching our expectations with our capabilities and in avoiding circumstances and relationships which can have an adverse effect on our ability to be healthy.

We fully recognize the importance of maintaining a balanced lifestyle that enables renewal and refreshment physically, socially, and emotionally. We recognize that work is demanding of our minds and bodies and that the work we do is of great value to our well being if it is pleasurable, i.e. something that we truly want to do.

We believe in the free enterprise system.
We support this belief by accepting competitiveness and societal acceptance as the measures for determining our existence in the marketplace. We strive to be the best at what we do and earnestly desire to have and maintain a respected reputation for effectiveness, quality, value, and integrity. We earn this respect by ensuring that our research is issue-centered and focused on the real world needs and desires of our clients, and our services are offered in a logical, understandable, and usable format.

We believe in being responsible for ourselves.
We support this belief with a management philosophy which encourages accountability as a positive process for planning and decision-making. We are always willing to take responsibility for our actions, and we encourage a willingness to seek help and guidance when alternative choices are present.

INTRODUCTION

TARGET TRAINING INTERNATIONAL, LTD.: About TTI

We respect each other's uniqueness and believe that people are our most important asset and that our future growth and development are governed by this fact. We are strong by being responsible for ourselves. Our operating policies and procedures are intended to make us flexible enough to withstand external pressures and to make us cohesive enough to deal with internal disagreements without compromising our personal values.

We strive, with management disciplines founded upon supportive forms of social influence, to create work environments which support people in the performance of their tasks, accurately reflect their intentions, and encourage self-direction.

We believe in the right to earn fair profit.
We support this belief by preventing waste of time, energy, and ability in the pursuit of activities and relationships, which fail to produce the financial returns necessary to sustain our growth. We live within our means and avoid the temptations of ego-centered expenditures, which cannot be translated into measurable returns on the investment. We practice budget-driven disciplines, which encourage accountability for financial contributions to the health of TTI.

We believe that our moral and legal responsibilities are one and the same.
We will strive to practice the disciplines associated with this value by the avoidance of coercive practices, which encourage irresponsible control over circumstances and events, which can have a harmful effect on the parties involved.

CHAPTER 1
What is DISC?

Chapter Objective:
To define and establish the parameters of the DISC language:

A. What DISC is NOT
B. What DISC IS

To explain maximum use of the language and prevent abuse or overextension of the model.

Chapter Contents:
- DISC Defined
- What DISC is NOT
- What DISC IS
- DISC Language Rules
- Objectives Revisited

"Communication is EVERYTHING!"
-Lee Iacocca in "Iacocca"

DISC DEFINED

Once upon a time, in a faraway land, a man (of unknown name or origin) was sitting on a rock, watching people. We're not sure why he was watching people, but one thing we do know for sure, he was content watching for hours.

As he watched, an unusual thing began to happen, he began to notice incredible similarities in the people who passed by. Although each one physically looked different, there were great similarities in how they acted. Some seemed talkative and friendly, while others were all business. Some talked more than they listened while others just listened. He was fascinated and was learning so much about people just by watching.

Then an idea popped into his mind, "If I become like the person I am talking to, maybe I can get to know more people and really make a difference in their lives. Hmm! Will it work?"

Methodically, he jotted down all the similarities and found four ways people acted. He wrote detailed descriptors for each one (not knowing what a descriptor was, he simply wrote down what he saw):

1. **Some people were forceful, direct, results-oriented**
2. **Some were optimistic, fun, talkative**
3. **Some were steady, patient, relaxed**
4. **Some were precise, accurate, detail-oriented**

He found that many people had characteristics of two or even three of the behaviors, but one behavior seemed to be the strongest. To test his theory, he was outgoing and friendly to the talkative, fun people. He put on a serious face and discussed the deep details of life with those of precise, accurate behavior. To those who were direct, he picked up his pace and got right to the point. Last of all, to those of steady, patient behavior he laid back, relaxed and listened. Incredible! Fantastic! He noticed his communication became more and more effective and people began to seek him out!

DISC DEFINED

He soon realized that a man who understood people was in great demand. To make a long story short, he became a well-respected citizen of the community, making many contributions to better the lives of the people around him. One thing people always said about him was that they felt so good when talking to him. Later in life as he pondered his accomplishments, he smiled and said, "All this I have done just because I took the time to open my eyes and watch people."

DISC is the universal language of observable human behavior. Just watching people proves its validity. Every day we live in a wonderful laboratory where we can observe people and learn how to communicate better. Scientific research has proven that people, in terms of "how they act" universally, have similar characteristics. By learning these characteristics, we can increase communication: therefore, increasing our understanding of each other. DISC is the universal language of observable human behavior.

The focus of this chapter is to define the parameters of what DISC is and what it is not. To define DISC, we will first define what DISC is NOT.

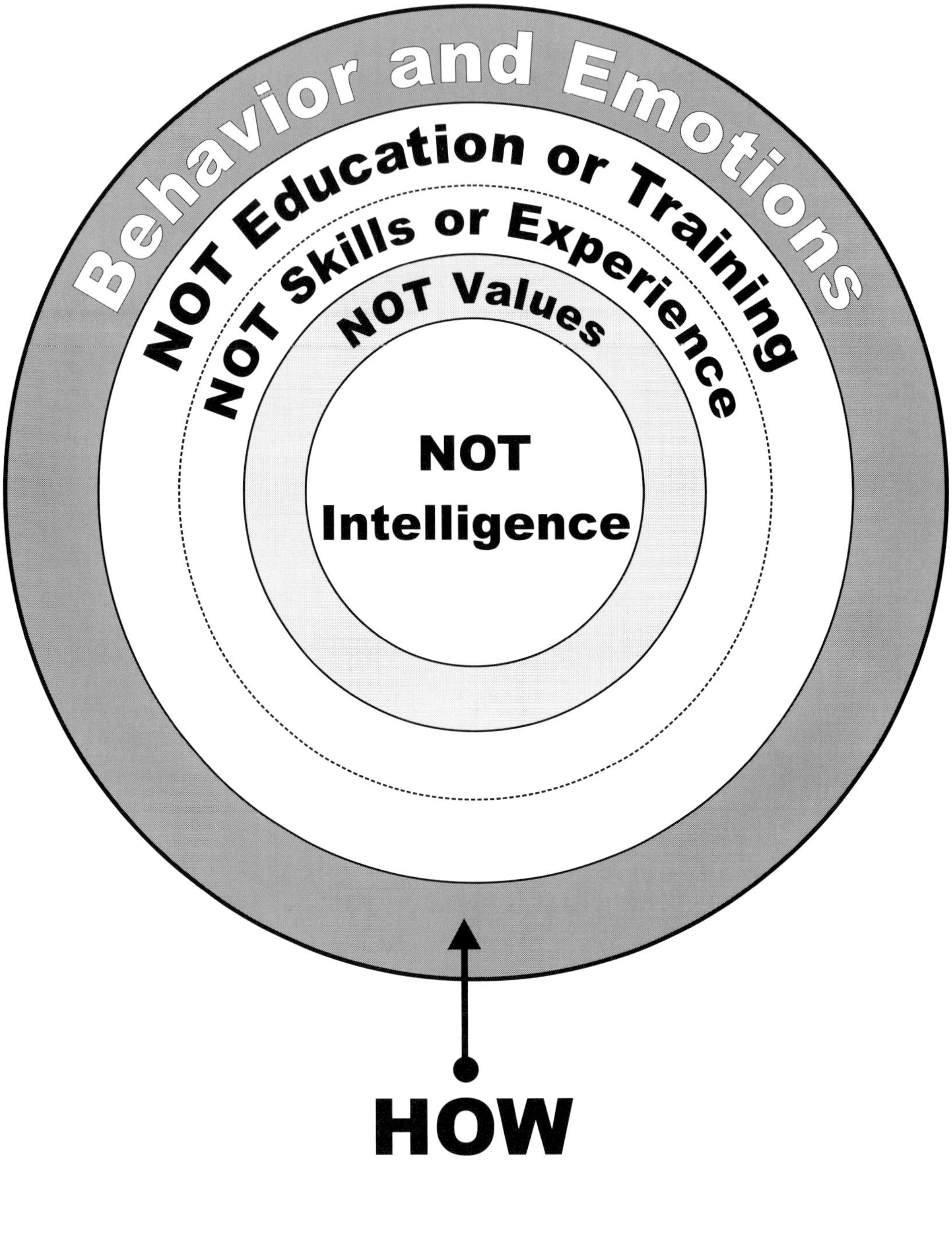
Behavior and Emotions
NOT Education or Training
NOT Skills or Experience
NOT Values
NOT
Intelligence
HOW

WHAT DISC IS NOT

1. DISC is NOT a measurement of a person's INTELLIGENCE!
Intelligence is very difficult to measure, if it can be measured at all. The DISC language gives us no indication of a person's intelligence.

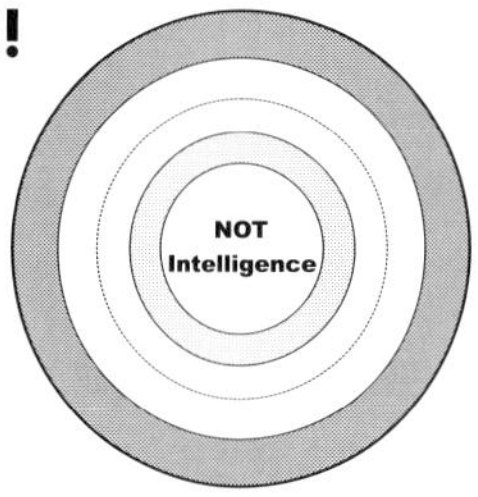

2. DISC is NOT an indicator of a person's Values!
Values are the why of a person's behavior! Why do we do what we do? Values are not observable, but must usually be dialogued.
DISC is not a measurement of values!

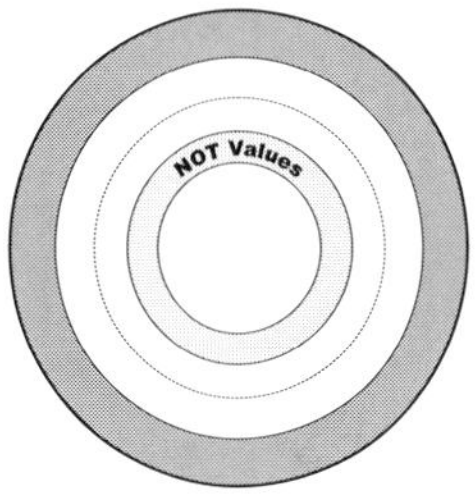

3. DISC is NOT a measurement of SKILLS AND EXPERIENCE!
Skills and experience are two of the primary focuses of an employer; what can you do and what have you done! Skills and experience are outside the realm of the DISC model!

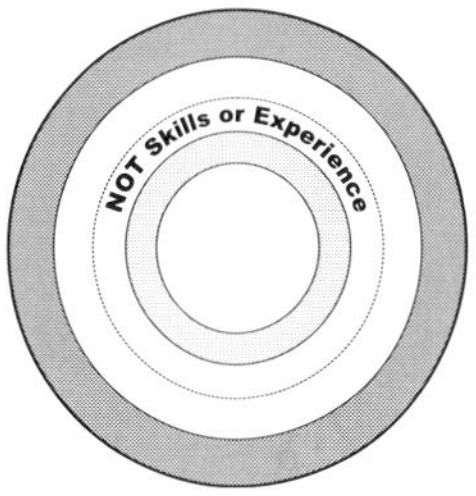

4. DISC is NOT a measurement of EDUCATION & TRAINING!
Two other primary focuses of an employer are education and training. Again, this is outside the realm of the DISC model!

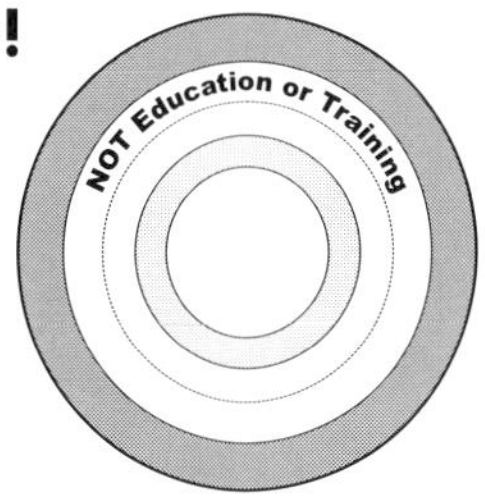

DISC is none of the above; and yet, as we shall see, DISC has an inescapable bearing on all of the above. An awareness and proper application will affect all four of the above areas: intelligence, values, skills and experience, education and training. So, what is DISC and why is it so important?

WHAT DISC IS

**DISC IS THE UNIVERSAL LANGUAGE OF:
BEHAVIOR AND EMOTIONS**

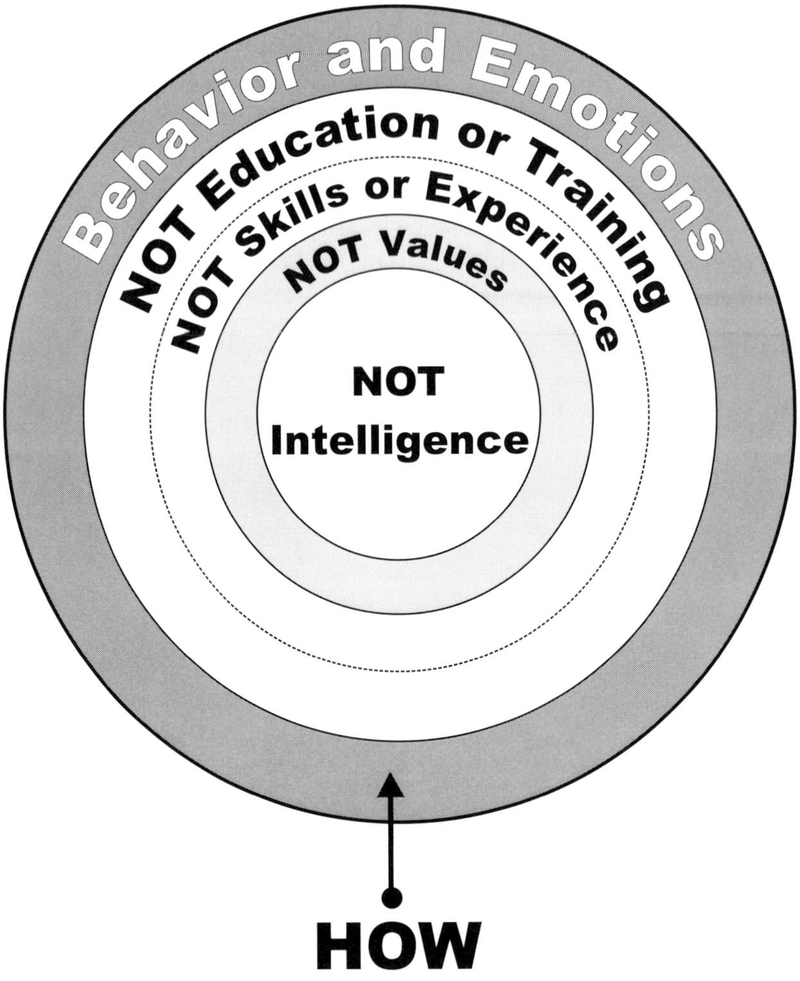

It is the language of "how we act," or our behavior. Research has consistently shown that behavioral characteristics can be grouped together into four quadrants, or styles. People with similar styles tend to exhibit specific types of behavior common to that style—this is not acting. A person's behavior is a necessary and integral part of who they are. In other words, much of our behavior comes from "nature" (inherent), and much comes from "nurture" (our upbringing). The DISC model merely analyzes behavioral style; that is, a person's manner of doing things.

DISC IS AN OBSERVABLE LANGUAGE

Everything learned in the DISC language is totally observable. Often those who have taken the Style Insights™ Instrument are amazed at the accuracy of the information obtained. Still, we are only looking at observable behavior. By applying the DISC language we stand a greater chance of learning about a person's beliefs, skills and experience, education and training, and even intelligence; but the scope of the DISC language extends only to behavior and emotions.

Some consultants have advertised seminars encouraging people to find their inner strength or reclaim their self. Upon dialogue with seminar participants, it was found that the trainer was using (or abusing) the DISC model or another four-factor model. The DISC model categorizes how we act—period! To extend it beyond its scope is to abuse a very powerful communication tool. Conversely, not to give it credence is to guarantee continued communication problems. In the building industry, tools allow for better and more efficient work. In the people business, which we all are in, the DISC language is a powerful tool for increasing communication effectiveness.

DISC IS A UNIVERSAL LANGUAGE

In every culture studied, the DISC model has been found to be valid. Reports are now available in several different languages. It is a universal language. This is easily observed by asking a few questions:

1. **Have you encountered people of a certain cultural background who are expressive, animated, outgoing, verbal or "touchy-feely"?**

2. **Have you encountered people of a certain cultural background who seem to be cool, aloof, hard to read, introverted or analytical?**

Nearly all seminar participants easily answer the above questions quickly. DISC is an observable language and is universal.

DISC IS A NEUTRAL LANGUAGE!

This point is so important that we are asking you to repeat it three more times.

1. DISC IS A NEUTRAL LANGUAGE!

2. DISC IS A NEUTRAL LANGUAGE!

3. DISC IS A NEUTRAL LANGUAGE!

Right and wrong has nothing to do with the DISC language. Right and wrong is based on values and beliefs. DISC is a NEUTRAL language only describing the differences in how people approach problems, other people, pace and procedures. Winners come from all styles of behavior.

Michael Jordan has a dominant behavior style on the basketball court, and people view him as a role model not because he is a dominant player, but because of his values. Saddam Hussein also has a dominant behavior style, but people view him as a tyrant not because he is dominant, but because he has such a low respect (if any) for human life.

Interestingly enough, the behavioral style people prefer is usually similar to their own-"birds of a feather flock together."

In extreme cases, we have seen heads of organizations not hire someone based on their behavioral style. Having nothing to do with a bona fide job selection process, the people making the hiring decisions simply did not like certain behavioral styles and wanted only people around who were like them. This is called "behavioral blindness." The thinking behind this point of view is narrow-minded, but can be changed by learning the DISC language.

A person's behavioral style is NOT what makes them good or bad, right or wrong. It is their beliefs and values only that has everything to do with good or bad, right or wrong.

DISC IS A NEUTRAL LANGUAGE!

Pursuing this further:
Why would a person mistreat another person? Only two answers are possible:

1. **Lack of awareness of their behavior!**

2. **Awareness of their behavior, but believing and acting on a bad set of beliefs!**

Lack of awareness of their behavior is simply solved by making the person aware of their behavior. If they then correct their behavior, you know they have a good set of beliefs. If they do not, then a values problem is present. Value conflicts always escalate in intensity–they do not go away. For example, when we pick up the paper and read pro-abortion vs. anti-abortion, we see a values-based conflict that tends to escalate and get even bigger. Value conflicts, if left unresolved, always escalate and will be at a high personal price for one or both parties, causing damage to one, both or all parties involved in the conflict (and often innocent people pay the price).

A person with a high respect for human life and who values people may still err in the treatment of others; but when aware of their behavior will apologize and make it right.

When you observe the negative side of behavior you are seeing values conflict, or a person under enough stress to overextend their behavioral strengths to the point where those strengths become a weakness. A person's behavioral style is totally neutral being made positive or negative based on their basic beliefs.

DISC IS A SILENT LANGUAGE

People do not like to be labeled! The DISC language, when understood and used properly, is a silent language. A person well trained shows their knowledge of the language in the way they interact with others. Read the following conversation.

Person 1: "Oh, you're a High I!"
Person 2: "I'm a what?"
Person 1: "A High I! There are four styles, D, I, S, and C.
You're a High I—talkative, chatty, fun."
Person 2: "Okay! I guess! Now, what are the others?"

Unfortunately, this type of conversation occurs much too often. Several points must be made:

1. **A person's behavior is the sum of the intensity of all four factors (DISC), and should not be labeled as a High I.**

2. **Person 2 had no knowledge of the language, much like speaking Spanish when in Japan. Little communication was taking place.**

3. **DISC only looks at observable behavior. People are much more complex than the DISC model shows.**

This reference manual gives the language basics in order for you to learn the language. As the language is learned, it should not be discussed with those who don't know the language. In other words, do not have the above conversation with people who do not know the styles. Do not openly refer to people as high or low D, I, S or C.

DISC LANGUAGE RULES

RULE #1
Use and discuss the DISC language only with those who know the language.

RULE #2
Exhibit your knowledge of the language by knowing your behavioral style, silently recognizing other people's styles and then adapting for greater communication.

RULE #3
Teach others the language in a setting where appropriate time is available for understanding.

OBJECTIVES REVISITED

The DISC language does NOT measure:

- Intelligence
- Values
- Skills and Experience
- Education and Training

The DISC language DOES measure:

- BEHAVIOR AND EMOTIONS

The DISC language IS:

- An Observable Language
- A Universal Language
- A Neutral Language
- A Silent Language

AUTHORS' NOTE:

To properly use the language and teach it, we must understand the parameters of what DISC IS and what DISC is NOT. By remaining within the confines of the language, the user will be free to see that we do not need to extend the model beyond its scope. It is incredibly powerful within its truthful parameters. In a manner of speaking, we have set the boundaries of the DISC "pond" that we can now swim in and explore. In training and education of the DISC language, people must be made aware of these boundaries to prevent overextension of the model. Now that the "pond" has been defined, freedom is given to explore the far reaches of correct application of the language. Its power, within its proper parameters, is astounding.

CHAPTER 2

Why Should I Learn the DISC Language?

Chapter Objective:
To provide solid, logical reasons for the necessity of learning the language, and to assist in the understanding of why behavior may need to be modified.

Chapter Contents:

- What's in it for Me?
- Benefits of Learning the Language
- Elements that Impact Your Endorsement
- Steps to Greater Endorsement
- Prerequisites to Learning the Language
- Motivation Principles
- Objectives Revisited

"You must first make an investment before you can expect a return. Investment always precedes return. Always."
–Judy Suiter

WHAT'S IN IT FOR ME?

PEOPLE DO THINGS FOR THEIR REASONS, NOT YOURS!

"What's in it for me?" is a fair question. Rephrased, this question appears in this way, "If I'm going to make an investment, what kind of return am I going to get?" Investors all over the world ask this question daily and no one raises an eyebrow. In the arena of consulting and training this question must be answered, otherwise how can change occur? A wise person once correctly stated, "I cannot change a person's behavior unless I can change his thinking." Another man stated, "As a man thinketh in his heart, so is he." To gain results in people development, the "What's in it for me?" question must be answered. If you do not believe learning DISC is worthwhile, you will not make the necessary time investment to learn. The objective of this chapter is to change your thinking to where you realize you MUST learn the DISC language because it is essential to your success!

"Connie and the Caddy"

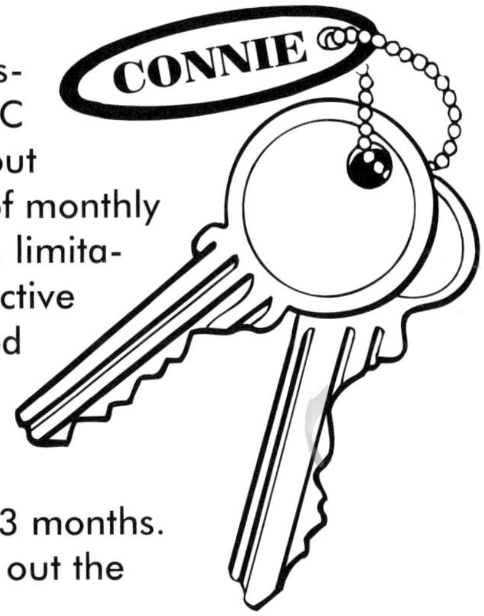

Connie, an Independent Sales Director for Mary Kay Cosmetics, invested her time and money learning the DISC language in August of 1993. At that time, she had about 65 business associates doing approximately $7,000.00 of monthly retail volume. After learning her strengths and possible limitations, Connie began to consciously become more directive and goal-oriented. In November of 1993, Connie reported she now had 78 business associates and a monthly retail volume over the $18,000.00 mark, well on her way to driving a new pink CADILLAC. Just so you know, those numbers equate to 157% increase in sales in only 3 months. Connie uses the DISC language daily to effectively bring out the best in her business associates.

BENEFITS OF LEARNING THE DISC LANGUAGE

1. GAINING COMMITMENT AND COOPERATION

People tend to trust and work well with those who seem like themselves. The most effective way to gain the commitment and cooperation of others is to "get into their world" and "blend" with their behavioral style. Observe a person's body language, "how" they act and interact with others. Notice clues in their work or living area. By applying the DISC language, you will immediately be able to adapt to their style.

2. BUILDING EFFECTIVE TEAMS

People tend to be too hard on each other, continually value judging behavior; therefore, team development tends to be slowed or halted due to people problems. An awareness of behavioral differences has an immediate impact on communication, conflict resolution and motivation for the team. Investment always precedes return. Investment in training the team on the DISC language gets an immediate return in team development. According to a specialist in team development, most teams never make it to high performance without training in a behavioral model and commitment to using it from the top management down.

3. RESOLVING AND PREVENTING CONFLICT

Understanding style similarities and differences will be the first step in resolving and preventing conflict. By meeting the person's behavioral needs, you will be able to diffuse many problems before they even happen. People prefer to be managed a certain way. Some like structure and some don't. Some like to work with people and some prefer to work alone. "Shot in the dark" management does not work in the 21st century. The DISC language, combined with TTI software, will teach you more about a person in 10 minutes than you can learn in a year without DISC.

4. GAINING ENDORSEMENT

Other words for endorsement are "credibility" or "influence." Every interaction you have with a person either increases or decreased your endorsement. Have you ever met a person who won't stop talking and relates his whole life story to you? When you see that person coming, do you dread the interaction? If so, it is because their behavior has caused them to lose endorsement with you, and, therefore, that person does not get the benefit of your time. Conversely, a person who you can't wait to see daily has gained your endorsement and, therefore, is deserving of your time. The DISC language allows you to behaviorally "stack" the deck in your favor. By knowing a person's behavioral style, you can immediately adapt to their style and gain endorsement.

ELEMENTS THAT IMPACT YOUR ENDORSEMENT

The following six elements greatly impact your endorsement, or how much "sanction" or "approval" others will give you. **HUMAN PERFORMANCE IS DIRECTLY PROPORTIONAL TO ENDORSEMENT.**

POSITION

An individual's position affects their endorsement. A president of a company will gain a certain amount of endorsement simply because of his position as president. If the president calls a meeting, people will completely change their schedule in order to be there. A person's position gives them a certain amount of endorsement. This endorsement can then be increased or decreased based on "how" they act and "what" they believe. Position can be earned. Most good executives that have worked their way to the top have developed good people skills.

APPEARANCE

Appearance greatly affects endorsement. People notice the way you dress, your stationery, briefcase, eye contact, handshake, walk, etc. Anything a person "sees" can positively affect your endorsement. Often, we see salespeople who send an unprofessional message just by the way they dress. Wearing tennis shoes with a suit, unmatched shirts and ties, coffee stained paperwork, and a messy briefcase are a few examples of things that can negatively affect your endorsement. Note: The intention here is not to dictate what a person should wear, but to inform you that whether you like it or not, appearance does affect your endorsement. The elements of professional appearance can be learned.

BELIEFS

Your beliefs impact your level of endorsement either positively or negatively. People who do what they say and say what they do will develop greater endorsement than people who are "wishy-washy" in their actions. A straight shooter will develop a greater level of endorsement because of his/her reliability and trustworthiness. Quality is important, and a quality person will gain more endorsement than a person who does not have a strong set of positive, consistent beliefs.

ELEMENTS THAT IMPACT YOUR ENDORSEMENT

COMPETENCE (TECHNICAL, SYSTEMS AND PEOPLE RELATIONS)

Technical ability impacts endorsement. A specialist in the field is the one to listen to in order to solve the problem. He/She has endorsement because of his/her level of learning in the specific field. Organizations all over the world look for those who can motivate people, transforming a common team into a great one. Collegiate and professional coaches who can lead the team to victory are in great demand. Those who continually post losing records lose their jobs. The great coaches such as Phil Jackson and Mike Krzyzewski have the ability to form strong people relations. The ability to develop good people skills can be learned.

ORAL PRESENTATION SKILLS

Have you ever sat through a lecture or seminar that put you to sleep? Was it because of the constant, boring, droning of the presenter? Have you ever sat through a seminar where the time just flew by? Was it because of the excitement, knowledge and skill of the presenter? The first presenter described will lose your endorsement. The second will gain it, and you will recommend the course to others. Many companies require their people to take a people course such as "The Dale Carnegie Course" to help increase oral presentation skills. A person who stands up and is unable to effectively present his ideas will have trouble gaining endorsement. Oral presentation skills can be learned.

ELEMENTS THAT IMPACT YOUR ENDORSEMENT

FEEDBACK (TWO-WAY COMMUNICATION)

Feedback is the giving, receiving and acting upon various forms of information from others. The ability to give effective feedback (one-on-one) greatly impacts endorsement. A manager or parent who can effectively communicate to an employee or child with positive information on their performance or lack of performance knows the power of feedback. Many employees receive little feedback on their performance, and therefore cannot make appropriate adjustments. The manager then loses the employee's endorsement and the relationship eventually ends. Most people want to do a good job. The manager's task is to give effective feedback allowing the employee to make appropriate changes. The ability to give effective feedback can be learned.

Position can be EARNED. The other five elements impacting endorsement can be LEARNED. The DISC language can assist you in the area of values, people relations and oral presentation skills. DISC is very powerful in one-on-one communications. Why should you learn the language? You should learn the language in order to be successful in your field of choice. Not to communicate behaviorally is to "shoot in the dark," hoping to hit the target. Understanding the DISC language will cause your communications to be more on target. We daily adapt our behavior to those around us, so behavioral adaptation is nothing new. The DISC language merely provides a valid model allowing for immediate adaptation to others.

ANALOGY: The DISC language is to communication what a turbo charger is to a fine-tuned engine. You can do well without the turbo charger, but if you want to be on the fast track, put the turbo charger on. The DISC language is the turbo charger for your communication skills. As long as you have to interact with people, you need to acquire a basic knowledge of the language.

STEPS TO GREATER ENDORSEMENT

The following steps will assist you in achieving greater endorsement with those around you.

KNOW YOURSELF

Awareness of your own behavioral tendencies provides the basic foundation for increased communication. Each of us has certain inherent behavioral tendencies that make us unique, and to be aware of these provides us with the knowledge to modify our behavior. For example, some people interrupt when others are talking, if the interrupter is aware of this, they can consciously learn to listen more and wait before responding. The DISC language, with the TTI software, provides you with basic information on your behavioral tendencies. Knowledge is power—if you apply it.

CONTROL YOURSELF

Once you have developed a heightened awareness of your behavior, you can begin to consciously control your behavior. For example, if you like to verbalize and you meet a person who also likes to verbalize, you can consciously choose to listen more and ask questions, knowing that the person will enjoy the opportunity to verbalize even more.

KNOW OTHERS

Know yourself first, and then learn to recognize behavioral differences in others. This heightened awareness allows you to take the third crucial step of application of the DISC language, creating more win/win situations.

APPEAL TO OTHERS' BASIC NEEDS

Before you can appeal to a person's basic needs, you must know their needs. By knowing their basic needs, you can intentionally do something that will appeal to their basic needs, giving you greater endorsement. For example, if you know a person likes punctuality (behavioral trait), then you can make sure you are on time for his/her meetings. Another example, if you know a person likes to direct, you can put him/her in charge of a project.

STEPS TO GREATER ENDORSEMENT

PROVIDE A CLIMATE FOR MOTIVATION

There are three types of motivation. The first is FEAR MOTIVATION, a "do it or else we can replace you" approach. This motivation in negotiating is basically the "take it or leave it" approach. Fear motivation is the easiest form of motivation; however, it is a motivation based on intimidation and power. The person in power, unable to effectively create a climate for other types of beneficial motivation, resorts to fear tactics. "Take it or leave it" often gets results because the person will do what's asked for fear of loss. Fear motivation always results in inner anger and resentment against the person using the fear tactics. Sometimes the threat of loss or punishment must be used, but should only be used when all other methods have failed. Fear motivation is the lowest form of motivation and usually results in "when the cat is away, the mice will play."

The second form of motivation is INCENTIVE MOTIVATION. Incentive motivation is the "carrot" held out that causes the person to want to run the race. "If you do this, then we will do this for you." Incentive motivation can be very powerful and should be a part of a compensation plan; however, it is not the strongest or highest form of motivation.

The third type, CAUSAL MOTIVATION, is the highest form of motivation. Causal motivation occurs when an environment is created that causes people to WANT to work and be the best they can be. As the title implies, causal motivation is working toward a "cause." People will work their hardest for something or someone they believe in. To develop causal motivation, there must first be a cause in which your team can believe in, and then the environment must be created that will cause the team to want to work toward the vision or goal. A causally motivated environment is unafraid to answer the question, "What's in it for me?" People naturally want a return on their investment of time, talent, money, etc. To expect people to work for your cause and your shareholders' cause without concern for their dreams and goals, is blindness to the way we are. People do things for their reasons, not yours.

The DISC language is the door to more effective communication. To not learn it is to behaviorally "shoot in the dark." Increasing endorsement has direct correlation with "how" people interact with and treat each other.

PREREQUISITES TO LEARNING THE DISC LANGUAGE

1. **You must want to find your strengths.**

2. **You must be willing to look at possible limitations in your behavior.**

3. **You must have a desire to bring out the best in others, to win through a people focus.**

In other words....

"If you want to change others, you must first change yourself."
–Judy Suiter

MOTIVATION PRINCIPLES

You may not agree with these discussion statements, so take time to discuss them with others and get their viewpoint on each statement.

1. **YOU CANNOT MOTIVATE ANOTHER PERSON; YOU CAN ONLY CREATE AN ENVIRONMENT IN WHICH PEOPLE BECOME SELF-MOTIVATED.**

2. **ALL PEOPLE CAN BE MOTIVATED.**

3. **PEOPLE DO THINGS FOR THEIR REASONS AND NOT YOURS!**

4. **AN INDIVIDUAL'S STRENGTHS OVEREXTENDED MAY BECOME A WEAKNESS.**

5. **IF I UNDERSTAND ME BETTER THAN YOU UNDERSTAND ME, THEN I CAN CONTROL THE COMMUNICATION OR THE SITUATION!**

6. **IF I UNDERSTAND ME, AND I UNDERSTAND YOU BETTER THAN YOU UNDERSTAND YOURSELF, I CAN CONTROL YOU!**

"Control" in statement 5 and 6 is not a negative word. In each conversation someone is controlling the conversation. Sales tapes say the person asking the questions is in control. People tend to have an aversion to the word "control." Most committees and boards are controlled by one or two people, in the sense that one or two people will have the tendency to exert more influence than others in the group.

After intense discussion, seminar participants usually agree to all six principles as being true. By using the DISC language, participants have seen an increased ability in creating a causal environment where people want to move forward and become the best they can. Sales have increased. Team development has increased. Staff unity and understanding has increased. Most of all, communication has increased dramatically.

OBJECTIVES REVISITED

Benefits of learning the language:

- Gain commitment and cooperation
- Build effective teams
- Resolve and prevent conflict
- Gain endorsement
- Increase sales
- Better time management

AUTHORS' NOTE:

Understand that people have accomplished great things without using the DISC language. Businesses are constantly looking for new technology–ways to increase productivity and efficiency. The DISC language, combined with the TTI software, is the newest and best technology available for efficiency and productivity increases related to your human resources.

"Why is it that so many companies invest millions in buildings and equipment, and yet invest so little in the development of their most important asset—people? It would seem we should take care of the people first and then they will take care of the company."

–Judy Suiter

CHAPTER 3
History of the Language

Chapter Objective:
To provide a partial history of the DISC language, establishing its validity.

Chapter Contents:
- History of the Language
- Emergence of Target Training International, Ltd.
- Objectives Revisited

"Nothing is so powerful as an insight into human nature... What compulsions drive a man, what instincts dominate his action... If you know these things about a man you can touch him at the core of his being."

-William Bernbach
(1911-1982)

HISTORY OF THE LANGUAGE

The DISC language is based on observable behavior. The objective of this chapter is to show that long, long ago people were watching people and noting observable behavioral differences. Throughout history, scientists and researchers have observed basic behavioral similarities, and now these have been clearly validated by companies such as Target Training International, Ltd. Instruments have been developed to assist people in maximizing their personal potential and the potential of their human resources. The lineage of the DISC language, although not then called DISC, takes us all the way back to Empodocles in 444 B.C.

EMPODOCLES
444 B.C.

Empodocles was the founder of the school of medicine in Sicily. He stated that everything was made up of four "roots" or elements. These were: earth, air, fire and water. These four elements, he stated, can be combined in an infinite number of ways, just as painters can create a great many pigments with only four different colors.

HIPPOCRATES
400 B.C.

Hippocrates was an observer of people. He noticed the effect of the climate and the terrain on the individual. Defining four types of climates, he categorized behavior and appearance for each climate, even suggesting which people would conquer others in battle, based on the environmental conditions in which they were raised. Hippocrates believed the climate and terrain affected behavior and appearance.

1. **CLIMATE and TERRAIN:** Mountainous country. Rugged. Elevated and well watered. Changes of season are very great.
   PEOPLE: Savage and ferocious in nature. Many shapes. Warlike disposition.

2. **CLIMATE and TERRAIN:** Low-lying places. Meadows. Uses warm waters. More hot winds than cold, ill-ventilated. Seasons are fine.
   PEOPLE: Not of large stature. Not well proportioned. Broad and fleshy. Black-haired. Not courageous. Less phlegmatic and more bilious. Emotional. Not given to much labor. Short fused.

3. **CLIMATE and TERRAIN:** High country. Level. Well watered. Windy.
   PEOPLE: Of large stature. Like one another. Gentle and unmanly.

HISTORY OF THE LANGUAGE

4. **CLIMATE and TERRAIN:** Thin, bare soils, ill-watered. Great changes of seasons. Not fenced. Blasted by the winter and scorched by the sun. **PEOPLE:** Hard. Well-braced. Blonde. Haughty and self-willed.

According to Hippocrates, a seldom-changing climate brings forth indolence whereas a climate with great changes causes the mind to labor, causing for courage. Frequent excitement of the mind induces "wildness, extinguishing sociableness and mildness of disposition." Current research validates Hippocrates' thinking, in the sense that environment can cause change in behavior.

NOTE: The TTI Graph I is called "RESPONSE TO THE ENVIRONMENT." For more information on graphs refer to Chapter 5.

SANGUINE **MELANCHOLIC** **CHOLERIC** **PHLEGMATIC**

Hippocrates pursued his thinking further. After identifying four types of climate and terrain and their effect on behavior, he identified four temperaments (sanguine, melancholic, choleric, phlegmatic) and associated them with four bodily fluids (blood, black bile, bile, mucous). He then made this statement, "I think the inhabitants of Europe to be more courageous than those of Asia." In the history of conflict throughout the world, does history prove him to be correct?

GALEN
130 A.D. – 200 A.D.

Galen, of Rome, spoke of four body fluids and their effect on behavior and temperament. They were: blood, yellow bile, black bile and phlegm. He also stated that our bodies act upon and are acted upon by warm, cold, dry and moist.

C.G. JUNG
1921

In 1921, Jung published "Psychological Types" in Germany. He identified and described four "types". These four types are primarily oriented by the four psychological functions: thinking, feeling, sensation and intuition. These four are further divided into two divisions that Jung called "libido" or "energy." These two divisions are "extroverted" and "introverted." Jung believed the extroverted and introverted types were categories over and above the other four functions.

HISTORY OF THE LANGUAGE

WILLIAM MOULTON MARSTON
1893-1947

The major developer of the DISC language is Dr. William Moulton Marston. Born in Cliftondale, Massachusetts, in 1893, Dr. Marston was educated at Harvard University. He also received three degrees from that institution, an A.B. in 1915, and LL.B in 1918 and a Ph.D. in 1921.

Most of Dr. Marston's adult life was spent as a teaching and consulting psychologist. Some of his assignments included lecturing at The American University, Tufts, Columbia and New York University. A prolific writer, Dr. Marston was a contributor to the *American Journal of Psychology,* the *Encyclopedia Britannica,* the *Encyclopedia of Psychology,* all while authoring and/or co-authoring five books.

Marston's most well-known contribution was his success in lie detection. His work was done at Harvard University and in 1938 his book, *The Lie Detector,* was published. Lie detectors, including Dr. Marston's, have been used by law enforcement and crime detection officials in various countries for many years.

Marston continued his career as a consulting psychologist, but using the pen name of Charles Moulton, he spent most of his time during the last five years of his life as the originator, writer and producer of Wonder Woman. First published in book form, this endeavor turned out to be a most successful and enduring comic strip. After having been stricken with polio in 1944, Dr. Marston was partially paralyzed until his death at age 53 in 1947.

In 1928 he published a book, *The Emotions of Normal People,* in which he described the theory we use today. He viewed people as behaving along two axes with their actions tending to be active or passive depending upon the individual's perception of the environment as either antagonistic or favorable.

By placing these axes at right angles, four quadrants were formed with each circumscribing a behavioral pattern.

1. **Dominance (D)** produces activity in an antagonistic environment
2. **Inducement (I)** produces activity in a favorable environment (called influence in the system).
3. **Steadiness (S)** produces passivity in a favorable environment.
4. **Compliance (C)** produces passivity in an antagonistic environment.

HISTORY OF THE LANGUAGE

Dr. Marston believed that people tend to learn a self-concept, which is basically in accord with one of the four factors. It is possible, therefore, using Marston's theory, to apply the powers of scientific observation to behavior and to be Objective and Descriptive rather than Subjective and Judgmental.

Marston did not invent the DISC behavioral measurement system, nor did he foresee the potential applications of his work. In the nearly 70 years since Marston published his research findings and observations, behavioral research has modified his ideas considerably. To the modern scientist, much of Marston's work may seem stilted and antiquated. Yet, the importance of his contribution in dividing human behavior into four distinct categories and using measurements of the strength of these responses as a means to predict human behavior remains undiminished.

Using Marston's theory it is possible to apply the powers of scientific observation to behavior, and then be objective and descriptive rather than subjective and judgmental. The Style Insights™ form and its various uses are all derived from the work of Dr. William Moulton Marston.

Despite the contributions made to the field of behavioral research since Marston, the modern categories of DISC (Dominance, Influencing, Steadiness and Compliance) owe much to his research. Thus it is helpful in understanding the working of the DISC system to keep Marston's categories and their original meaning in mind. The premise of the modern day DISC system is that all people demonstrate some behavior in each dimension. The four dimensions used as the basis for the Style Insights™ Instrument (and its various forms and applications) fall into the following categories:

DOMINANCE – CHALLENGE
How you approach and respond to problems and challenges and exercise power.

INFLUENCING – CONTACTS
How you interact with and attempt to influence others to your point of view.

STEADINESS – CONSISTENCY
How you respond to change, variation and pace of your environment.

COMPLIANCE – CONSTRAINTS
How you respond to rules and procedures set by others and to authority.

HISTORY OF THE LANGUAGE

The DISC measurement system analyzes all of these factors and reveals one's strengths and weaknesses, one's actual behavior, and tendencies toward certain behavior. Behavioral research suggests that the most effective people are those who understand themselves and others. The more one understands personal strengths and weaknesses coupled with the ability to identify and understand the strengths and weaknesses of others, the better one will be able to develop strategies to meet the demands of the environment. The result will be success on the job, at home or in society at large.

WALTER CLARK
1950s
Walter Clark was the first person to build a psychological device based on the Marston theory. His instrument was called the "Activity Vector Analysis." Some of Clarke's original associates subsequently left his company, further refining the format as they created their own "adjective check-list forms."

The following individuals and companies have contributed to the DISC model:

1960s
J.P. Cleaver
Leo McManus

1970s
Bill J. Bonnstetter
John Geier

1980s
Michael O'Conner
Resource Analysis
Judy Suiter
Target Training International

1990s
Resource Analysis
Target Training International
Judy Suiter
Dr. David Warburton

THE EMERGENCE OF TARGET TRAINING INTERNATIONAL, LTD.

Target Training International, Ltd. (TTI), under the direction of Bill J. Bonnstetter, has staged a 20-year blistering pace in the innovation and development of the DISC language. Combined with continuing, intensive research validation, TTI has become the clear leader in product development and research in the area of behavior and values. Listed below is the track record of TTI development:

1980
Bonnstetter validates a correlation between the appearance of a person's premises (personal or business) and their behavioral style.

1981
Bonnstetter validates that salespeople tend to sell to styles similar to their own and buyers tend to buy from salespeople with a similar style to the buyer. He validates that if the salesperson adapts to the style of the buyer sales will increase. Bonnstetter develops the "Buyer Profile Action Plan" to assist salespeople of all fields in recognizing and "blending" their styles.

1984
Target Training International is the first company to develop and introduce computerized and personalized reports on the DISC model.

TTI identifies Graph III as not providing valid information when there is a significant disparity between Graphs I and II.

TTI develops the most accurate validated truck driver selection program in the world. The program is based on the DISC model (see Page 254).

1985
The introduction of Managing for Success® and Employee-Manager software versions.

1986
The reading level on the instrument is lowered to a ninth grade high school level. Other instruments were at a college junior reading level.

The introduction of Sales Profile, Family Talk, Personal Insights, and Successful Career Planning software.

THE EMERGENCE OF TARGET TRAINING INTERNATIONAL, LTD.

1987
Introduced Telesales, Lawyer's Version, and Team Building software.

1988
The introduction of Job Analysis and Interviewing Insights software.

1990
The introduction of the Behavioral Factor Indicator.
Trademark granted for Managing for Success® software.

1991
The introduction of the Graph Reader Program, Personal Interests, Attitudes and Values Software. TTI clearly validates the universal application of the DISC language worldwide. DISC became a universal language.

Develops and introduces Customer Service Software, the Work Environment Analysis and the Executive Software.

1992
TTI, under Bonnstetter's direction developed and patented the Success Performance Index, the first software on the market to merge behavior and values into one report.

TTI funds an outside study by Dr. David Warburton and Judy Suiter to investigate the effects of Graph I and Graph II disparity on job satisfaction, mental health, stress and substance abuse (see Chapter 11).

The introduction of Communicating with Style, Healthcare Insights, Time P.L.U.S., and education software for administrators, teachers and students.

TTI creates 60-section, Success Insights Wheel® and applies for patent.

1993
TTI translates *The Universal Language, DISC* into Finnish, Swedish, German, Dutch, French, Italian, Spanish and Polish. Software reports are now available in each of these languages.

TTI is the first company to design and introduce DISC software that allows you to select a multi-lingual response form and a multi-lingual report.

THE EMERGENCE OF TARGET TRAINING INTERNATIONAL, LTD.

1994
Mentoring program introduced.

1995
Sales Strategy Index™ introduced to the marketplace.

1996
New 11,000 square foot office building was built to accommodate corporate headquarters. Patent granted for the Employee Success Predictive System.

1997
Developed the first 360 Feedback Instrument.

1998
Research comparing US and German top sales performers using both behaviors and values.

1999
Bill Bonnstetter writes the book, *If I Knew Then What I Know Now,* published by Forbes.

Internet Delivery Service™ (IDS) created for sending and receiving assessments plus distributing the results; patent applied for.

2000
www.ttidisc.com and www.ttied.com created.

Trademark granted for bicycle depicting Success Insights Wheel®.

2001
Introduced Interactive Reports and Blueprint for Success.

Success Insights spun off as a separate, international division of TTI.

THE EMERGENCE OF TARGET TRAINING INTERNATIONAL, LTD.

2002

Introduction of Attribute Index™.

TriMetrix™ System developed co-authored with William Brooks.

Created e-learning courses.

Assisted over 4000 distributors start their consulting business.

2003

Validated that some of the words used on the questionnaire were no longer valid and new words that are valid were added leading to new questionnaires: Style Insights and Motivation Insights.

Drs. Peter Klassen and Russell Watson commissioned to perform validity studies on the new instruments (see Chapter 11).

Updated logo and report layout.

ODsurveys Plus™ introduced.

2004

IDS generates 1 report every 10.7 seconds. Developed new research software, TTI Success Insights Collection. Instruments translated into 23 languages and sold in 50 countries. TTI celebrates its 20th anniversary with a record attendance at the Winter Winners' Conference. Success Journey, interactive debriefing video game show developed. Completed research study for predicting superior performance in a very specific job for a major employer, which showed the system to be 91% predictable classifying people into superior performer or inferior performer categories.

THE EMERGENCE OF TARGET TRAINING INTERNATIONAL, LTD.

What We've Learned Using DISC Over the Years:
Discovered that D's think they have more personal skills than I's; I's think they have more personal skills than S's; S's think they have more personal skills than C's. Safety research indicates that high D's and low S's have a higher chance of accidents in certain occupations.

TTI IN THE FUTURE
TTI leads the way with continued development in the area of interactive, multi-media training and skill-based questionnaires. Continued research is being conducted in the area of values and attitudes.

OBJECTIVES REVISITED

Importance of the History:

- People have observed others as early as 444 B.C.
- DISC is based on observable behavior.
- Marston describes the theory we use today.
- Clark was the first to develop an instrument.
- Bill J. Bonnstetter validated communication style.

AUTHOR'S NOTE:
To record all the people who have made contributions to the field of human behavior would require volumes of research beyond the scope of this book. This chapter shows that as early as 400 B.C., people were being observed and similarities were being recorded. Those who have made contributions specifically to the DISC language have been mentioned. TTI is extensively chronicled due to their emergence in the field as the pacesetter. The reader should have a better appreciation of the history of DISC and those who have contributed to its development.

"To avoid criticism, do nothing, say nothing, be nothing."
–Elbert Hubbard

CHAPTER 4
Defining & Learning the Language

Chapter Objective:
To recognize the observable characteristics of the four pure behavioral styles, High D, I, S and C, providing the solid foundation for proper, effective usage of the language.

Chapter Contents:
- Introduction
- Pure Behavioral Styles
- Research Proof
- The High D
- The High I
- The High S
- The High C
- Objective Revisited

"In order to understand our relationships with our people, we must first understand ourselves."
–Bill J. Bonnstetter

INTRODUCTION

Albert Einstein stated, "Everything should be reduced to its simplest form, but not simpler." Such is the purpose of this chapter, to provide the reader with clear definition of the DISC language, allowing you to "compartmentalize" four distinct behavioral styles in your mind:

High D

High I

High S

High C

Once these four styles have been mastered, by opening your "behavioral eyes," you will begin to see others differently and appreciate those differences. The ability to adapt your behavior to each of the styles will increase the effectiveness of communication allowing for greater understanding and appreciation of our similarities and differences.

When discussing human behavior, the issue of "right" vs. "wrong" is a non-issue. The "D" is not better than the "I," nor is the "S" better than the "C." Each behavioral style brings strengths and weaknesses to the situation. Each can be a winner, and the team needs all four styles to win. Right and wrong issues relate to values, which is not in the realm of the DISC language.
DISC is a NEUTRAL language!

"All people exhibit all four behavioral factors in varying degrees of intensity."
–W.M. Marston

PURE BEHAVIORAL STYLES

In this chapter pure behavioral styles are being defined.
Definitions: A style is "pure" if only one point is above the energy line. For more information on graph reading refer to Chapter 5.

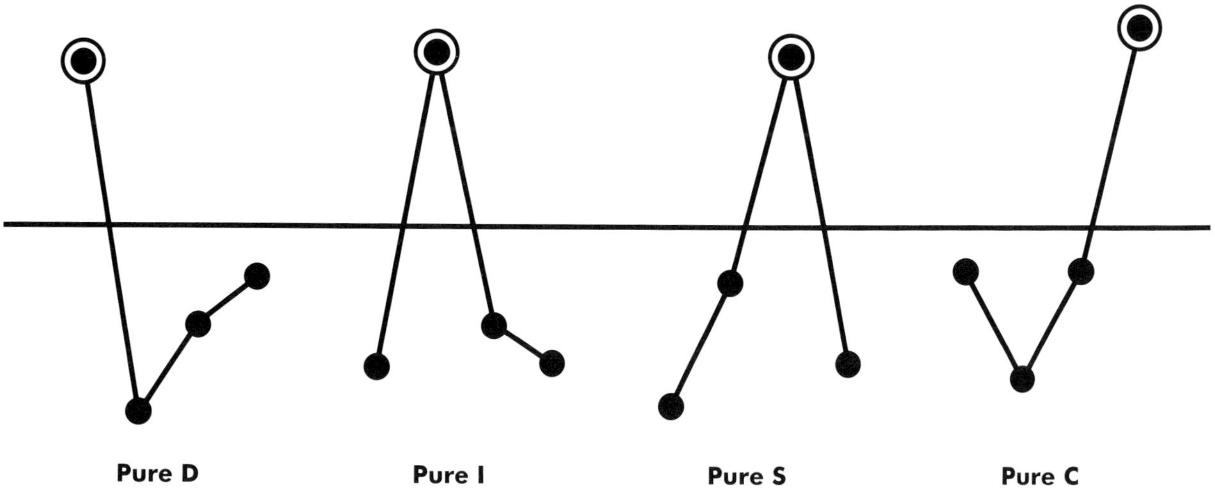

Pure behavioral styles represent a very small percentage of the population, according to recent research by TTI.

Pure High D	**about 2% of the population**
Pure High I	**less than 1% of the population**
Pure High S	**less than 1% of the population**
Pure High C	**about 1% of the population**

The behavior of most of the population is a combination of two or more styles; therefore, to refer to someone merely as a High D is useful in describing their primary behavior only. The language should be mastered in order to see and understand the relationship of four factors. Step 1 of learning the DISC language is to learn the Pure Styles and be able to recognize a person's primary behavior and adapt accordingly.

By learning the pure DISC language, you will have a strong foundation to build on to understand the interrelationships of the four factors of the language. You are literally learning a new language of behavior, which, if learned properly, will open your "behavioral eyes" to a much greater understanding of those around you.

RESEARCH PROOF

D	I	S	C
Ambitious	Expressive	Methodical	Analytical
Forceful	Enthusiastic	Systematic	Contemplative
Decisive	Friendly	Reliable	Conservative
Direct	Demonstrative	Steady	Exacting
Independent	Talkative	Relaxed	Careful
Challenging	Stimulating	Modest	Deliberative

RESULTS: OVER 85% PREDICTIVE ACCURACY. In other words, the behavioral style the judges assigned to a particular individual proved to be accurate over 85% of the time when the individual responded to the DISC instrument. To explain from another angle: When the judges assigned the High D descriptors to a person, that person also viewed himself as a High D over 85% of the time.

The DISC language is based on OBSERVABLE behavior. When we are observing a person, we can easily apply the DISC language if we know the characteristics of each of the four factors. Each person has one PRIMARY or BASIC behavioral style. As we interact with people on a daily basis, without using an instrument, we can recognize the PRIMARY style and adapt accordingly. Advanced users of the language will be able to recognize the interrelationships of the four factors and greatly increase communication and understanding.

THE HIGH D

D

The dominant director, the driver, the "D"
Unconquerable, demanding, aggressive, free
Brave, decisive, competitive, tough
Up to the task, direct, sometimes rough!

Quick to the draw, flip with the lip
You'll get it direct, straight from the hip
They'll climb any mountain, nothing's too high
They aim to succeed, whatever they try!

Results is the focus, press on to new heights
Along the way, expect a few fights
Don't take it personal, they just speak their mind
So pick up the pace, or get left behind!

You may smirk a little when you hear them rant
Of all that they'll win if their wish you grant
Give them a challenge that's brave and bold
Stand back and watch as they "bring home the gold"!

–Randy Widrick

Definition:
The "D" factor is the highest plotting point on Graph II, the Basic Response.

THE HIGH D

Dominant, Driver, Choleric

DESCRIPTORS

Direct	**Results-Oriented**	**Inquisitive**
Daring	**Domineering**	**Demanding**
Forceful	**Aggressive**	**Impatient**
Innovative	**Strong Ego Strength**	**Authoritative**
Blunt	**Goal-Oriented**	**Adventuresome**
Decisive	**Problem Solver**	**Responsible**
Competitive	**Quick**	**Risk Taker**
Strong-Willed	**Challenge-Oriented**	**Power**
Bold	**Persistent**	**Self-Starter**

FAMOUS HIGH D'S

Barbara Walters, TV news anchor
Michael Jordan, basketball player extraordinaire

BARBARA WALTERS

When any celebrity agrees to do the interview with Barbara Walters, one thing is sure—the tough questions will get asked. Barbara Walters is unafraid of asking the hard personal questions. Her directness has taken her to the peak of her industry. Most celebrities consider it a career milestone to be asked on a Barbara Walters' special.

MICHAEL JORDAN

Is there any mountain in the annals of basketball history that Michael Jordan has not conquered? Anytime an opponent burned Air Jordan on one end of the court, you could easily predict that person would immediately see the bottom of Jordan's Nikes on the other end of the court, as the ball went smashing through the hoop. In an issue of *Time Magazine,* the press covered Michael Jordan's early retirement. Jordan said, "When I lose the sense of motivation and the sense to prove something as a basketball player, it's time to step down."

THE EMOTION OF THE "D" FACTOR: ANGER

Each of the four factors has an emotion linked to it. The emotion of the "D" factor is anger. A High D will tend to be quick to anger and have a "short fuse." A person whose "D" factor is low, will be slow to anger and have a "long fuse." The higher the "D," the shorter the fuse. By observing the intensity of the "D's" emotion of anger, the "D" factor can be quickly assessed as high or low when observing someone.

OUTSTANDING CHARACTERISTICS OF THE HIGH D

NEED TO DIRECT

High D's have an inherent need to direct. Extroverted persons, High D's, will usually give their opinion in clear specific language. If the group or discussion is moving a little slowly, expect the High D to step up to the plate and push the group along. Given the authority and responsibility, High D's can take you to new heights that previously were considered impossible.

CHALLENGE

If a job loses challenge, expect the High D to become somewhat bored. High D's must have a continual challenge—a mountain to climb! If there is no challenge, the High D will create one. When basketball no longer offered a challenge to Michael Jordan, he left the game.

DESIRE TO WIN

Living is winning. The High D is driven to win, both in the corporate world, as well as on the golf course. Vince Lombardi's famous quote, "Winning isn't everything, it's the ONLY thing," is picturesque of the High D's approach to each situation. Other profiles desire to win but for different reasons. The High D's desire to win is related to being on top of the heap, proving it can be done.

DIRECT COMMUNICATION

In dealing with people, High D's will be direct and to the point. The flowery words will usually not be present as they say what they think. High D's may unintentionally come across as being too blunt to some other behavioral styles. High D's will take issue if they disagree, even heatedly, but will seldom hold a grudge. After they have spoken their mind, they tend to forget about it—no harm done. The High D is task-oriented, looking for results.

OUTSTANDING CHARACTERISTICS OF THE HIGH D

HIGH RISK

The thrill of victory; the agony of defeat. The High D can be a high risk-taker, perhaps not considering the consequences. Not intentionally trying to hurt others, the High D does not consider failure as an option. Because of the high risk factor, the "D" needs others to supply enough facts and data to make sure the "jump" is a relatively safe one. Oftentimes the high risk factor allows the High D to take you "where no man has gone before."

The High D has the ability to juggle many balls at one time, but may lose interest in a project if the challenge ceases. Interested in the new, the unusual, and the adventurous, High D's will usually have a wide range of interests and be willing to try their hand at anything.

By utilizing the Descriptors on Page 42, the famous examples, and the outstanding characteristics, the High D behavioral style should be developing clearly in your mind. The DISC language is based on observable behavior. By opening your "behavioral eyes," you will begin to notice the High D's around you.

PEOPLE READING: RECOGNIZING THE HIGH D

Understanding that the DISC language interprets how we act, behavioral observation has proven that the following attributes usually apply to the High D behavioral style. Employ these cues to assist in quick recognition of the High D.

QUICK HIGH D OBSERVABLE INDICATORS

Extroverted/Introverted:	Extroverted
People- or Task-Oriented:	Task
More Direct or Indirect:	Direct
Overextensions:	Impatient
Geared to/Looking for:	Results/Efficiency
High D emotion:	Anger/Short fuse
Low D emotion:	Slow to anger/Long fuse

OBSERVABLE BEHAVIOR: "HOW HIGH D'S ACT"

Buy:	Quick decision makers; new and unique products.
Change:	Love change.
Conflict response:	Fight back.
Drive:	Fast, always somewhere to get to in a hurry.
Decorate an office:	Status conscious, large desk, efficiency.
Gesture:	A lot of hand movement when talking, big gestures.
Goal setting:	Sets many goals, usually high risk and not written down.
Letter writing:	Direct, to the point. Results-oriented.
Organization:	Efficient, not neat.
Read:	Cliff notes, executive book summaries.
Risk factor:	High risk-taker.
Rules:	May tend to break the rules. The end justifies the means.
Stand:	Forward leaning. Hand in pocket.
Stress relief:	Physical activity, preferably of a competitive nature.
Talk on the phone:	Little chitchat. To the point. Results.
Talk to others:	Direct. While others are talking may do other activities, as well as interrupt or jump to their next response.
Walk:	Fast, always going somewhere.
Magazines they may read:	*Fortune, Forbes, Money.*

RECOGNIZING THE HIGH D

Refer often to these cues, until you have a clear picture of the High D style. Any one of these observable cues can instantly tell you that you are relating to a High D. You must invest the time learning the language in order to use it effectively.

Pure styles are being described in this section! The High D style is definitely affected by the intensity of the "I," "S," and "C" response. Effective language learning will give you the skills to recognize the effect of the other factors and adapt accordingly.

THE VALUE OF THE HIGH D TO THE TEAM

1. **Bottom-line organizer**
2. **Self-starter**
3. **Forward looking**
4. **Places high value on time**
5. **Challenge-oriented**
6. **Competitive**
7. **Initiates activity**
8. **Challenges the status quo**
9. **Innovative**
10. **Tenacious**

1. Bottom-line organizer
High D's are results-oriented. If given the authority, they will cut through all the needless steps and get the job done. Many of the paper pushing activities done in organizations add nothing to the value of the product turned out. Give the High D the job, set broad boundaries, and watch it happen.

2. Self-starter
Given the task, the responsibility and the authority, High D's will work long hours to show you they can make it happen. No need to push them to get them going.

3. Forward looking
High D's focus on the possibilities of what can happen. Obstacles represent a challenge to be overcome, not a reason to stop. Expect them to go for the GOLD.

4. Places high value on time
High D's are driven for efficiency: quicker, faster, better. How much can be accomplished in the least amount of time. They will speed up others and the process, but expect other styles to resist the change and fast pace of High D's.

5. Challenge-Oriented
A challenge is not an option for High D's. They MUST have a challenge. If there is a challenge, a High D will take it on. Regardless of how impossible, they will focus all their energies on making it happen. If the High D does not have a challenge they will create one.

THE VALUE OF THE HIGH D TO THE TEAM

6. Competitive
Winning is everything. A competitive situation, sales competition, family competition and sports competition all motivate the High D to perform even better.

7. Initiates activity
The High D is the running back saying, "Give me the ball." Not one to sit around and discuss options, the High D wants to (and will) initiate activity to get desired results.

8. Challenges the status quo
Unconcerned with the "way we've always done it," the High D will reinvent the old way focusing on one goal—results. High D's will "rock the boat" in their quest for results, and will find more efficient ways to get the job done.

9. Innovative
A fast mover, the High D's focus on efficiency causes them to be constantly looking for shortcuts to get the desired results.

10. Tenacious
Driven to results, challenges, and winning, the High D is forceful and direct. Anything other than winning is obviously losing, so the High D will be tenacious in overcoming obstacles to reach a goal.

Example:
Captain Kirk, on *Star Trek,* altered the Star Fleet computer program in the "NO WIN SITUATION," and became the only cadet to ever win the "NO WIN." When asked why he altered the computer program he stated, "I don't believe in no win situations."

It's very easy to see the value of High D's to the team. Their fast pace, results-oriented approach is often misunderstood; but with the proper understanding and management, the High D is a tremendous person to have around. Not having or wanting a High D on the team puts the team at a great disadvantage.

Based on the verbiage and descriptors given to this point, make a list of your associates who have a High D in their profile.

IDEAL ENVIRONMENT FOR THE HIGH D

- Freedom from controls, supervision and details.
- Evaluation based on results, not process or method.
- An innovative and futuristic oriented environment.
- Non-routine work with challenge and opportunity.
- A forum for them to express their ideas and viewpoints.

COMMUNICATING WITH THE HIGH D

Be clear, specific and to the point.
Don't ramble on, or waste their time.

Stick to business.
Don't try to build personal relationships, or chitchat.

Come prepared with all requirements, objectives and support material in a well-organized package.
Don't forget or lose things, be unprepared, disorganized or messy.

Present the facts logically; plan your presentation efficiently.
Don't leave loopholes or cloudy issues if you don't want to be zapped!

Ask specific (preferably "What?") questions.
Don't ask rhetorical questions, or useless ones.

Provide alternatives and choices for making their own decisions.
Don't come with the decision made, or make it for them.

Provide facts and figures about probability of success or the effectiveness of options.
Don't speculate wildly or offer guarantees and assurances where there is a risk in meeting them.

If you disagree, take issue with the facts.
Don't take issue with the High D personally.

Provide a win/win opportunity.
Don't force the High D into a losing situation.

COMMUNICATING WITH THE HIGH D

Motivate and persuade by referring to results.
Don't try to convince by personal means.

Support and maintain.
Don't direct or order.

MOTIVATING THE HIGH D

- Allow them to control their own destiny and the destiny of others.
- Give them the power and authority to achieve results.
- Provide prestige, position and titles.
- Provide them with a vehicle to obtain money and material things that indicate success.
- Allow opportunity for rapid advancement.
- Maintain their focus on the bottom line.
- Follow communication tips listed above, always.
- Allow freedom from controls, supervision and details.
- Allow efficiency in people and equipment.
- Provide new and varied experiences.
- Provide challenges with each task.
- Provide a forum for verbalizing.

MANAGING THE HIGH D

- Clearly explain results expected.
- Negotiate commitments one-on-one.
- Define rules.
- Confront face-to-face in all disagreements.
- Provide challenging assignments.
- Train on understanding and being easier on people.
- Assist them in learning to pace self and relax.
- Train on understanding teamwork and participation.
- Train on listening skills.
- Make sure their emotional intensity fits the situation.
- Plan advancement and a career path.

Refer to your list of those whom you believe to be High D's. Carefully examine your communication strategies and motivation techniques to determine if there are areas in which you are mismanaging the High D. High D's will always be High D's. Your task is to bring out the best in them and to channel those energies to a win/win situation for all of the people involved.

POSSIBLE LIMITATIONS OF THE HIGH D

The limitations listed for the High D are tendencies for the pure High D, which represent a very small percentage of the population. Each of these tendencies are altered by the position of the "I," "S," and "C" factors and by the individual's values.

THE HIGH D MAY:

- Overstep authority.
- Be too directive.
- Be impatient with others.
- Be argumentative.
- Not listen well; be a one-way communicator.
- Take on too many tasks.
- Push people rather than lead them.
- Lack tact and diplomacy.
- Focus too heavily on task.

The possible limitations of the High D are the opportunities for growth. The very strengths of the "D" overused can become weaknesses. The task is to make the High D aware of his/her strengths and weaknesses and train him/her to cognitively make the correct VALUE choices needed for everyone to win.

CHAPTER APPLICATION

To effectively begin to use the language of the High D defined in this chapter, use the following steps:

1. Review the chapter for 15 minutes each day for 3 weeks cementing the High D characteristics in your mind.

2. Memorize the High D descriptors used in Dr. Warburton's studies.

   Ambitious
   Forceful
   Decisive
   Direct
   Independent
   Challenging

3. Apply the descriptors above and the High D characteristics in this chapter to those whom you contact regularly. Make a list of those whom you believe, by observation, to have a High D in their profile.

4. Refer often to Page 46 and adapt your style for better communication and understanding with the High D's you know.

5. As you meet new people, using the descriptors above, notice those who may be High D's and adapt your behavior for greater communication.

6. Stand back and watch the results! You'll be amazed at your newly found effectiveness by using DISC, the Universal Language.

"If you invest the pennies from your pocket into your mind, your mind will fill your pocket!"
–Tom Hopkins

THE HIGH I

Influencer, expressive, sanguine, the "I"
Life's full of hope, the limit's the sky
Enthusiastic, fun, trusting, charming
Confident, optimistic, popular, disarming.

Words smooth as cream as they talk to you
Winning you over to their point of view
A sparkling eye, a smile that's bright
In the dark of night, the "I" sees the light.

A people person with a need to be liked
Inspiring the team to continue the fight
Talking a lot while getting work done
Don't worry a bit, work should be fun.

A joke or two, expect a high five
The High I adds humor, keeps things alive
Turn them loose and watch what's done
The team is inspired to work as ONE.

–Randy Widrick

Definition:
The "I" factor is the highest plotting point on Graph II, the Basic Response.

THE HIGH I

Influencer, Expressive, Sanguine

DESCRIPTORS

Enthusiastic	**Persuasive**	**Emotional**
Trusting	**Affable**	**Generous**
Charming	**Convincing**	**Personable**
Popular	**Inspiring**	**Optimistic**
Gregarious	**Spontaneous**	**Self-Promoting**
Influential	**Sociable**	**Poised**
Confident	**Effusive**	**Good Mixer**
Open-Minded	**Talkative**	

FAMOUS HIGH I'S

Robin Williams, actor comedian
Arnold Palmer, professional golfer
Former President Bill Clinton

ROBIN WILLIAMS

An expressive, outgoing, incredibly funny man with a thousand faces and voices, Robin Williams delights audiences all over the world. His portrayal of the Genie in Disney's "Aladdin" lets us see his incredible verbal ability. Outgoing and social, Robin Williams has no trouble blending in with any crowd. An expert at improvising, many of his roles are loosely defined allowing him the opportunity to ad-lib, which he does very well–as do all High I's.

ARNOLD PALMER

Arnold Palmer is a people person. He values not only the recognition and friendship of other performers, but the adulation of an adoring public. His goal is not only to win games, but also to win and maintain friendships. Palmer is a charger who can come from behind to win a tournament with several spectacular holes, or who can "stink up the course" if his game is off and his gambles don't pay off. Arnold Palmer's ability to inspire others and win them to his cause is the stuff of a great legend.

FORMER PRESIDENT BILL CLINTON

Could anyone watch President Clinton and NOT see that he is clearly a High I, behaviorally? Throughout the campaign in1992, reporters continually commented on the way people energized then Governor Clinton. Verbally persuasive, optimistic, friendly and trusting, President Clinton, as leader of the United States, attempted to be very persuasive in his efforts to direct the country. President Clinton is clearly an extrovert, unafraid to show his emotion or express his concern. Even his foes state that he clearly cares about people, even if they disagree with his agenda.

THE EMOTION OF THE HIGH I: OPTIMISM

The higher the "I" plotting point on Graph II, the more optimistic the person will be. High I's believe the impossible can be done and will hold incredible optimism as to the future. This extreme optimism may not be grounded totally in data and facts. Conversely, a person with a Low I in their profile will tend to be pessimistic and more skeptical, requiring proof.

Example statement made to a High I and a Low I:
"If you invest with us, we can return 15% on your investment."

High I: "Really? That's a fantastic return."
Low I: "Yeah, Right! Prove it!"

OUTSTANDING CHARACTERISTICS OF THE HIGH I

NEED TO INTERACT

The High I has an inherent need to interact, loving opportunities to verbalize. The High I has a tendency to talk smoothly, readily and at length, using friendly contact and verbal persuasion as a way of promoting a team effort. They will consistently try to inspire you to their point of view.

NEED TO BE LIKED

Fundamentally, the High I wants to be liked and usually likes others... sometimes indiscriminately. Preferring not to be alone, the High I has a need for social affiliation and acceptance. Possessing a high level of trust in others, the High I may be taken advantage of by people.

Social rejection is the fear of the High I. "Praise in public and rebuke in private" is true for all people, but especially the High I. Incredibly optimistic, High I's will build on the good in others and see the positive side of a negative situation.

INVOLVEMENT

Expect the High I to be involved in just about everything. At their best, High I's promote trust and confidence and feel they can persuade people to the kind of behavior they desire. Usually, they perform very well in a situation where poise and smoothness are essential factors.

OUTSTANDING CHARACTERISTICS OF THE HIGH I

EMOTIONAL

Emotion is very difficult for High I's to contain. They do wear their "heart on their sleeve," and their face is very expressive of the emotions they are experiencing. This positive enthusiasm of the High I is very contagious, causing others to jump on whatever bandwagon the "I" is on.

Utilizing the descriptors on Page 56, the famous examples, and the outstanding characteristics the High I behavioral style should be beginning to develop clearly in your mind. The DISC language is based on observable behavior. By opening your "behavioral eyes" you will begin to notice the High I's around you.

VALUE OF THE HIGH I: TRUST

The DISC language does not measure a person's values. However, an interesting value is integrated in the "I" profile. Research has shown that the higher the "I" plotting point, the greater tendency the person has to "trust" others. Conversely, the lower the "I," the greater the tendency for distrust. When you meet optimistic people who seem to trust others, be assured they have a High I in their profile.

Note: TTI, under the direction of Bill J. Bonnstetter, is in the process of researching further correlations between behavioral style and values.

PEOPLE READING: RECOGNIZING THE HIGH I

Understanding that the DISC language interprets HOW we act, behavioral observation has proven that the following attributes usually apply to the High I behavioral style. Employ these cues to assist in quick recognition of the High I.

QUICK HIGH I OBSERVABLE INDICATORS

Extroverted/Introverted:	Extroverted
People or Task Oriented:	People
More Direct or Indirect:	Indirect
Overextensions:	Disorganization
Geared to/Looking for:	Fun, the experience
High I emotion:	Optimism
Low I emotion:	Pessimism
High I value:	Trust*
Low I value:	Distrust*

OBSERVABLE BEHAVIOR: "HOW THE HIGH I's ACT"

Buy:	Quick decision makers; showy products; impulse buyer.
Change:	May not notice change.
Conflict response:	Flight, run.
Drive:	Visual, looking around, radio on.
Decorate an office:	Contemporary, memorabilia of experiences.
Gesture:	A lot of big gestures and facial expressions when talking.
Goal setting:	Not good at setting goals. Intention is present, planning is not.
Letter writing:	More wordy letters, warm people focus.
Organization:	Disorganized. A lot of piles.
Read:	Fiction, self-improvement books.
Risk factor:	Moderate risk-taker.
Rules:	May not be aware of rules and break them unintentionally.
Stand:	Feet spread. Two hands in pockets.
Stress relief:	Interaction with people.
Talk on the phone:	Long conversations. A great deal of tone variation in voice.

***This is the only value that consistently correlates with behavior.**

PEOPLE READING: RECOGNIZING THE HIGH I

Talk to others: Verbal, at length. Personal with others. May have poor listening skills.

Walk: Weave, people focus, may run into things.

Magazines they may read: *People, Psychology Today.*

Refer often to these cues, until you have a clear picture of the High I pure style. Any one of these observable cues can instantly tell you that you are relating to a High I. You must invest the time learning the language in order to use it effectively.

Pure styles are being described in this section! The High I style is definitely affected by the intensity of the D, S, and C response. Effective language learning will give you the skill to recognize the effect of the other factors and adapt accordingly.

VALUE OF THE HIGH I TO THE TEAM

1. **Optimism and enthusiasm**
2. **Creative problem solving**
3. **Motivates others toward goals**
4. **Positive sense of humor**
5. **Team player**
6. **Negotiates conflict**
7. **Verbalizes with articulateness**

1. Optimism and enthusiasm
The High I is the people person, possessing a great ability to motivate and get the team excited. When the going gets tough, the optimism and enthusiasm of the High I will keep the team together.

2. Creative problem solving
High I's possess a very creative mind and if allowed, will be ingenious in their ability to come up with new, creative ideas and solutions to problems.

3. Motivates others toward goals
Leadership is the ability to move people toward a common goal. Although all four styles can do this, the High I motivates people through positive interaction and persuasion. This High I's ability causes others to want to work together as a team.

4. Positive sense of humor
The High I adds fun to the team and to the task. Studies have proven that productivity is increased as the team begins to have fun. The High I adds that natural fun, humorous element to the team.

5. Team player
Needing much people interaction, the High I is a very good team player. Working together means having fun while getting the job done.

THE VALUE OF THE HIGH I TO THE TEAM

6. Negotiates conflict

A natural mediator (not liking conflict), the High I can verbally persuade both sides to come to an agreement. Part of this is due to their ability to focus on the bright side of the issues. Also, if both factions know the High I mediator, both probably like him/her. People buy from people they like.

7. Verbalizes articulately

If there is a presentation to be made, an argument to be won, someone who needs to be persuaded into something that is good for all, send in the High I's. In these situations they will paint an optimistic picture of the possibilities and have a greater chance of achieving the desired results, not to mention the fact that they will enjoy the opportunity of being energized by the chance to verbalize. However, make sure they have the necessary data.

The High I is a tremendous asset. Their warm, friendly, fun demeanor adds an optimistic hope to the team. When the hard times hit, as they always do, the High I can bring a light to the dark night.

Based on the verbiage and descriptors given to this point, make a list of your associates who have a High I in their profile.

IDEAL ENVIRONMENT FOR THE HIGH I

- Assignments with a high degree of people contact.
- Tasks involving motivating groups and establishing a network of contacts.
- Democratic supervisor with whom they can associate.
- Freedom from control and detail.
- Freedom of movement.
- Multi-changing work tasks.

COMMUNICATING WITH THE HIGH I

Plan interaction that supports their dreams and intentions.
Don't legislate or muffle.

Allow time for relating and socializing.
Don't be curt, cold or tight-lipped.

Talk about people and their goals.
Don't drive to facts, figures and alternatives.

Focus on people and action items. Put details in writing.
Don't leave decisions up in the air.

Ask for their opinion.
Don't be impersonal or task-oriented.

Provide ideas for implementing action.
Don't waste time in "dreaming."

Use enough time to be stimulating, fun, fast moving.
Don't cut the meeting short or be too businesslike.

Provide testimonials from people they see as important or prominent.
Don't talk down to them.

Offer special immediate and extra incentives for their willingness to take risks.
Don't take too much time. Get to action items.

MOTIVATING THE HIGH I

The High I wants:

- An environment free from control data.
- Popularity and social recognition.
- Freedom of speech, people to talk to.
- Favorable working conditions.
- Group activities outside the job.
- Identification with the team.
- Public recognition of their ability.
- Monetary rewards.

MANAGING THE HIGH I

- Assist in setting realistic goals.
- Work with on-time management.
- Develop a friendship and make time for interaction daily.
- Open door policy for High I to discuss any issues.
- Train on Behavioral Styles to increase effectiveness of people interactions.
- Station them in a people area where they can interact and get the job done.
- Allow them freedom of movement, without control.
- Set clear objectives of task to be accomplished.
- Look for opportunities for them to utilize their verbal skills.

Refer to your list of those whom you believe to be High I's. Carefully examine your communication strategies and motivation techniques to determine if there are areas in which you are mismanaging them. The High I will always be a High I. Your task is to bring out the best in him/her and to channel those energies to win/win situations for all parties involved.

POSSIBLE LIMITATIONS OF THE HIGH I

The limitations listed for the High I are tendencies for the pure High I, which represents a very small percentage of the population. Each of these tendencies may be negated by the position of the "D," "S," and "C" factor and/or the beliefs of the individual. DISC is a NEUTRAL language.

The High I may:
- Oversell.
- Act impulsively, heart over mind.
- Trust people indiscriminately.
- Be inattentive to detail.
- Have difficulty planning and controlling time.
- Overestimate their ability to motivate others or change behavior.
- Under instruct and over delegate.
- Tends to listen only situationally.
- Overuse hand motions and facial expressions when talking.
- Rely too heavily on verbal ability.

The possible limitations of the High I are the opportunities for training and growth. Managing is "getting things done through people." The task, then, is to make the High I aware of his/her strengths and weaknesses and train him/her to cognitively make the correct VALUES choices needed for everyone to win.

CHAPTER APPLICATION

To effectively begin to use the language of the High I defined in this chapter, use the following steps:

1. Review the chapter for 15 minutes each day for 3 weeks cementing the High I characteristics in your mind.

2. Memorize the High I descriptors used in Dr. Warburton's studies.

    Expressive
    Enthusiastic
    Friendly
    Demonstrative
    Talkative
    Simulating

3. Apply the descriptors above and the High I characteristics in this chapter to those whom you contact regularly. Make a list of those whom you believe, by observation, to be High I's.

4. Refer often to Page 60 and adapt your style for better communication and understanding with the High I's you know.

5. As you meet new people, using the descriptors above, notice those who may be High I's and adapt your behavior for greater communication.

6. Stand back and watch the results! You'll be amazed at your newly found effectiveness by using *The Universal Language, DISC*.

"Treat people as if they were what they ought to be and you help them to become what they are capable of being."
–Johann Wolfgang von Goethe

THE HIGH S

S

The steady relater, amiable, High "S"
Mild, laid back, patient, no stress
Stable, sincere, passive, serene
Great listening skills, an "ace" on the team.

Hard at work behind the scenes
Helping to do what's best for the team
Others will tire, the "S" will finish
Determined to stay till the task has diminished.

Loyal, devoted, they'll be here awhile
Jumping around just isn't their style
Won't leave a job until it is over
Finish one first, you're not a rover.

Acutely aware of people's needs
Responding to personal hurts on the team
Although appearing slow in the jobs they do
When it comes to a team, the S is the "glue."

–Randy Widrick

Definition:
The "S" factor is the highest plotting point on Graph II, the Basic Response.

THE HIGH S

Steady, Relater, Amiable, Phlegmatic

DESCRIPTORS

Passive	**Mild**	**Sincere**
Possessive	**Inactive**	**Non-demonstrative**
Amiable	**Friendly**	**Team player**
Steady	**Systematic**	**Patient**
Predictable	**Serene**	**Stable**
Understanding	**Good listener**	

FAMOUS HIGH S's

First Lady Laura Bush
Rodney Rogers, professional basketball player

LAURA BUSH

Gentle, calm, relaxed, with a deep concern for others, Laura Bush is also a High S. Close ties to the family, she seems always willing to help others. She endears the hearts of America to her causes and adds a distinction to her office as First Lady. America respects and loves the gentle, calm, stability of Laura Bush.

RODNEY ROGERS

Professional basketball player Rodney Rogers is a classic example of a High S. He won the 6th Man of the Year award in the NBA. As a true S he was able to observe from the bench what was happening on the floor. Coming off the bench, he went in and immediately made a contribution. As a starter, he never made as great a contribution because he couldn't see what his role was.

EMOTION OF THE HIGH S: Non-emotional

Read carefully to avoid misunderstanding. High S's are very emotional. So why are we saying non-emotional? High S's have an inherent ability to "mask" their emotions. Whether they are going through a terrible personal ordeal or have just won the lottery, you may not know. High S's do not express their emotions. If you play a game where bluffing is involved (we recommend you don't), you will experience the power of the "non-emotion" of the High S. The strong side of this trait is that the High S can build a great team while going through tough personal events. The weak side of this trait is that internalized emotion is not physically or mentally healthy. High S's will open up and share their concerns with people they trust.

Conversely, Low S's openly display their emotions wearing their "heart on their sleeve."

OUTSTANDING CHARACTERISTICS OF THE HIGH S

NEED TO SERVE

The High S has an inherent need to serve. Always the one to help out, the High S lends a hand to get the job done. Other styles may serve for differing reasons, but the High S has a natural tendency to serve. In other words, serving and helping energizes the High S.

LOYALTY

High S's do not switch jobs very often, preferring to remain in one company as long as possible. Also, the High S will tend to stay in a relationship a long time, be it business or personal for reasons of security and also harmony. With the goal of harmony, High S's become very adaptable to the situation, modifying their behavior in order to achieve a sense of stability and harmony.

PATIENT, RELAXED

Showing a cool, relaxed face, High S's are not easily triggered or explosive in nature. Although they are very active emotionally, they do not show their emotion. An introverted personality, they will hide their problems and not wear their "heart on their sleeve." High S's have been known to lead their teams to great heights, even while going through incredible personal struggles.

LONG-TERM RELATIONSHIPS

High S's will develop strong attachments to their work group, family, club or association. They operate very well as members of a team and coordinate their efforts with others easily. They will strive to maintain the status quo, since they do not want change that is unexpected or sudden.

CLOSURE

Closure is essential for the High S. In other words, they must be allowed to finish what they start. To start several jobs and leave them undone is stressful to the High S. In a task-oriented situation, they should be given a few tasks and allowed to complete them before moving on. Having to "juggle" many balls at once is also stressful to the High S. The tendency observed is for High S's to read one book before they start another. High S's have been observed to dislike watching a movie or television if they have missed the start of the program.

OUTSTANDING CHARACTERISTICS OF THE HIGH S

High S's, once in an established "groove" or pattern, can follow it with unending patience. They have the ability to do routine work, at all skill levels, and develop good work habits.

Amiable, easygoing, and relaxed, the High S will build strong relationships with a few close people. Sensibility, low risk, steadiness, and serenity mark the High S Style.

Utilizing the descriptors on Page 70, the famous examples and the outstanding characteristics, the High S's behavioral style should be beginning to develop clearly in your mind. The DISC language is based on observable behavior. By opening your "behavioral eyes," you will begin to notice the High S's around you.

PEOPLE READING: RECOGNIZING THE HIGH S

Understanding that the DISC language interprets HOW we act, behavioral observation has proven that the following attributes usually apply to the High S behavioral style. Employ these cues to assist in quick recognition of the High S.

QUICK HIGH S OBSERVABLE INDICATORS

Extroverted/Introverted:	Introverted
People or Talk Oriented:	People
More Direct or Indirect:	Indirect
Overextensions:	Possessiveness
Geared to/Looking for:	Trust
Emotion of the High S:	Non-emotional
Emotion of the Low S:	Emotional

OBSERVABLE BEHAVIOR: "HOW THE HIGH S's ACT"

Buy:	Slow decision maker: traditional products
Change:	Does not like change. Needs much preparation.
Conflict response:	Tolerate, put up with it.
Drive:	Relaxed pace, no hurry.
Decorate an office:	Family snapshots, "homey" atmosphere.
Gesture:	Will gesture with hands, not large sweeping gestures.
Goal setting:	Goals are short-term, low risk. May use daily to do lists.
Letter writing:	Long letters giving lots of information.
Organization:	Usually some type of system. A little on the sloppy side.
Read:	People stories, fiction and nonfiction.
Risk factor:	Moderately low risk-taker.
Rules:	Will usually follow time-tested, proven rules.
Stand:	Leaning back, hand in pocket.
Stress relief:	Rest time/sleep. Hot baths.
Talk on the phone:	Warm conversationalist, friendly and concerned.
Talk to others:	Warm, not pushy. Will listen before talking.
Walk:	Steady, easy pace.
Magazines they may read:	*Reader's Digest, National Geographic.*

PEOPLE READING: RECOGNIZING THE HIGH S

Refer often to the behavioral cues until you have a clear picture of the High S's pure style. Any one of these observable cues can instantly tell you that you are relating to a High S. You must invest the time learning the language in order to use it effectively.

Pure styles are being described in this section! The High S style is definitely affected by the intensity of the "D," "I," and "C" response. Effective language learning will give you the skill to recognize the effect of the other factors and adapt accordingly.

VALUE OF THE HIGH S TO THE TEAM

1. Dependable team worker
2. Work hard for a leader and a cause
3. Great listener
4. Patient and empathetic
5. Good at reconciling factions, calming and stabilizing
6. Logical and step-wise thinker
7. Will finish tasks started
8. Loyal, long-term relationships

1. Dependable team worker

Always willing to help out, the High S will be a great team player. Usually stays in a situation a long time, the High S loyalty has a stabilizing effect on the team.

2. Work hard for a leader and a cause

If the High S believes in the leader and the cause, they will work extremely hard to make it happen (other styles will also work hard, but for different reasons). High S's will be quick to assist others in areas they are familiar with. When the High S accepts the task, expect them to be around for a while and to logically move toward completion.

3. Great listener

Listening skills are natural behavior for High S's. Even when interrupted, they will stop and look you in the eye and listen. Great listening ability makes them natural at helping people work through problems. Combined with their logical thinking, they become great assets to have on the team.

4. Patient and empathetic

Combined with great listening skills, High S's are very patient. Really trying to understand the situation the other person is in, they sometimes can become too adapting. Usually they will give the other person the benefit of the doubt, and may stay in a situation or relationship too long, hoping against hope that it will get better.

5. Good at reconciling factions, calming and stabilizing

Driven by a desire for harmony and peace, High S's can be a great asset in stabilizing a conflict situation. Again, their patience, listening ability, and logical approach can bring them back into harmony and focus.

VALUE OF THE HIGH S TO THE TEAM

6. Logical and step-wise thinker
Involved in the planning process, High S's are a great asset. Oftentimes goals are set and the plans to get there are never thought out. High S's can bring lofty ideas back to the realm of the real world and point out gaps and flaws in the plan, due to their logical thinking process.

7. Will finish tasks started
Closure is of utmost importance to High S's. They can, but do not enjoy juggling a lot of balls. A task that is started must be finished. The High S will finish the first task and then move on to the next. Also having the ability to organize effectively, the High S will develop a system to get the job done.

8. Loyal, long-term relationships
High S's on the team will form loyal, long-term relationships with whom they associate. When the going gets tough, the High S may be able to hold the team together because of the close relationships they have nurtured and developed.

High S's bring some incredible strength to the team. Their loyalty and ability to form close relationships has a cementing effect on the people around them, pulling everyone together for a common goal.

Based on the descriptors and verbiage to this point, make a list of your associates who have a High S in their profile.

IDEAL ENVIRONMENT FOR THE HIGH S

- Jobs for which standards and methods are established.
- Environment where long standing relationships can be, or are developed.
- Personal attention and recognition for tasks completed and well done.
- Stable and predictable environment.
- Environment that allows time for change.
- Environment where people can be dealt with on a personal, intimate basis.

COMMUNICATING WITH THE HIGH S

Start with personal comments. Break the ice.
Don't rush headlong into business or the agenda.

Show sincere interest in them as people.
Don't stick coldly or harshly to business.

Patiently draw out their personal goals and ideas. Listen and be responsive.
Don't force a quick response to your objectives.

Present your case logically, softly, non-threateningly.
Don't threaten with positional power, or be demanding.

Ask specific (preferably "How?") questions.
Don't interrupt as they speak. Listen carefully.

Move casually, informally.
Don't be abrupt and rapid.

If the situation impacts them personally, look for hurt feelings.
Don't mistake their willingness to go along for satisfaction.

Provide personal assurances and guarantees.
Don't promise something you can't deliver.

If a decision is required of them, allow them time to think.
Don't force a quick decision; provide information.

MOTIVATING THE HIGH S

The High S wants:

- Logical reasons for change.
- Identification with team members.
- Harmony. A happy home and work life.
- Procedures that have been proven.
- A road map to follow.
- Closure on tasks.
- Time to adjust to change.
- Appreciation.
- Recognition for loyalty and service.
- To know you care.
- To work with a small group of people, develop relationships.

MANAGING THE HIGH S

- Clearly explain upcoming changes in order to prepare them.
- Give rewards in terms of things.
- Make an effort to get to know them and their needs.
- Allow them the opportunity to finish the tasks started.
- Assign them fewer, larger projects.
- Encourage their contribution in meetings.
- Involve them in the long-term planning.
- Work to stretch them carefully to new heights.
- Create a non-threatening environment, allowing disagreement.
- Reward them for good work habits.
- Clearly define parameters and requirements of the task.
- Assign them to work with a small group of people.
- Do not switch them from team to team.
- Praise in public, rebuke gently in private.

Refer to your list of those you believe to be High S's. Carefully examine your communication strategies, motivation techniques and see if there are areas in which you are mismanaging him/her. The High S will always be a High S. Your task is to bring out the best in him/her and to channel those energies to win/win situations for all parties involved.

POSSIBLE LIMITATIONS OF THE HIGH S

The limitations listed for the High S are tendencies for the Pure High S, which represent a very small percentage of the population. Each of these tendencies may be negated by the position of the "D," "I," and "C" factor or the values of the individual.

The High S may:

- Take criticism of work as a personal affront.
- Resist change just for change sake.
- Need help getting started on new assignments.
- Have difficulty establishing priorities.
- Internalize feelings when they should be discussed.
- Wait for orders before acting.
- Give false sense of compliance.
- Be too hard on themselves.
- May stay involved in a situation too long.
- Not project a sense of urgency.

Studies have shown that when persons focus on overcoming their weaknesses, they also diminish their strengths. The most effective people are those who understand themselves and surround themselves with people who are lovingly honest. All people have strengths and weaknesses. Our task is to build on the strengths, "two heads are better than one," "many hands make light work" and "a strand of three is not easily broken."

CHAPTER APPLICATION

To effectively begin to use the language of the High S defined in this chapter, use the following steps:

1. Review the chapter for 15 minutes each day for 3 weeks cementing the High S characteristics in your mind.

2. Memorize the High S descriptors used in Dr. Warburton's studies.

    Methodical
    Systematic
    Reliable
    Steady
    Relaxed
    Modest

3. Apply the descriptors above and the High S characteristics in this chapter to those whom you contact regularly. Make a list of those whom you believe, by observation, to be High S's.

4. Refer often to Page 74 and adapt your style for better communication and understanding with the High S's you know.

5. As you meet new people, using the descriptors above, notice those who may be High S's and adapt your behavior for greater communication.

6. Stand back and watch the results! You'll be amazed at your newly found effectiveness by using DISC, the Universal Language.

"I have yet to find the person, however exalted his station, who did not do better work and put forth greater effort under a spirit of approval than under a spirit of criticism."
–Charles Schwab

THE HIGH C

C

Compliant, analytical, melancholic, the "C"
Methodical, courteous, complete accuracy
Restrained, diplomatic, mature and precise
Accurate, systematic, those standards are nice.

Planning and organizing done to perfection
The smallest detail is no exception
Consistently clear and objective thinking
Gives the team top-notch results without blinking.

And when it comes time to make a decision
You'd best have the facts to accomplish the mission
The C at your side with all the correct facts
Will assure the return on your investment won't lack.

Go by the book, follow the rules
Procedures are written, use the right tools
Standards are crucial, both now and later
In God we trust, all others use DATA!

–Randy Widrick

Definition:
The "C" factor is the highest plotting point on Graph II, the Basic Response.

THE HIGH C

Compliance, Analytical, Melancholic

DESCRIPTORS

Perfectionist	**Fact-finder**	**Systematic**
Courteous	**Restrained**	**Analytical**
Mature	**Precise**	**Methodical**
Accurate	**Diplomatic**	**Conventional**
Conscientious	**High standards**	**Sensitive**
Evasive	**Patient**	**Exacting**

FAMOUS HIGH C's

Actress Courtney Cox as Monica Geller on *Friends*
Former Vice President Al Gore

COURTNEY COX

As the character Monica Geller on TV's *Friends*, Courtney Cox is the classic example of a High C. Monica is always concerned with neatness and gets really upset when things are moved from their regular place.

FORMER VICE PRESIDENT AL GORE

With an analytical approach, Vice President Gore laid out the facts and figures of government waste, focusing on systems and procedures of how things are handled (or mishandled). Whether one agrees with his thinking or not, Vice President Gore is well thought out and analytical in his approach to the environment as well as government. *Time Magazine* gave an account of Gore's success in a debate with Ross Perot over NAFTA (North American Free Trade Agreement). Gore was urged by his advisors to play to his strength--to be "wooden," not animated. Typical of a High C, he spent many hours studying alone. He analyzed all of Perot's claims, looking for flaws. Then he had a group of aides fire questions at him for over two hours and then held a mock debate. Gore took control of tactics and strategy. Gore told his team that he wanted to hammer Perot with facts. On all accounts, Vice President Al "Wooden" Gore won the debate.

EMOTION OF THE HIGH C: FEAR

The emotion of the "C" factor is fear. The higher the "C" factor the more the individual will be low risk, following procedures and going "by the book." Research by TTI in this area has proven conclusively that a person with a High C in their profile is a better driver than a person with a Low C in their profile. Also observed is the fact that parents who are High C's tend to be more protective of their children, due also to the emotion of fear. Conversely, the lower the "C" factor, the more the person will be high risk and tend to break rules and procedures.

OUTSTANDING CHARACTERISTICS OF THE HIGH C

NEED FOR PROCEDURES

High C's strive for a stable and orderly life and tend to follow procedures in both their personal and business lives. Dependent upon procedures, they will usually stick to methods that have brought success in the past.

BY THE BOOK

"Going by the book" is the first rule of conduct for High C's. They are very aware of and sensitive to the dangers of mistakes and errors, preferring a professional disciplined approach to problem solving. They are often the "quality" people who will write proven procedures to ensure the proper outcome.

PERFECTIONIST

Preferring to compete with themselves, the High C is constantly striving toward better ways of doing things. There is a right way to do things and a wrong way. High C's have the desire to be right, which usually means that they will come down on the safe side of a problem, where there is less risk. They would rather be cautious than brash, conventional than bold. The lower the "I" the higher the tendency towards being a perfectionist.

PRECISE AND ATTENTIVE TO DETAIL

High C's are data gatherers and will gather all possible facts (maybe too many) related to a specific problem. They are systematic thinkers, precise and attentive to detail. When called upon by other styles, the "C" will tend to ask questions to clarify the data, and go to the heart of the issue. The High C is very careful in thought and deed.

OUTSTANDING CHARACTERISTICS OF THE HIGH C

PROOF AND EVIDENCE

Statements made with little or no proof will not fly with the High C. "Prove it" is the calling card of the High C.

"In God we trust, all others use data," depicts the High C very well. This drive for proof and facts can save a company a great deal of money that would have been wasted in inconclusive speculation.

High C's tend to be loyal and dedicated, doing whatever is expected of them to the best of their ability. They are more tacticians than strategists.

Utilizing the descriptors on Page 84, the famous examples, and the outstanding characteristics, the High C behavioral style should be beginning to develop clearly in your mind. The DISC language is based on observable behavior. By opening your "behavioral eyes" you will begin to notice the High C's around you.

PEOPLE READING: RECOGNIZING THE HIGH C

Understanding the DISC language interprets HOW we act. Behavioral observation has proven that the following attributes usually apply to the High C behavioral style. Employ these cues to assist in quick recognition of the High C.

QUICK HIGH C OBSERVABLE INDICATORS

Extroverted/Introverted:	Introverted
People- or Task-Oriented:	Task
More Direct or Indirect:	Direct
Overextensions:	Critical
Geared to/Looking for:	Procedures/information
Emotion of the High C:	Fear
Emotion of the Low C:	No fear

OBSERVABLE BEHAVIOR: "HOW THE HIGH C's ACT"

Buy:	Very slow buyers: proven products.
Change:	Concerned of the effects of change.
Conflict response:	Avoidance.
Drive:	Careful, follow rules. Best drivers.
Decorate an office:	Graphs, charts, functional.
Gesture:	Very reserved, little or no gestures.
Goal settings:	Good at setting safe goals, probably in many areas. Goals may be safe with little risk or reach.
Letter writing:	Direct, to the point, with appropriate data.
Organization:	Everything in its place. Perfectly organized.
Read:	Nonfiction, technical journals.
Risk factor:	Very low.
Rules:	"By the book." Knows and follows rules.
Stand:	Arms folded, one hand on chin.
Stress relief:	Alone time.
Talk on the phone:	Little chitchat. To the point. May be short or long depending on data needed.
Talk to others:	Direct. Questioning, clarifying.
Walk:	Straight line.
Magazines they may read:	*Consumer Reports.*

PEOPLE READING: RECOGNIZING THE HIGH C

Refer often to these cues until you have a clear picture of the High C style. Any one of these observable cues can instantly tell you that you are relating to a High C. You must invest the time learning the language in order to use it effectively.

Pure styles are being described in this section! The High C style is definitely affected by the intensity of the "D," "I," and "S" response. Effective language learning will give you the skill to recognize the effect of the other factors and adapt accordingly.

VALUE OF THE HIGH C TO THE TEAM

1. **Objective thinker**
2. **Conscientious**
3. **Maintains high standards**
4. **Defines, clarifies, gets information, criticizes and tests**
5. **Task-oriented**
6. **Asks the right questions**
7. **Diplomatic**
8. **Pays attention to small details**

1. Objective thinker

When dialoguing with High C's, the real world is the arena. They deal in the area of objective fact and will make you prove your case. The High C brings a reality to plans, analyzing and testing the data for accuracy.

2. Conscientious

High C's take their work personally, almost as an extension of their being. The finished task is a reflection of their attention to small details. They are usually very loyal and will go the extra mile to get the job done.

3. Maintains high standards

In a book called "The Wisdom of Team," one characteristic was found on all high performance work teams, they were committed to the highest standards. The High C will even assist in writing the standards. With a quality focus, the High C assists the team in consistency of standards and operation, adding order to the scenario.

4. Defines, clarifies, gets information, criticizes and tests

A great objective thinker, the High C will blow holes in plans that are not well thought out. Their skeptical nature looks at all possibilities before they buy into the plan. Utilized in this way, the High C can be a great asset to any team. Oh, and don't argue with a "C" unless you are sure you have your "ducks in a row." Collectors of data, the High C is a walking computer, always analyzing, testing, and clarifying.

5. Task-oriented

The world is not all touchy-feely. We need people on the team that place urgency on doing the tasks that are needed. For years, the High C's have made significant contributions to such events as going to the moon. The "I's" would still be planning the party for the arrival.

VALUE OF THE HIGH C TO THE TEAM

6. Asks the right questions

One of the most significant contributions the High C's make to any organization is asking the rough questions. This talent often leads to distraction of a shallow plan.

7. Diplomatic

If given the opportunity, High C's will be very diplomatic in sharing the data to support their conclusions. They prefer discussions void of emotional appeal.

8. Pays attention to small details

Many projects would be a total disaster if it weren't for the High C's attention to detail. Every organization needs a "C" on their team for those projects where the little things make a big difference.

In summary, the High C sets the standards for the team and maintains them. In a world of fast pace and change, the High C keeps us closer to reality with their objective thinking processes. High C's, with their questioning, analyzing and clarifying style do not allow us to get away with "sloppy thinking." Sometimes misunderstood, they can take ideas that are too "lofty" and bring them back to a state of realism. Based on the verbiage and descriptors given to this point, make a list of your associates who you believe to have a High C in their profile.

IDEAL ENVIRONMENT FOR THE HIGH C

- Where critical thinking is needed and rewarded
- Assignments can be followed through to completion
- Technical, task-oriented work, specialized area
- Noise and people are at a minimum
- Close relationship with small group of people
- Environment where quality and/or standards are important

COMMUNICATING WITH THE HIGH C

Prepare your case in advance.
Don't be disorganized or messy.

Approach them in a straightforward, direct way.
Don't be casual, informal or personal.

Use a thoughtful approach. Build credibility by looking at all sides of each issue.
Don't force a quick decision.

Present specifics, and do what you say you can do.
Don't be vague about expectations or fail to follow through.

Draw up an "Action Plan" with scheduled dates and milestones.
Don't over promise as to results, be conservative.

Take your time, but be persistent.
Don't be abrupt and rapid.

If you disagree, prove it with data and facts or testimonials from respected people.
Don't appeal to opinion or feelings as evidence.

Provide them with the information and the time they need to make a decision.
Don't use closes, use incentives to get the decision.

Allow them their space.
Don't touch them.

MOTIVATING THE HIGH C

The High C wants:

- Operating procedures in writing.
- Safety procedures.
- To be part of a quality-oriented team.
- No sudden or abrupt changes.
- Reassurance that the job is being done correctly.
- Information and data available.
- Time to think.
- Objective, tough problems to solve.
- Manager who follows company policy.

MANAGING THE HIGH C

- Involve them in defining standards that are undefined.
- Involve them in implementation of the standards.
- Clearly define requirements of the job and expectations.
- Allow them the opportunity to finish the tasks started.
- Set goals that have "reach" in them.
- Encourage their contribution in meetings.
- Involve them in the long-term planning.
- Train them in people skills and negotiating.
- Respect their personal nature.
- Allow them to work with a small group of people, in a less active area.
- Do not criticize their work unless you can prove a better way.

Refer to your list of those you believe to be High C's. Carefully examine your communication strategies and motivation techniques to see if there are areas and be willing to be the one who has to adapt.

POSSIBLE LIMITATIONS OF THE HIGH C

The limitations listed for the High C are tendencies for the pure HIGH C, which represent a very small percentage of the population. Each of these tendencies may be negated by the position of the "D," "I," and "S" factor.

The High C may:

- Hesitate to act without precedent.
- Overanalyze: analysis paralysis.
- Be too critical of others.
- Get bogged down in details.
- Not verbalize feelings, but internalize them.
- Be defensive when criticized.
- Yield position to avoid controversy.
- Select people much like themselves.
- Be too hard on themselves.
- Tell ideas as opposed to sell ideas.

As stated, the intensity of the "D," "I," and "S" factors can offset the limitations of the "C" factor. As with all styles, their very strengths are the cause of their weaknesses. The challenge, knowing you need the strengths of all four styles on your team, is to grow and learn to bring out the best in each style, maximizing strengths and minimizing the weaknesses of each style.

CHAPTER APPLICATION

To effectively begin to use the language of the High C defined in this chapter, use the following steps:

1. Review the chapter for 15 minutes each day for 3 weeks cementing the High C characteristics in your mind.

2. Memorize the High C descriptors used in Dr. Warburton's studies.

   Analytical
   Contemplative
   Conservative
   Exacting
   Careful
   Deliberative

3. Apply the descriptors above and the High C characteristics in this chapter to those whom you contact regularly. Make a list of those whom you believe, by observation, to be High C's.

4. Refer often to Page 88 and adapt your style for better communication and understanding with the High C's you know.

5. As you meet new people, using the descriptors above, notice those who may be High C's and adapt your behavior for greater communication.

6. Stand back and watch the results! You'll be amazed at your newly found effectiveness by using DISC, the Universal Language.

"People rarely get fired for incompetence. It's not getting along that is almost always the underlying reason for dismissal."
–Stuart Margulies
Industrial Psychologist

FAMOUS EXAMPLES

High "C"
Bernard Shaw
Clint Eastwood (in real life)
Diane Sawyer
Spike Lee
Ivan Lendl
Kevin Costner
Ted Koppel
Monica Seles
Mr. Spock (in Star Trek)
Bjorn Borg
Jack Nicklaus
Barbara Stanwyck

High "D"
Ross Perot
Cher
Hillary Clinton
Charles Barkley
Jimmy Connors
Michael Douglas in "Wall Street"
Barbara Walters
Roseanne Arnold
Madonna
John McEnroe
Sam Donaldson
Fidel Castro
Lee Iaccoca

High "S"
John Denver
Tom Brokaw
Michael J. Fox
Magic Johnson
Ted Danson
Danny Glover (in "Lethal Weapon")
Martina Navratilova
Mr. Rogers (Children's TV Host)
Ladybird Johnson
Mother Teresa
Gandhi

High "I"
Bette Midler
Liza Minnelli
Arsenio Hall (as TV Host)
Arnold Schwarzenegger
Tony Danza
Oprah Winfrey
Andre Agassi
Chi Chi Rodriquez
Dolly Parton

Comic Characters of:
Steve Martin
Eddie Murphy
Robin Williams

OBJECTIVES REVISITED

Once this chapter has been learned, you should be at the following stage:

A. Definition and learning

Having properly reviewed each segment of this chapter, you will have four distinctly differrent "compartments" in your memory. Each compartment will have:

1. Visual pictures of famous examples.
2. Visual pictures of people you know.
3. Descriptors of the "compartment style" (DISC).
4. Behavioral style indicators.

B. Observation

By observing and opening your "behavioral eyes," you will see "how" people act. Now that the language is "compartmentalized," you will be able to identify the "primary" behavioral style as you observe people. Then by referring to the communication sections in this chapter, you will be able to increase your effectiveness immediately.

They look like...?

CHAPTER 5
Reading the DISC Language

Chapter Objective:
To provide you with information and instructions to become proficient in graph reading using the Style Insights™ Instrument.

Chapter Contents:
- The Style Insights™ Instrument
- Scoring Method
- Understanding Graph I
- Understanding Graph II
- The Energy Line
- Graph Reading
- Four-step Plan
- Unusual Graphs
- TTI's Success Insights Wheel®
- Objectives Revisited

APPROACH:

Individual Customized Graph Reading

Many behavioral models classify behavior into 16 basic types. Although this is a good approach and provides useful information, it is not the best. Each person is a unique creation and we approach graph reading with that uniqueness in mind. The 16 common types only represent 64% of the population, and to "fit" the remaining present 36% of the population into one of the 16 types does not give the reading accurate information.* Therefore, we will present a step-by-step approach to customized graph reading, taking into account the uniqueness of each person's behavior allowing us to understand each person better and not "fit" them into an established pattern.

*Information based on data collected in 2004

"He who knows others is learned, he who knows himself is wise."
–Lao Tse

THE INSTRUMENT: STYLE INSIGHTS™

Based on the individual's responses to the 24 "most" words, over 20,000 different graphs can be plotted, and over 20,000 different graphs can be plotted for the "least" responses. The magnitude of those numbers makes it impractical to write an evaluation of each potential graph, so, for evaluation purposes, these possible graphs are condensed into one of 384 graphs. The computer-generated reports are based on evaluating the 384 graphs from both the "most" and the "least" responses.

Current research indicates that 64% of the population will fall into 16 basic graphs. The remaining 36% of the population is distributed across the remaining 368 graphs. This is why it is so difficult to compare the Style Insights to other psychological instruments. As a result of this, the Style Insights instrument is far more sophisticated than instruments that only measure one factor against another in each question. This leads to a discussion of face validity.

Taking the Style Insights Instrument:

To ensure highest accuracy, the following instructions should be given to the individual taking the instrument:

1. **Focus on how you act at work**
2. **Take ten minutes or less to complete the response form, uninterrupted**
3. **There are no right or wrong answers**
4. **Don't over analyze**

Style Insights™

Ten Minutes to Increased Success!

In just ten minutes you can complete the Style Insights Response Form and begin a process of self-understanding that will benefit you both personally and professionally. After completing the instrument, the **Internet Delivery Service**™ (IDS) will be used to generate a valuable report full of information that may change the rest of your life.

Your report merges sophisticated behavior analysis with computer software operations to provide you with unique personal insights. This comprehensive report will help you discover qualities about yourself that could be the key to opening new doors of opportunity. You will be able to better understand your work and/or management style from the information provided, and develop an action plan that can enhance your personal and professional growth.

Directions:

On the page you will see 24 boxes of words. Each box contains 4 lines of words. For each box select the line of words that best describes you and mark the oval in the **M**ost column of that line. Then, select the line of words that least describes you and mark the oval in the **L**east column of that line. Repeat this process for the remaining 23 boxes.

- While you are responding to the 24 questions, keep your focus on the descriptions that apply to yourself in the workplace.
- Be ruthlessly honest with yourself!
- Go with your *"gut"* instinct—don't over-analyze!
- Select **ONLY 1 Most and 1 Least** in each of the 24 numbered boxes.
- You should take no more than 10 minutes to complete the instrument and it should be done in one uninterrupted sitting.

Refer to the example below before proceeding:

Example

M	L	
●	○	Gentle, kindly
○	○	Persuasive, convincing
○	●	Humble, reserved, modest
○	○	Magnetic, attracts others

Only available on the Internet Delivery Service™.

Style Insights™

Name______________________________ Company ______________________________ Male ❑ Female ❑

FOCUS: Work ❑ Personal ❑

M	L			M	L		
◯	◯	Spontaneous	1	◯	◯	Well-disciplined, self-controlled	13
◯	◯	Contented, satisfied		◯	◯	Generous, willing to share	
◯	◯	Positive, admiting no doubt		◯	◯	Animated, uses gestures for expression	
◯	◯	Peaceful, tranquil		◯	◯	Persistent, unrelenting, refuses to quit	
◯	◯	Easily led, follower	2	◯	◯	Sociable, enjoys the company of others	14
◯	◯	Bold, daring		◯	◯	Patient, steady, tolerant	
◯	◯	Loyal, faithful, devoted		◯	◯	Self-reliant, independent	
◯	◯	Charming, delightful		◯	◯	Soft-spoken, mild, reserved	
◯	◯	Expressive	3	◯	◯	Gentle, kindly	15
◯	◯	Daring, risk-taker		◯	◯	Persuasive, convincing	
◯	◯	Diplomatic, tactful		◯	◯	Humble, reserved, modest	
◯	◯	Satisfied, content		◯	◯	Magnetic, attracts others	
◯	◯	Respectful, shows respect	4	◯	◯	Captivating	16
◯	◯	Pioneering, exploring, enterprising		◯	◯	Kind, willing to give or help	
◯	◯	Optimistic		◯	◯	Resigned, gives in	
◯	◯	Accommodating, willing to please, ready to help		◯	◯	Force of character, powerful	
◯	◯	Willing, agreeable	5	◯	◯	Companionable, easy to be with	17
◯	◯	Eager, impatient		◯	◯	Easygoing	
◯	◯	Methodical		◯	◯	Outspoken, speaks freely and boldly	
◯	◯	High-spirited, lively, enthusiastic		◯	◯	Restrained, reserved, controlled	
◯	◯	Logical	6	◯	◯	Factual	18
◯	◯	Obedient, will do as told, dutiful		◯	◯	Obliging, helpful	
◯	◯	Unconquerable, determined		◯	◯	Willpower, strongwilled	
◯	◯	Playful, frisky, full of fun		◯	◯	Cheerful, joyful	
◯	◯	Adventurous, willing to take chances	7	◯	◯	Attractive, charming, attracts others	19
◯	◯	Analytical		◯	◯	Systematic	
◯	◯	Cordial, warm, friendly		◯	◯	Stubborn, unyielding	
◯	◯	Moderate, avoids extremes		◯	◯	Pleasing	
◯	◯	Good mixer, likes being with others	8	◯	◯	Restless, unable to rest or relax	20
◯	◯	Structured		◯	◯	Neighborly, friendly	
◯	◯	Vigorous, energetic		◯	◯	Popular, liked by many or most people	
◯	◯	Lenient, tolerant of others' actions		◯	◯	Orderly, neat	
◯	◯	Competitive, seeking to win	9	◯	◯	Argumentative, confronting	21
◯	◯	Considerate, caring, thoughtful		◯	◯	Adaptable, flexible	
◯	◯	Outgoing, fun-loving, socially striving		◯	◯	Nonchalant, casually indifferent	
◯	◯	Harmonious, agreeable		◯	◯	Light-hearted, carefree	
◯	◯	Aggressive, challenger, takes action	10	◯	◯	Brave, unafraid, courageous	22
◯	◯	Life of the party, outgoing, entertaining		◯	◯	Inspiring, motivating	
◯	◯	Easy mark, easily taken advantage of		◯	◯	Avoid confrontation	
◯	◯	Fearful, afraid		◯	◯	Quiet, composed	
◯	◯	Stimulating	11	◯	◯	Cautious, wary, careful	23
◯	◯	Sympathetic, compassionate, understanding		◯	◯	Determined, decided, unwavering, stand firm	
◯	◯	Tolerant		◯	◯	Convincing, assuring	
◯	◯	Aggressive		◯	◯	Good-natured, pleasant	
◯	◯	Talkative, chatty	12	◯	◯	Jovial, joking	24
◯	◯	Controlled, restrained		◯	◯	Organized	
◯	◯	Conventional, doing it the usual way, customary		◯	◯	Nervy, gutsy, brazen	
◯	◯	Decisive, certain, firm in making a decision		◯	◯	Even-tempered, calm, not easily excited	

Only available on the Internet Delivery Service™.

THE SCORING METHOD

Certain descriptors used in the Style Insights Instrument do not meet the standard necessary to be classified as a strong "D", "I", "S" or "C" tendency. Because the correlation of the descriptors does not meet the standard, it remains in the instrument, but is not used in the scoring.

The graphs are statistically adjusted to account for the non-scoring adjectives, which are included in the instrument to ensure accurate scoring.

UNDERSTANDING GRAPH I

1. Graph I is generated from the MOST responses.
The MOST responses identify a person's responses to their environment. In other words, what behavior a person feels he/she needs to exhibit in order to survive and succeed at the job.

2. Graph I is our "MASK" graph.
A "mask" indicates we are "putting on" something to cover our true identity. We tend to adapt our behavior in order to survive or succeed in a specific environment Graph I is the behavior we allow others to see, even though it may not be our true behavior.

3. Graph I is the MOST CHANGEABLE.
We adapt our behavior to the environment. Graph I shows this adaptation. Graph I will change depending on the environment we focus on. For example, a person transferring from an accounting position to a sales position may need to utilize more people skills in order to succeed in the new environment. Adaptation of their behavior would appear in Graph I.

4. Graph I is our ADAPTED graph.
As we respond to the Style Insights Instrument, we are asked to focus on what we are like at work. Graph I indicates what we said we are MOST like and gives us our responses to our environment. If we focused on something other than work, like being a father, then Graph I would indicate the behavior we felt we needed to exhibit in order to succeed as a father. Graph I indicates the behavior of what ever focus was used.

UNDERSTANDING GRAPH II

1. Graph II is our basic behavior.

Poetically speaking, "Graph II is you." Graph II identifies a person's BASIC behavior, the core, the real you. By reading this graph, we can learn what you are like under pressure, or when you are totally at ease. When you are under stress or pressure the mask comes off and we see Graph II behavior, also, when things are going good and you can "let your hair hang down," we see Graph II behavior.

2. Graph II is generated from the LEAST responses.

The LEAST choices you select determine the plotting points for Graph II. Research tells us that people are most true in their responses when we ask what they are least like. In other words, we can get a better picture of you by asking you to tell us what you are not like, than we can by asking you to tell us what you are like.

3. Graph II is the LEAST CHANGEABLE.

Because Graph II is the real you, it is of utmost importance in understanding yourself. If you were a people person in high school, you will probably be a people person when in your rocking chair. Graph II will seldom change significantly.

4. Graph II can change when you experience a significant emotional event.

Often, when a person has taken a Style Insights Instrument in the past, they may say their Graph II is totally different. When questioned, we inevitably discover that the person has been through an emotional event such as surgery, car accident, death of a loved one, or some event that caused them to change. Otherwise, Graph II will remain fairly consistent throughout a person's lifetime.

THE ENERGY LINE

The Energy Line is the centerline of the graphs, the foundation from which intensity levels can be determined. When we discuss the DISC language, often we refer to a person as a High D, High I, High S, or High C. Simply stated, High D means that the "D" plotting point is furthest up from the Energy Line. High C would mean the "C" factor is the highest plotting point above the Energy Line and so on. A low D would indicate that the "D" factor is the lowest plotting point below the Energy Line.

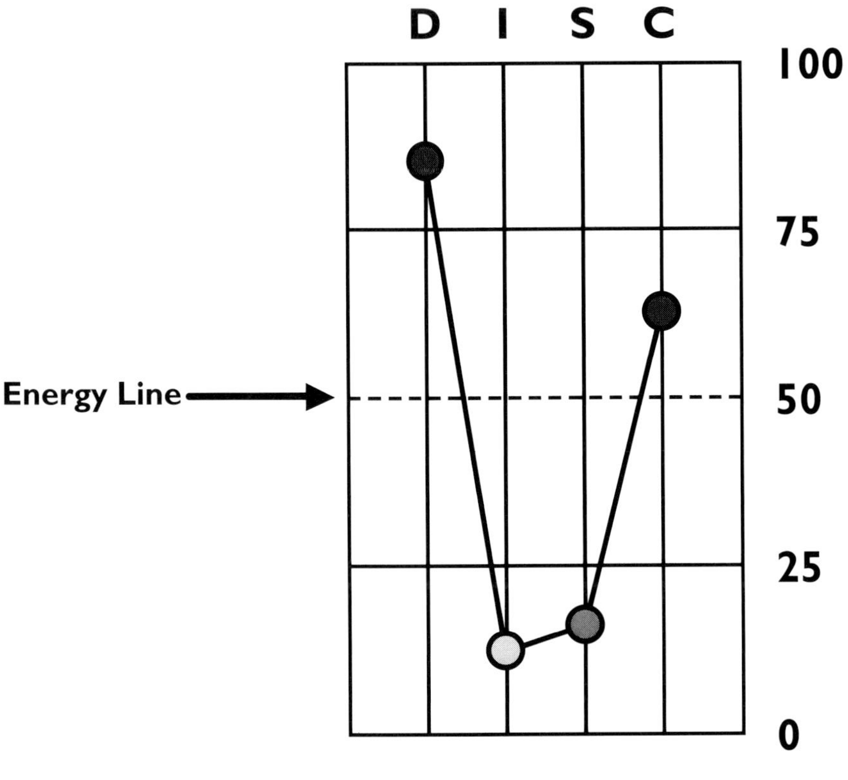

In the above example, the individual would be understood to be a High D because the D factor is the highest plotting point above the Energy Line.

However, in order to understand the behavior of the whole person, we would not only look at the characteristics of the High D, but also the intensity of the I, S, and C factors and their relationship, high or low, to the Energy Line and to each other.

At the end of this chapter you will be able to read any graph without reading the computer report.

Arnold Palmer: High I

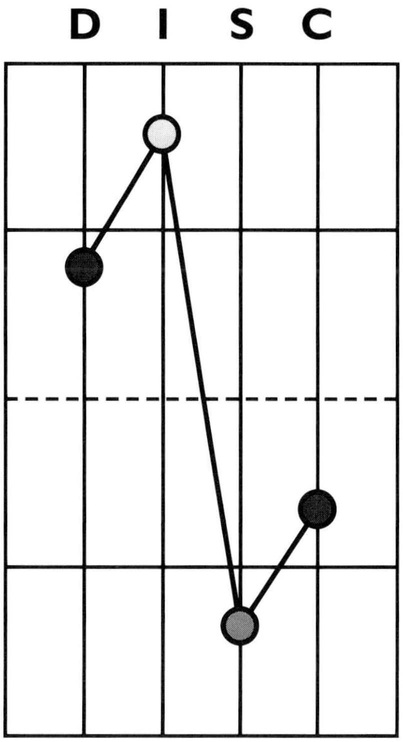

I	Optimistic, trusting
I/S	Sociable, contact ability
I/C	Projects self-confidence
I/D	Amiable, friendly
D/S	Results-oriented, sense of urgency
D/C	Ambivalent, vacillating, temperamental
C/S	Alert, sensitive to problems, controls, rules, mistakes

Jack Nicklaus: High C

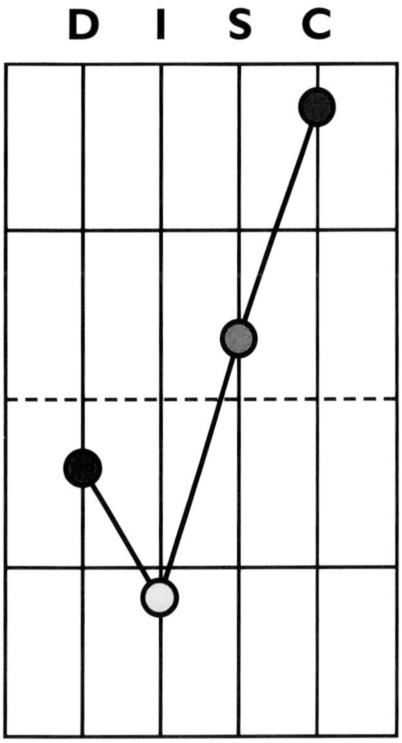

C	Compliance
C/I	Precise, perfectionist
C/D	Adaptable, dependable, soft-spoken
C/S	Alert & sensitive to problems, controls, rules, mistakes
S/I	Concentrating on details, reflective, intense
D/I	Incisive, argumentative, direct, analytical

Both win their own unique way!

GRAPH READING

A Four-Step Plan to Greater Behavioral Understanding

Step 1: Determine primary behavioral style and factor relationships for Graph II

Step 2: Give feedback

Step 3: Check for disparity between Graph I and Graph II

Step 4: Repeat process for Graph I

The graph reading process begins first with Graph II, the BASIC RESPONSE. After the behavior of Graph II has been analyzed, the same process can be applied to Graph I.

STEP 1

Determine Primary (above line) Behavioral Style and Factor Relationships of Graph II.

The Primary Behavioral Style is the highest plotting point above the Energy Line. In Example 1, the Primary Behavioral Style is a High C.

Example 1

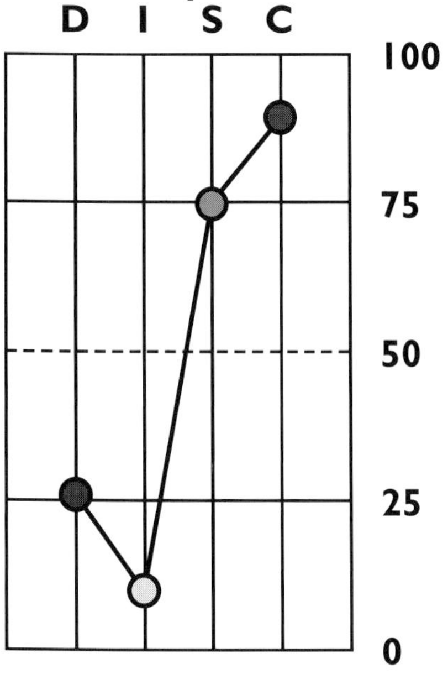

Primary C

Factor Relationships	Spread	Tendency
C/I	75	Strong
C/D	65	Strong
C/S	9	Weak
S/I	50	Strong
S/D	40	Strong
D/I	15	Moderate

GRAPH READING

Now that we know the Point Spread for each relationship, we can identify Strong, Moderate and Weak tendencies.

Strong, Moderate and Weak Tendencies
The rule to follow for identifying Strong, Moderate and Weak tendencies is as follows:

POINT SPREAD
STRONG tendency: Point Spread greater than or equal to 20
Associated verbiage will tend to be highly accurate; the absolute truth

MODERATE tendency: Point Spread of 10-19
Associated verbiage will explain a tendency toward a certain behavior

WEAK tendency: Point Spread of 9 or less
Verbiage may not be accurate; too close to call

STEP 2
Giving Feedback

C is the highest, so give feedback based on High C. Refer to the Example 1 for details.

C Feedback
Factor Relationship Feedback

C/I **Strong:** Precise, accurate, perfectionist

C/D **Strong:** Adaptable, dependable, soft spoken

C/S **Weak:** Alert and ready to adapt to systems, but cautious

S/I **Strong:** Concentrating on details, reflective, intense

S/D **Strong:** Patient, nonchalant, lackadaisical, resigned

D/I **Moderate:** Incisive, argumentative, direct, analytical, creative

GRAPH READING

Repeat Step 2 on the following Famous People's Graphs:

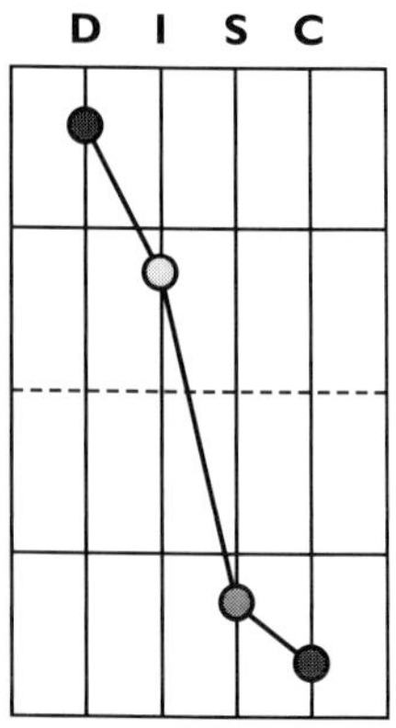

Charles Barkley

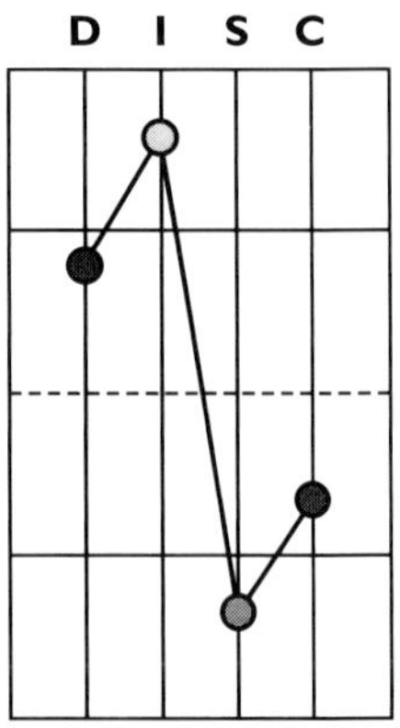

Arnold Palmer

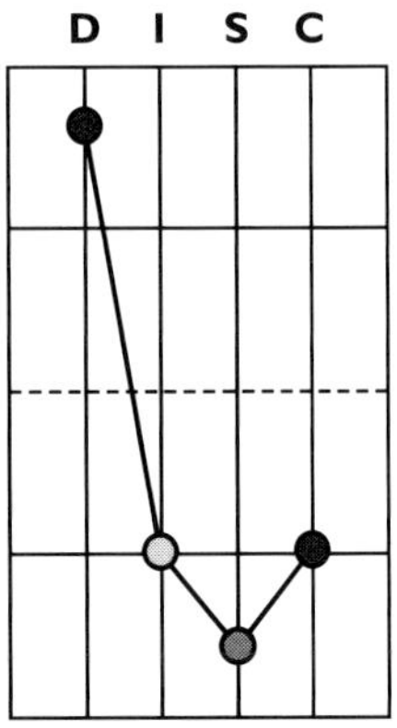

Donald Trump

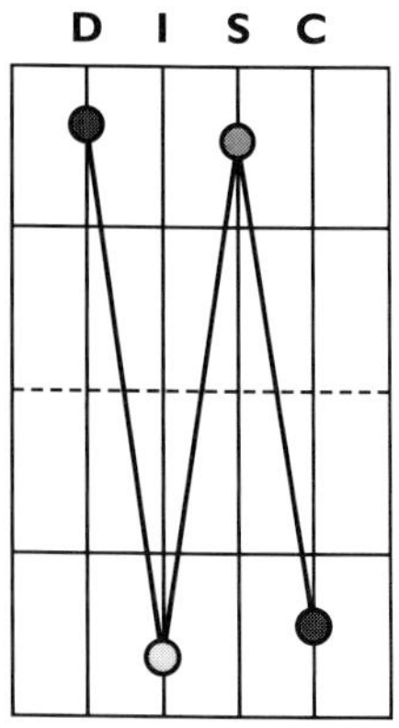

Richard Nixon

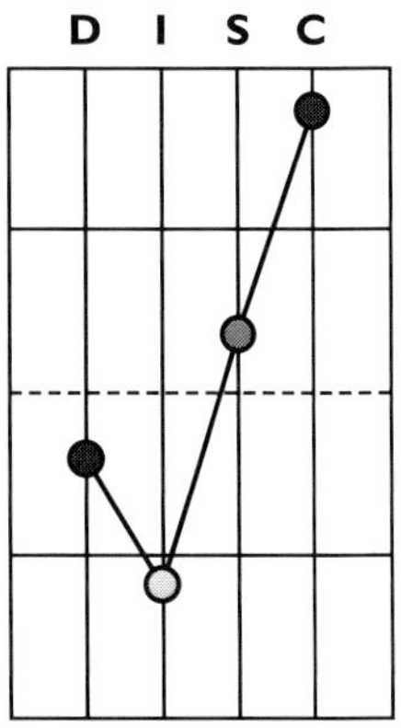

Jack Nicklaus

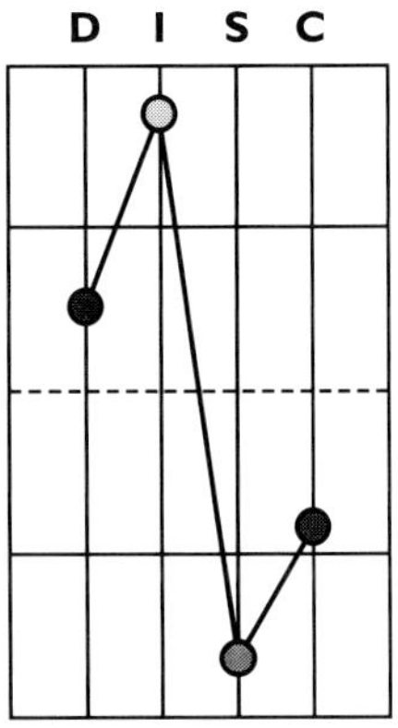

Bill Clinton

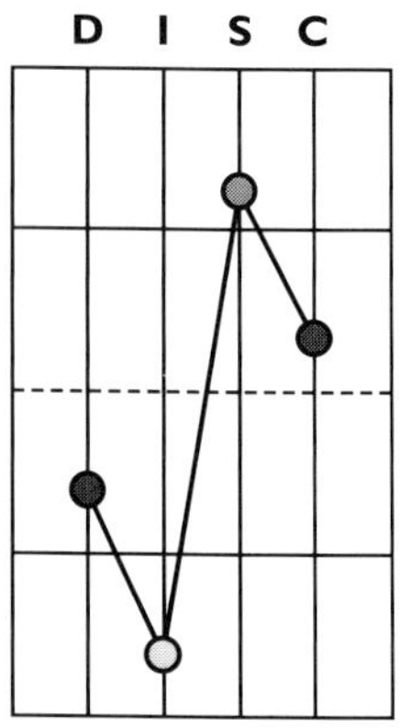

Rodney Rogers

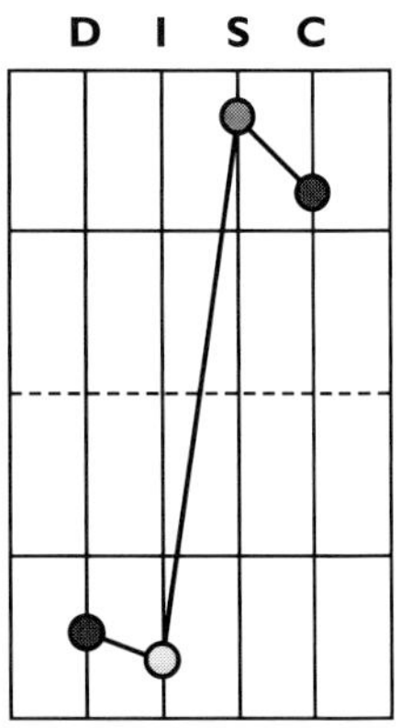

Tom Brokaw

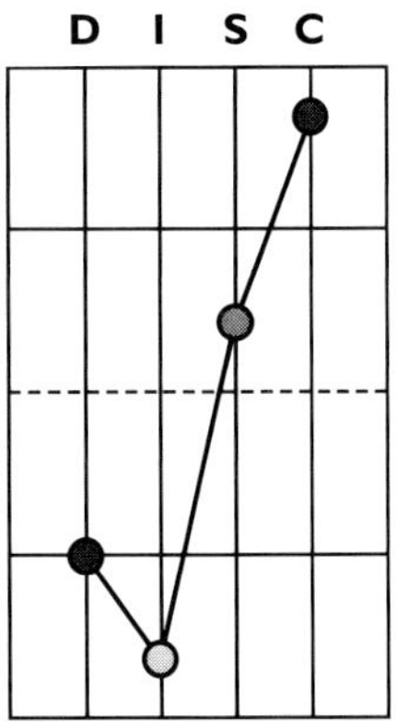

Penny Hardaway

GRAPH READING

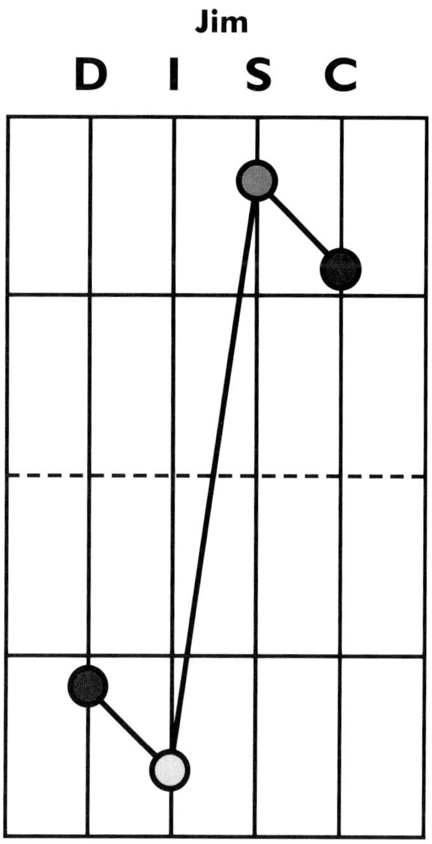

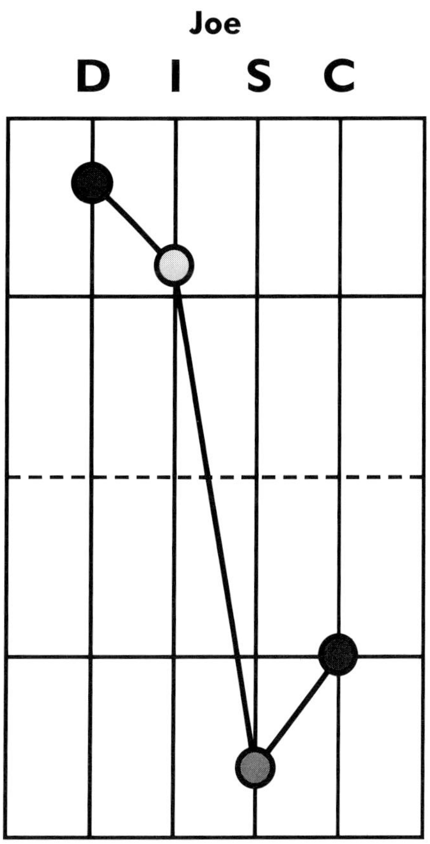

How will Jim communicate with Joe?

How will Joe feel about Jim's natural communication style?

How will Joe communicate with Jim?

How will Jim feel about Joe's natural communication style?

Communication is the key to managing, motivating, leading, parenting, etc. Use this process to demonstrate to both parties the power of TTI's assessments.

The following pages include the information needed to learn how to read all possible graphs.

HIGH D: DOMINANT

D

Quick to Anger "Short Fuse"

Demanding

Egocentric

Driving
Ambitious
Pioneering
Strong-willed
Forceful
Determined
Aggressive
Competitive
Decisive
Venturesome

Inquisitive
Responsible

Conservative

Calculating
Cooperative
Hesitant
Low-keyed
Unsure
Undemanding
Cautious

Mild
Agreeable
Modest
Peaceful

Unobtrusive

Slow to Anger "Long Fuse"

PROBABLE STRENGTHS *

Ego
Problem-solver
Likes challenging assignments
Drive for results
Positive, likes confrontation
Power and authority
Motivated by direct answers

POSSIBLE LIMITATIONS *

Overstep authority
Use fear as a motivator
Poor listener
Lack tact and diplomacy
Dislikes routine work
Over delegates, under instructs

* Possible because we are only discussing one factor — statements may change based on intensity of the other three factors.

TOP FACTOR "D" STYLE COMBINATIONS

DESCRIPTORS | **VERBIAGE**

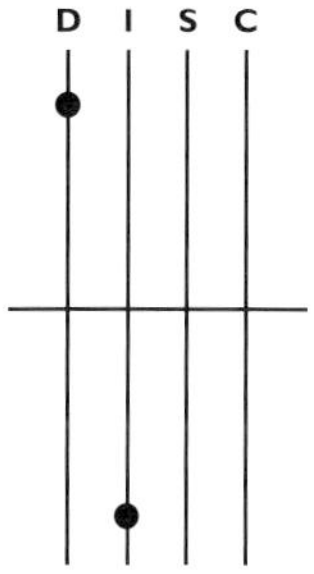

D1. D/I

Incisive, argumentative, direct, analytical, creative and/or innovative, straight-forward

Seeks and solves problems in an independent direct manner. Any situation can be faced and dealt with given time and technique.

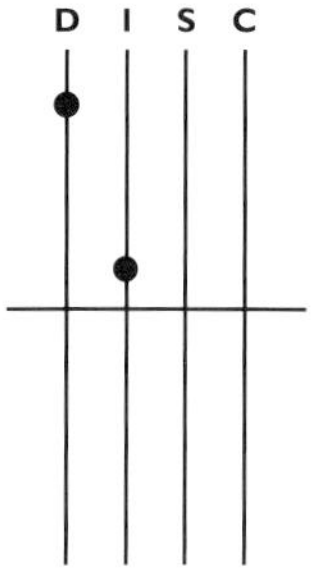

D2. D/I Both above line

Incisive, argumentative, direct, analytical, creative and/or innovative, straight-forward

Seeks and solves problems persuasively with the support of people. How to understand others and solicit their help represents an appealing challenge.

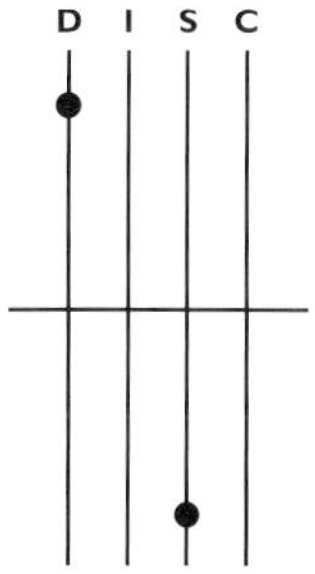

D3. D/S

Results-oriented, urgent, driving, deadline conscious, self-starter, wide scope of activities

Anxiously impatient to overcome obstacles and competition in the most expedient way, from the many choices of action available. Driven to succeed.

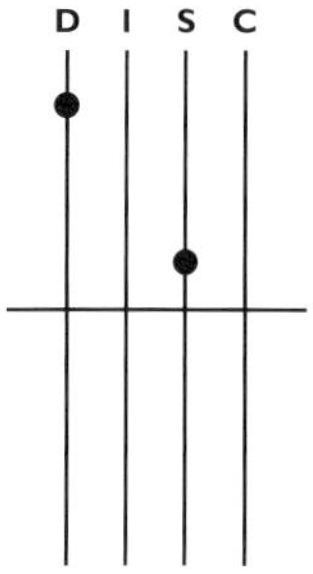

D4. D/S Both above line

Results-oriented, urgent, driving, deadline conscious, self-starter; good at fewer activities than the really Low S

Actively goal-oriented. Chooses to go after solutions to problems rather than wait to see how they come out.

TOP FACTOR "D" STYLE COMBINATIONS

DESCRIPTORS | **VERBIAGE**

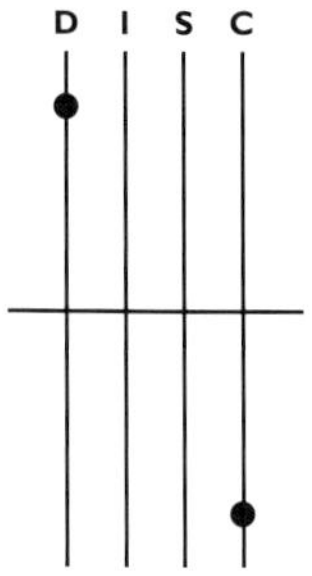

D5. D/C

Decisive individualist, daring, bold, gutsy, risk-taker, venturesome, pioneering

Aggressively and independently tackles problems with little regard for possible drawbacks in choice of solutions.

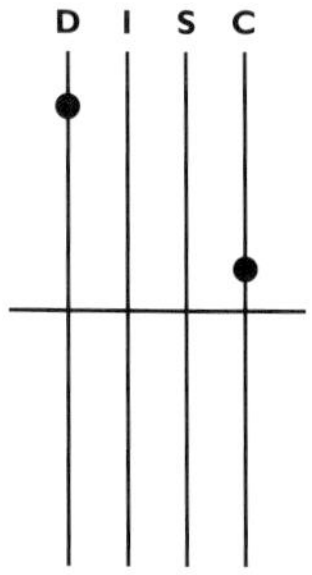

D6. D/C Both above line

Ambivalent, vacillating, temperamental, do it—do it right voices

Capable of decision making within a climate of uncertainty but may hesitate to act under heavy pressure.

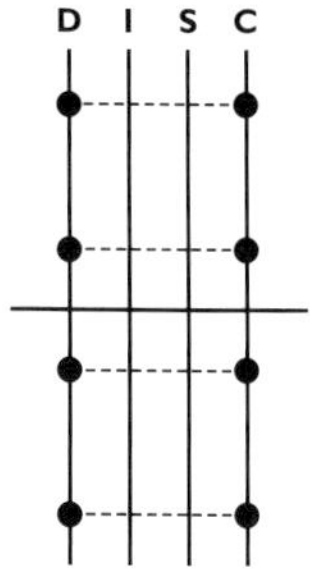

D7. D/C

Ambivalent, vacillating, temperamental

Capable of decision making within a climate of uncertainty but may hesitate to act under heavy pressure.

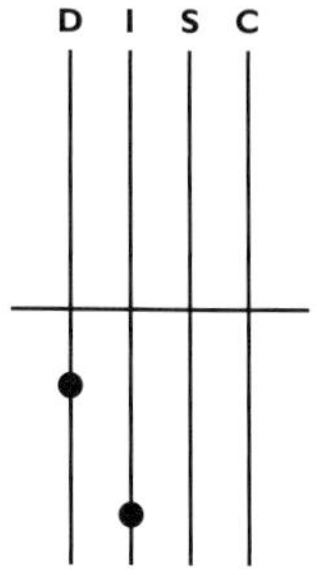

D8. D/I Both below the line

Internal heat, emotions internalized

Inner intensity felt, but not displayed to others, magnified if standards aren't met.

HIGH I: INFLUENCER

I

Optimistic, Trusting

Effusive

Inspiring
Magnetic
Political
Enthusiastic
Demonstrative
Persuasive
Warm
Convincing
Polished
Poised
Optimistic

Trusting
Sociable

Reflective

Factual
Calculating
Skeptical

Logical
Undemonstrative
Suspicious
Matter-of-fact
Incisive

Pessimistic
Moody

Critical

Pessimistic, Distrusting

PROBABLE STRENGTHS *
Socially and verbally aggressive
Very optimistic
Good at persuading people
Can see the "big dream" and communicate it
People-oriented
Team-oriented
Motivated by praise and strokes

POSSIBLE LIMITATIONS *
Acts impulsively – heart over mind
Unrealistic in appraising people
Inattentive to detail
Situational listener
Disorganized

* Possible because we are only discussing one factor — statements may change based on intensity of the other three factors.

TOP FACTOR "I" STYLE COMBINATIONS

	DESCRIPTORS	VERBIAGE
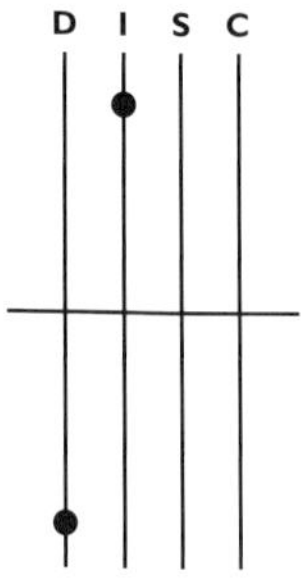	**I1. I/D** Obliging, conciseness, accommodating	Persuasively and emotionally looks to people for support and inner-satisfaction more than as a way to help reach personal goals.
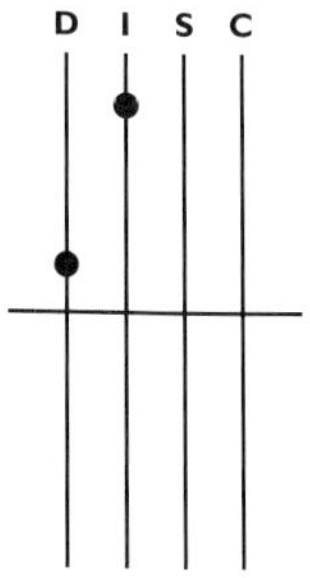	**I2. I/D Both above line** Amiable, friendly, affable	Cordially enterprising. Enjoys communicating with people, with an awareness for the supportive strength they provide to succeed. Convinces and promotes in a friendly, talkative manner to achieve goals.
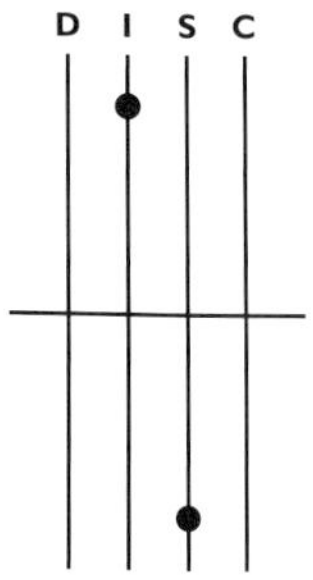	**I3. I/S** Sociable, contact ability, good mixer	Actively seeks communications and relationships with a variety of people. Extroverted in demeanor.
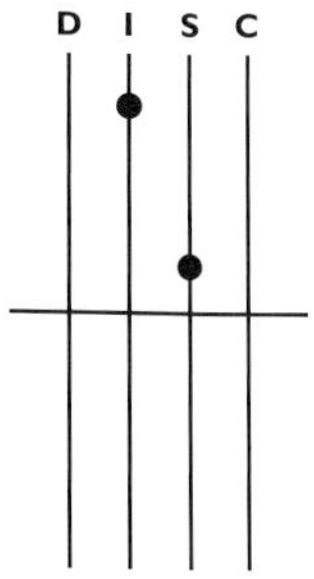	**I4. I/S Both above line** Contact ability, good mixer, gregarious and sociable	Openly friendly with others in many situations, but primarily with groups of established friends and associates. Sociable and enjoys the uniqueness of each human being.

TOP FACTOR "I" STYLE COMBINATIONS

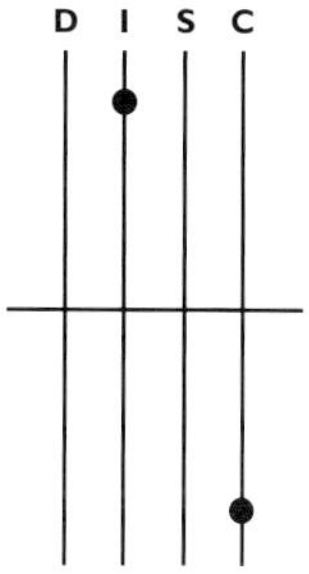

DESCRIPTORS

15. I/C

Projects well, self-assured, self-confident

VERBIAGE

Confident and relaxed with others, even in social situations that may seem risky and uncertain. Sees people for their qualities rather than as a threat.

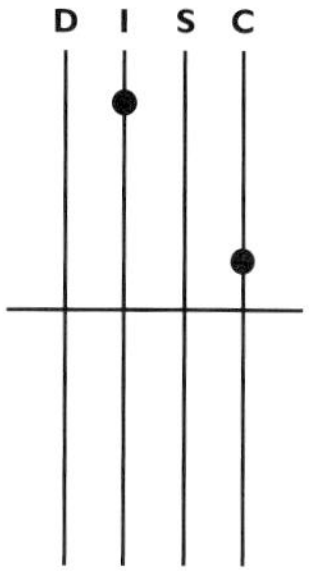

16. I/C Both above line

Diplomatic, quality social relations

Interacts with people in an assured and poised manner.

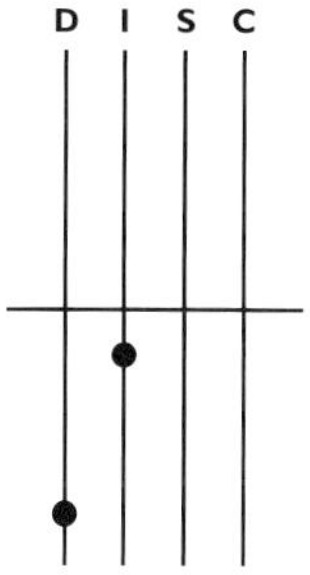

17. I/D Both Below Line

Gentle, shy, meek, timid, unobtrusive, reticent, complacent

Inner intensity of each situation felt but not displayed to others. Magnified if standards are not met.

HIGH S: STEADINESS

S

Non-emotional, Non-expressive

Phlegmatic

Relaxed
Resistant to Change
Non-demonstrative

Passive

Patient

Possessive

Predictable
Consistent
Deliberate
Steady
Stable

Mobile

Active
Restless
Alert
Variety-oriented
Demonstrative

Impatient
Pressure-oriented
Eager
Flexible
Impulsive
Impetuous

Hypertense

Emotional, Expressive

PROBABLE STRENGTHS *

Loyal to those they identify with
Good listener
Patient and empathetic
Likes to have team environment
Long service is deemed important
Oriented towards family activities
Motivated towards traditional procedures

POSSIBLE LIMITATIONS *

Tends to get in a "rut," maintain status quo
Resists change
Holds grudge
Lacks projected sense of urgency
Slow to act without precedent
Hesitates to move
Rather than delegate, may do work themselves

* Possible because we are only discussing one factor — statements may change based on intensity of the other three factors.

TOP FACTOR "S" STYLE COMBINATIONS

DESCRIPTORS	VERBIAGE

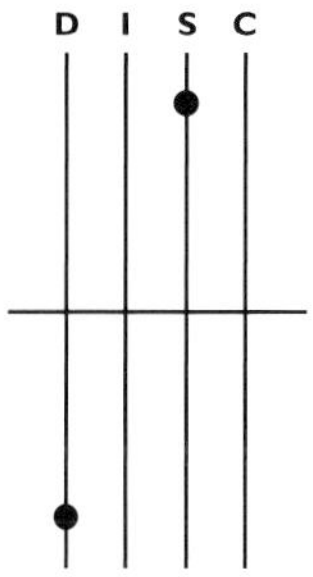

S1. S/D

Patient, nonchalant, lackadaisical, resigned; uses humor to avoid confrontation

Patient and stable under pressure. Prefers to wait out problems and difficult encounters rather than confront them.

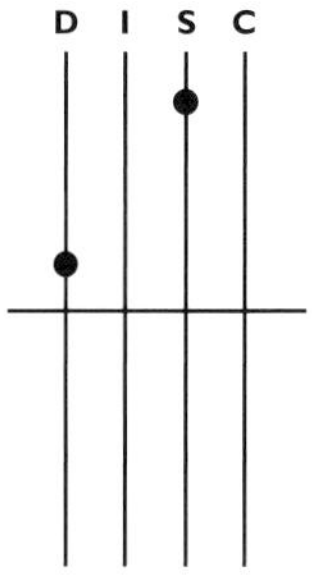

S2. S/D Both above line

Patient, nonchalant, lackadaisical, resigned; can become stubborn

Tolerates difficulty and relies on situations to eventually change for the better, in most cases.

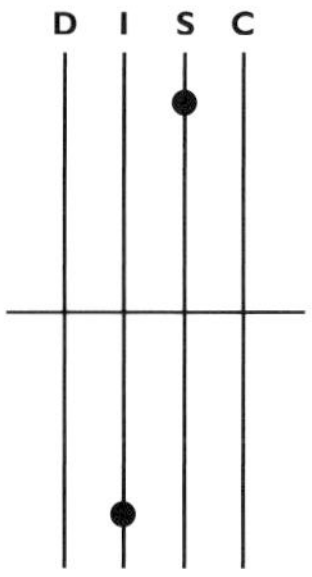

S3. S/I

Concentrating on details; reflective, intense, low trust

Able to focus and not be distracted for long periods of time. Will logically and systematically center all attention on current needs, with little concern for personal loneliness or being liked by others.

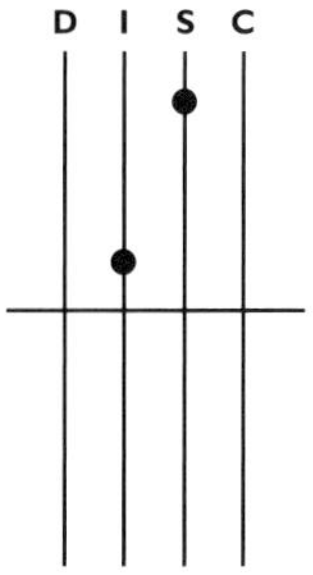

S4. S/I Both above line

Concentrating on details; reflective, intense

Is intent and reflective, but friendly. Accepts and depends on the support of selected individuals.

TOP FACTOR "S" STYLE COMBINATIONS

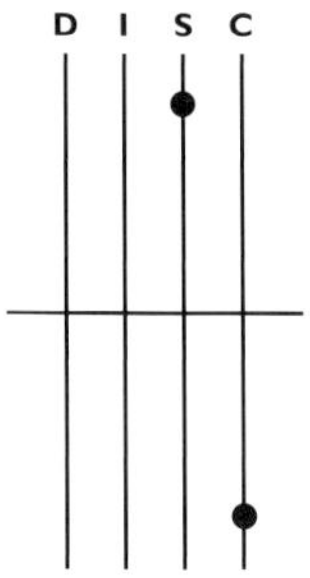

DESCRIPTORS

S5. S/C

Persistent, persevering; may display some independence.

VERBIAGE

Persistently holds to views, even when they are contrary to the opinions of others. May be dogmatic in nature and extremely resistant to change in approaches to problems and people.

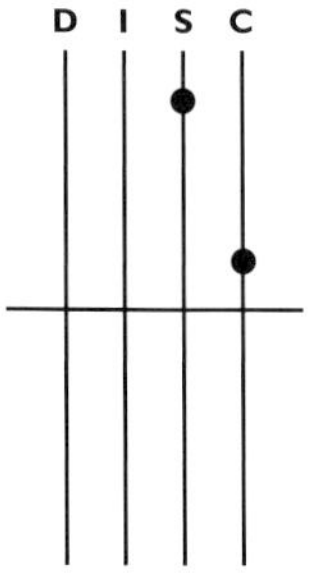

S6. S/C Both above line

Persistent, persevering

Determined to be "on course" with past procedures, but not at the expense of quality or with no regard for the expectations of others.

HIGH C: COMPLIANCE

C

Fear: Low Risk

Evasive

Worrisome
Careful
Dependent
Cautious
Conventional
Exacting
Neat

Systematic
Diplomatic
Accurate
Tactful

Open-minded
Balanced Judgment

Firm

Independent
Self-willed
Stubborn

Obstinate

Opinionated
Unsystematic
Self-righteous
Uninhibited
Arbitrary
Unbending

Careless with Details

No Fear: High Risk

PROBABLE STRENGTHS *
Critical thinker
High standards for self and subordinates
Well disciplined
Maintain high standards
Motivated by the right way to proceed
Accurate

POSSIBLE LIMITATIONS *
Leans on supervisor
Hesitates to act without precedent
Bound by procedures and methods
Will not risk stating new ideas without qualifying statement
Does not verbalize feelings
May do work themselves and not delegate
Yields position to avoid controversy

* Possible because we are only discussing one factor — statements may change based on intensity of the other three factors.

TOP FACTOR "C" STYLE COMBINATIONS

DESCRIPTORS | **VERBIAGE**

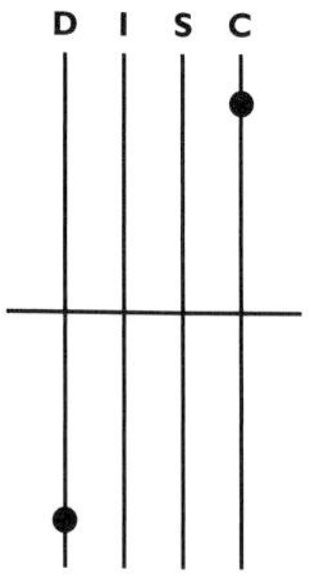

C1. C/D

Adaptable, dependable, soft-spoken. uses humor to avoid confrontation.

Willing to adapt rather than risk confrontation. Behaves according to established and respected systems and procedures.

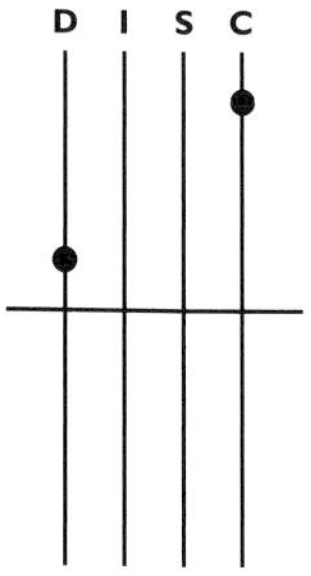

C2. C/D Both above line

Adaptable, dependable, soft-spoken; will confront when pushed.

Diplomatic and concerned with the approval of others, especially of supervisors and key associates. Probably will push quite hard to find correct, acceptable answers.

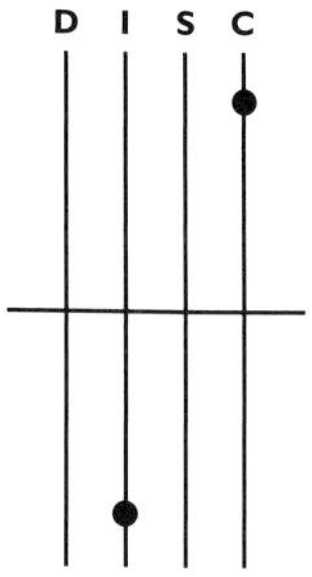

C3. C/I

Precise, accurate, perfectionist; careful with details; stickler for quality, system and order.

Precise, with utmost concern for quality. Analytical rather than persuasive in efforts to achieve correctness.

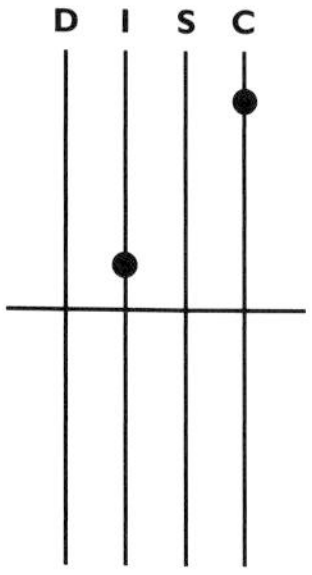

C4. C/I Both above line

Precise, accurate, perfectionist; careful with details; stickler for quality, system and order; situational with application of descriptors.

Organized, even in relationships. Polite and cooperative with people. Appreciates company of people with similar ideas and views as theirs who are organized and quality-conscious.

TOP FACTOR "C" STYLE COMBINATIONS

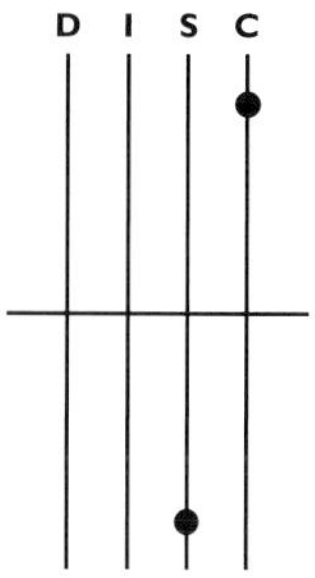

DESCRIPTORS

C5. C/S

Alert and sensitive to: problems, controls, dangers, mistakes, errors, rules, regulations, procedures; aware of social economic, and political implications of one's decisions.

VERBIAGE

Very sensitive to changes in the social and work environment, willing to adapt accordingly. Complying with what seems correct at the moment may result in being impulsive in actions.

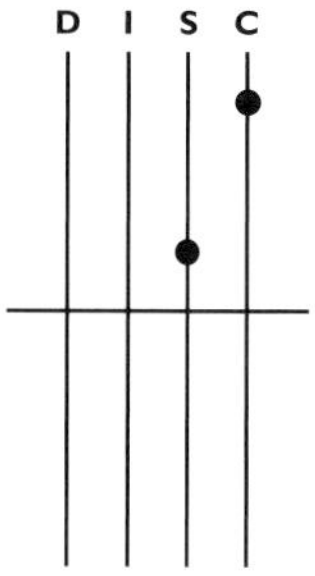

C6. C/S Both above line

Alert and sensitive to: problems, controls, dangers, mistakes, errors, rules, regulations, procedures, disciplines

Alert and ready to adapt to respected systems and procedures, but cautious and takes time to assess possible, consequences. Especially wary of making change, which may damage long-standing relationships and/or is contrary to deeply ingrained techniques and procedures.

EMOTIONS OF THE FOUR DIMENSIONS

"D" EMOTION: ANGER

The higher the plotting point, the more the person will tend to have a short fuse, or be impatient. This does not mean they will "blow up." They may be able to control the anger, but they definitely will become impatient and anger quickly.

The lower the "D" plotting point, the more the person will tend to be patient and slow to anger.

"I" EMOTION: OPTIMISM/TRUST

The higher the "I" plotting point the more the person will look on the bright side of things and exhibit a high trust level.

The lower the "I" plotting point, the more the person will tend to be pessimistic and exhibit a low level of trust.

"S" EMOTION: NON-EMOTIONAL

The "S" has feelings. However, the higher the plotting point of the "S," the more the person will not demonstrate or "show" their emotion, because they do not want to burden you with their problems. The person will internalize the emotion and tell you everything is all right when it isn't.

The lower the "S" factor, the more you will hear and see the emotion the person is going through.

"C" EMOTION: FEAR

The higher the "C" factor, the more the person will follow the rules due to a fear of getting caught, or of authority. A "C" factor above the midline will tend to go "by the book." The fear factor may be hidden and not shown.

The lower the "C" factor the more the person is likely to be a high risk-taker, showing little fear. May believe rules are just guidelines and will break them, if necessary.

GRAPH READING

STEP 3

Check Graph I and Graph II Disparity

Research by Judy Suiter and Dr. David Warburton has shown that adapting behavior in Graph I that is significantly different from Graph II can cause stress, mental health problems and job dissatisfaction. The larger the movement, the more significant the correlation. An example of disparity can be demonstrated by the following graphs:

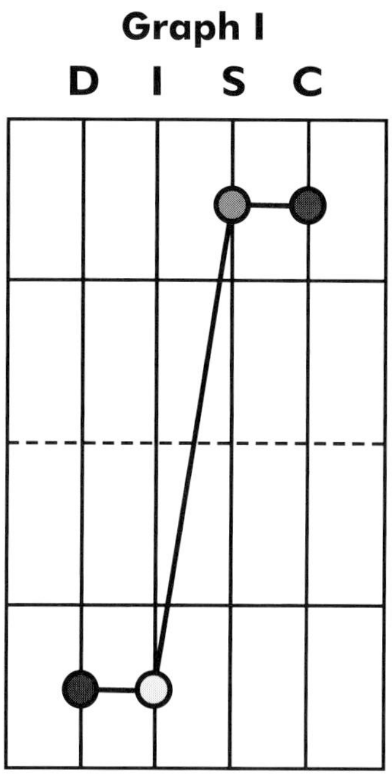

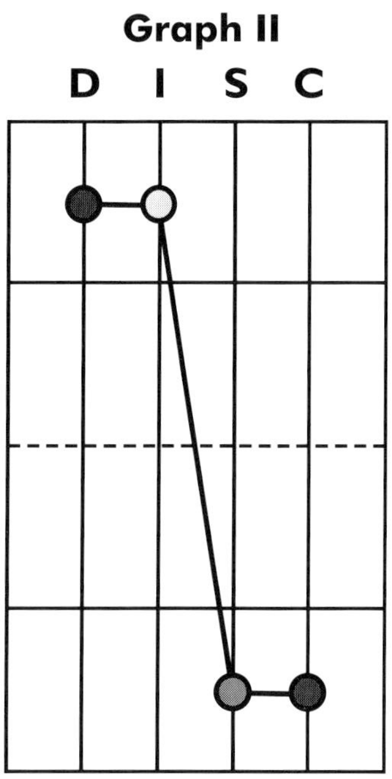

A High D, High I, Low S, Low C person goes to church. The environment calls for the person to adapt their behavior to Low D, Low I, High S, High C. A person can tolerate this type of change for a period of time. The time expands if the person's passion, beliefs and value needs are being met. The same person experiences the same adapted behavior when they work on doing their tax returns. Excessive time spent in an activity that a person sees of little or no value can cause stress. This is the reason many salespeople have resisted call reporting systems.

FACTOR MOVEMENT

Factor movement is the change between Graph I and Graph II – job related. By this we mean: Is Graph I mirroring the Work Environment Graph? If the answer is "yes," then the adapted behavior will enhance performance on the job.

If Graph I is significantly different from the Work Environment Graph, we must do a little detective work. The person could be adapting behavior for any of the following reasons:

1. **Trying to survive.**
2. **Guarding their rear-end.**
3. **Don't understand the behavior needed to be successful on the job.**
4. **Searching to discover who they really are.**

Any movement in a factor indicates you are adapting your behavior to meet the demands of your current environment. Always look at the direction of the movement from the intensity of each factor in Graph II (least).

The following information will provide insights into typically what the movement means. However, until you analyze the environment we can only give you some ideas as to what typical movement means. Why a person is adapting their style is important to discover. A person may adapt their behavior in Graph I (most) to survive or succeed. Care should be taken to discover the true motive behind the change. If it is job related, the person is adapting to succeed. If the change is not job related, then security may be an issue.

WHAT FACTOR MOVEMENT MEANS

Example One:

GRAPH I

D I S C

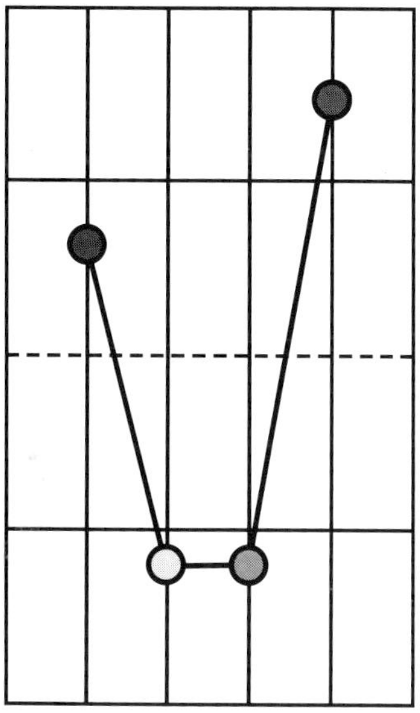

GRAPH II

D I S C

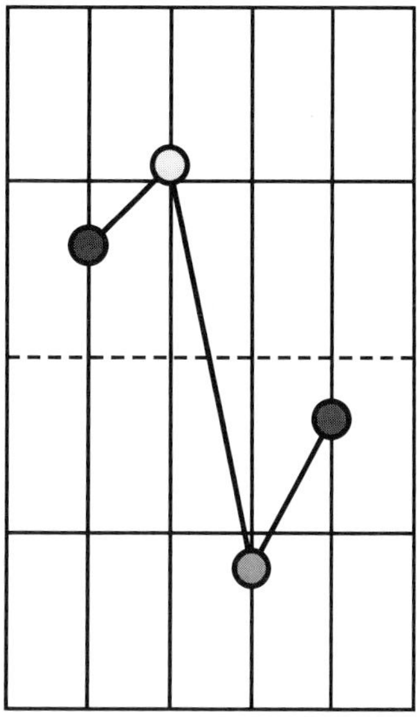

(Up or down movement based on change from Graph II)

D Not significant movement.
I Moves down.
S Not significant movement.
C Moves up.

Possible interpretation

I Lowering trust level.
C Responding to procedures (security, concerns).

Typically when we see this type of situation, the person has been hurt in a relationship or laid off from a job. They are lowering their "I" factor to guard from being hurt by being too trusting. This experience has led them to meet their security needs by following procedures or not taking risks.

WHAT FACTOR MOVEMENT TYPICALLY MEANS

Direction determined from Graph II (least) to Graph I (most).

D goes up	Become more assertive and challenge-oriented.
D goes down	Become less assertive.
I goes up	Become more outgoing and people-oriented.
I goes down	Become less trusting, guard what you share.
S goes up	Slow the world down.
S goes down	Increase activity level and pace.
C goes up	Respond to procedures, lower risk taking or protect security.
C goes down	Become more independent, be your own person.

Graph disparity should be a concern to all when the change is significant. An open discussion will usually lead to discovery of the real reason for adapting new behavior.

Note: Many or most unemployed people raise their "C" factor in Graph I. This is a response to society's rules. When unemployed you must call, write, interview, etc.

Currently, many employees who were fortunate enough not to get a pink slip or fired raise their "C" factor. They are adapting behavior so they are not the next person out the door. This is their response to their security needs.

DISPARITY & CORRELATION

Example Two:

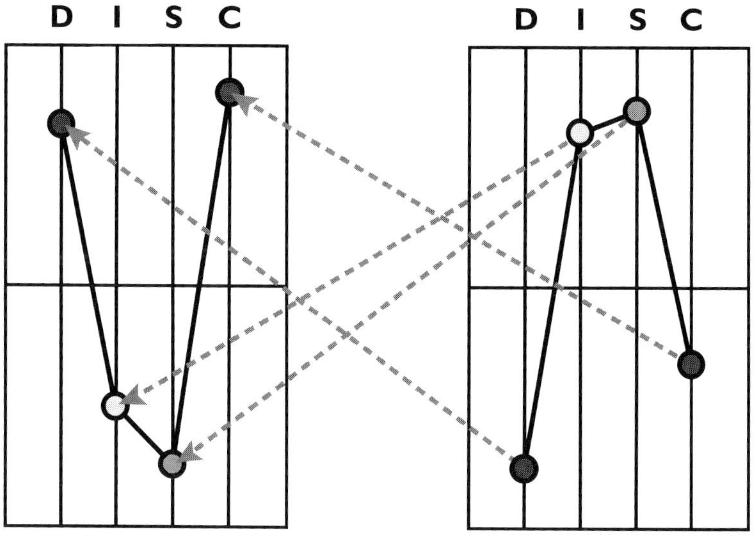

Research conducted by Dr. David Warburton and Judy Suiter indicates that the disparity between Graph I and Graph II has a correlation with job satisfaction, health problems and stress. Although further research needs to be completed, the initial finding shows that when there is disparity between Graphs I and II, job satisfaction goes down over a period of time and health problems increase. Common sense also tells us that an introverted person would probably not be very happy as an outside salesperson and an extroverted person would not fit into an accounting profession handling data all day long. The person in Example 2 masks their true behavior in order to succeed in their environment (Graph I). This person is expending a great amount of energy to maintain the mask and admitted to being under a great deal of stress.

DISPARITY & CORRELATION

Example Three:

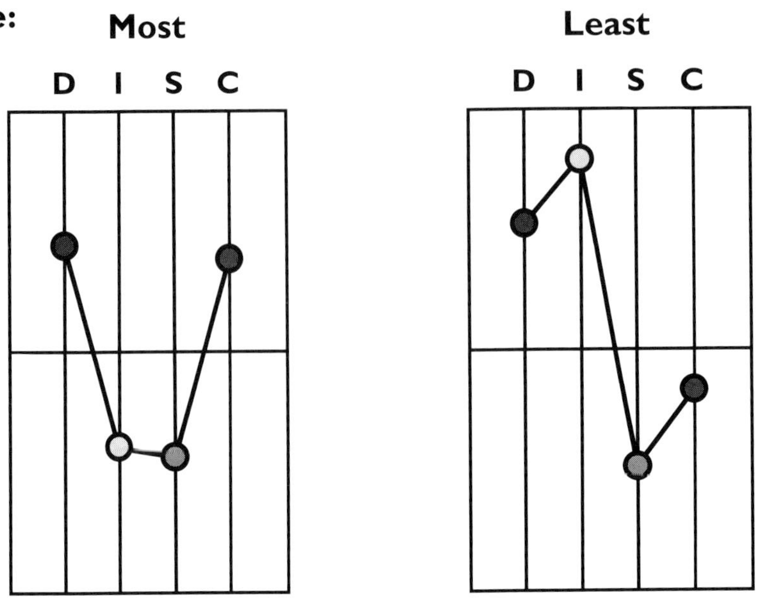

No Disparity:

D The plotting point of the D factor in both graphs is about the same.

S The plotting point of the S factor in both graphs is about the same.

Disparity:

I Note the High I in Graph II is a Low I in Graph I. Emotionally, this person normally displays a great deal of optimism and trust (Graph II), but in his work environment (Graph I) is displaying pessimism and distrust. Why?

This question should be asked, and dialogue can resolve the difference.

C Note the C movement from just below the Energy Line in Graph II to a very high intensity of Graph I. Naturally, this person tends to follow rules depending on the situation. However, in the work environment, this person is totally following established rules and procedures. Emotionally, the person is displaying in Graph I a high degree of fear. Why?

Again, the question should be asked and dialogued.

DISPARITY & CORRELATION

Note: It has been validated that when a person is afraid of losing his/her job, the C factor will rise to a high intensity in Graph I.

More research needs to be done on the effect masking has on mental and emotional health and well being. Graph I and Graph II disparity has a definite effect on stress, mental ill-health, and job satisfaction, as proven by research of Dr. David Warburton and Judy Suiter.

STEP 4

Repeat the Process for Graph I (adapted)

Use this 4-step process in conjunction with Style Insights™ Instrument Graph I for greater behavioral understanding of their adapted behavior. TTI software reads the graphs in a similar manner analyzing both the high and low intensity levels in Graphs I and II.

UNUSUAL GRAPHS

Although the Style Insights Instrument is designed to measure NORMAL BEHAVIOR, there are three graphs that can occur which indicate unusual behavior. The Style Insights Instrument is not a clinical instrument; however, it is used by many professionals as a tool to assist people in understanding their behavior. The three unusual patterns must be approached based on their occurrence in either Graph I or Graph II.

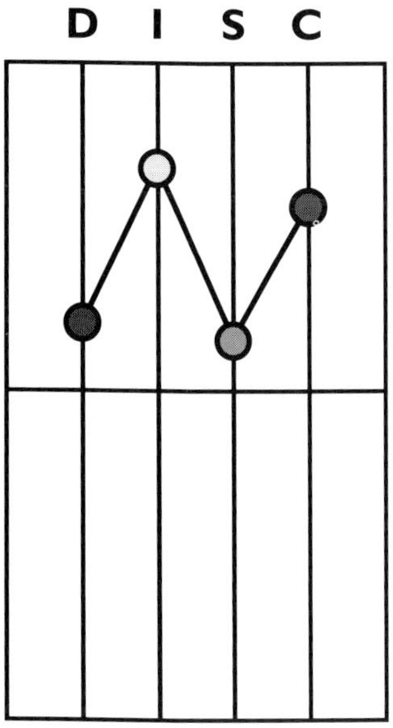

Over shift
All plotting points above the energy line.

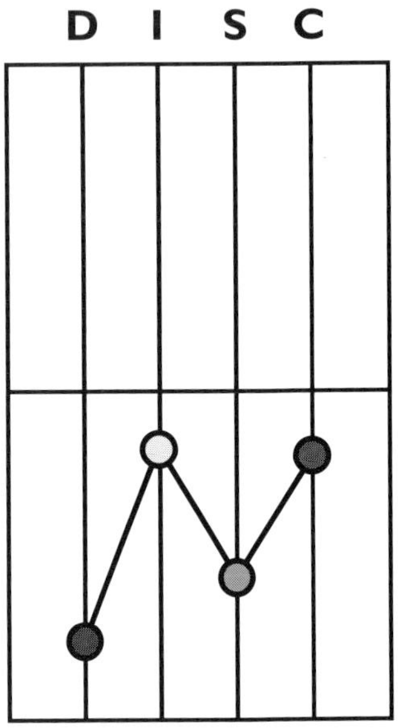

Under shift
All plotting points below the energy line.

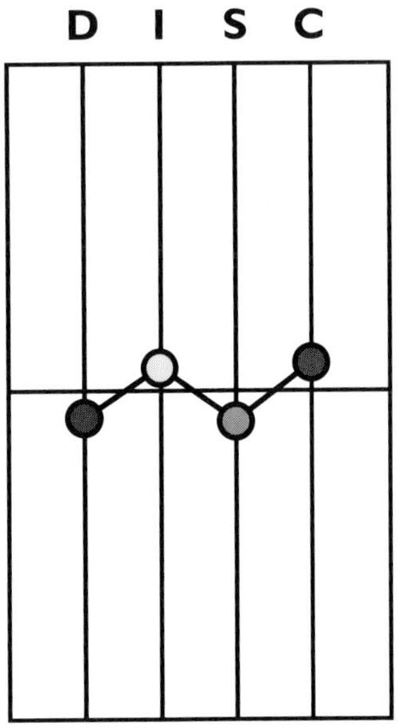

Tight
All plotting points near the energy line (40 to 60 percent).

When observing an unusual graph, first check to see if the instrument was scored properly. If proper scoring has occurred, another cause may be an inability to understand the word choices. The Style Insights Instrument has an sixth grade reading level, and therefore has virtually eliminated the problem with understanding word choices. Further causes must be investigated.

UNUSUAL GRAPHS

Unusual graphs (Over shift – Under shift –Tight) in Graph I may be caused by the following reasons:

1. **Attempting to outsmart the instrument.**
2. **Trying to be an overachiever.**
3. **Overanalyzing by taking too long to respond.**
4. **Being new to the job and not understanding the behavior required to be successful.**
5. **Transition from one environment to another.**

Unusual patterns in Graph I are usually temporary. Having the person respond to another instrument with a proper focus will usually develop the proper graph. Also, a person new to the job needs to wait a few weeks before responding to the second instrument, so they have the opportunity to determine the correct work behavior. Use the Work Environment Instrument to discover the behavior needed by the job and then discuss the results.

Unusual graphs (Over shift – Under shift – Tight) in Graph II can be caused by a person who is:

1. **Attempting to outsmart the instrument.**
2. **Overanalyzing by taking too long to respond.**
3. **Experiencing a significant emotional event or a personal trauma (Tight Graph only).**
4. **Under pressure to "be all things to all people" (Over shift Graph only).**

UNUSUAL GRAPHS

When an unusual pattern appears in Graph II, ask the person to retake the assessment. Then if the same pattern appears, it should be taken seriously. This person is experiencing discomfort and the result will have a direct effect on performance. Many times professional help is needed for this person to discover who he/she really is, or what factors are influencing his/her graph results.

Occurrence in population of Unusual Graphs (N = 22,771):

	Graph I	Graph II
Over shift	**3.45%**	**0.18%**
Under shift	**0**	**0**

In a sample of 22,771 people, the under shift pattern never occurred. Exact data is not available on the tight pattern, although it occurs less than 3% of the time.

TTI'S SUCCESS INSIGHTS WHEEL®

The Success Insights Wheel was added to reports to visually enhance the understanding of one's behavior both naturally and in the work environment. TTI is the first and only behavioral software company to use a wheel page to plot behavior. The Success Insights Wheel has proven its value by increasing the overall understanding of TTI reports, decreasing the time needed to train, and eliminating the need for clients to be able to read graphs.

Why was the Success Insights Wheel developed? TTI believes that visual aids are an important component in learning. People especially benefit from learning the DISC concept and language through a visual model that is easily understood, such as the Success Insights Wheel. The Wheel provides a visual format for plotting the data obtained from the Style Insights response form. The Wheel model is another, and, we believe, an easier method of introducing DISC.

The Wheel can be used to demonstrate the behavioral differences between a person's Natural Style, Adapted Style and Work Environment. In addition, the DISC professional can plot an entire team's behavioral composition and identify potential conflicts at a glance.

TTI is the first behavioral software company to use a wheel page to explain behavior. The Success Insights Wheel has been used by TTI's Success Insight's European Distributors for years. It has proven its value by eliminating the need for your clients to have graph reading skills.

TTI'S SUCCESS INSIGHTS WHEEL®

How to interpret the Success Insights Wheel

The Success Insights Wheel uses the 60 most common graphs. The graphs are plotted on the Wheel according to all points above the energy line. The Wheel model uses 48 basic graphs with 12 exceptions. A person's high factor determines the quadrant in which the graph will appear. (The TTI Success Insights reports are generated based on 384 graphs, which represent 324 more individualized graph interpretations.)

The Wheel is made up of eight different spokes, which are:

Relater	**I, S**
Supporter	**S**
Coordinator	**S, C**
Analyzer	**C**
Implementor	**D, C**
Conductor	**D**
Persuader	**D, I**
Promoter	**I**

WHEEL APPLICATIONS

Why is this person adapting?

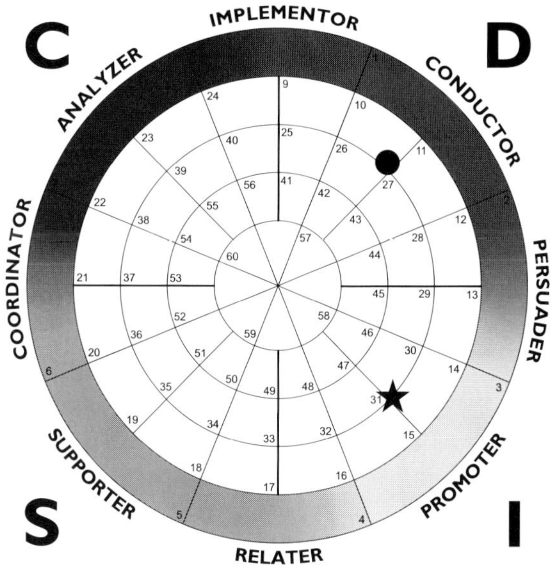

● **Natural**

★ **Adapted**

How will Person A and Person B get along?

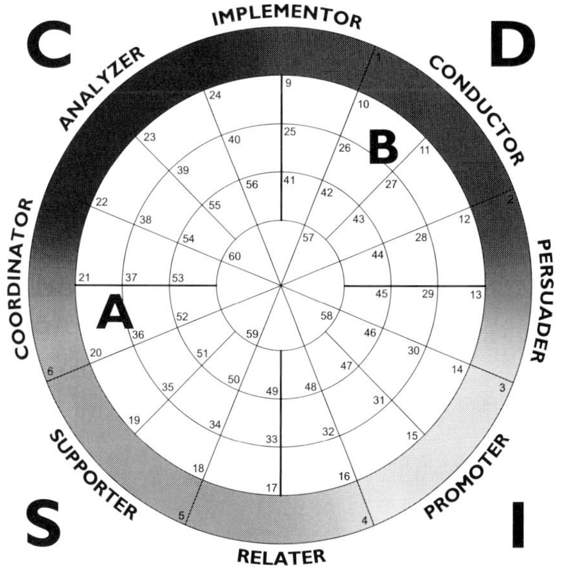

WHEEL APPLICATIONS

A person adapting behavior due to job related issues.

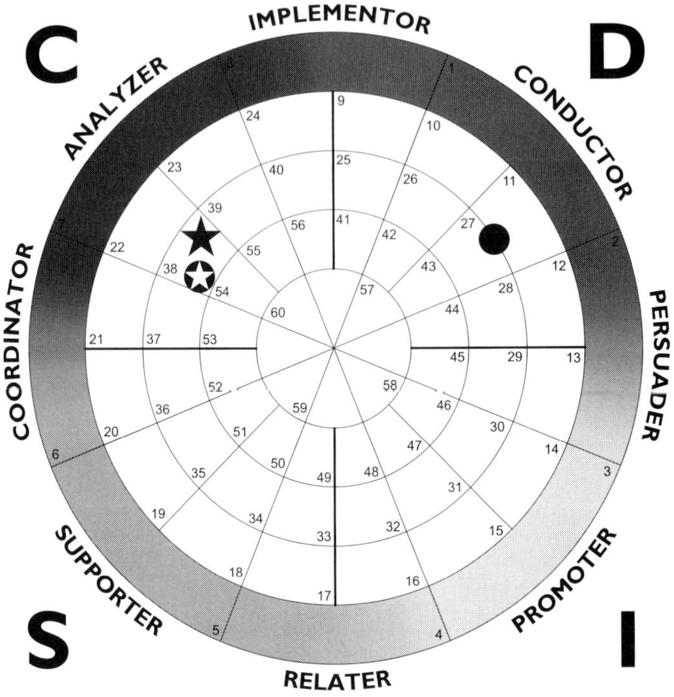

● **Natural**

★ **Adapted**

✪ **Job**

OBJECTIVES REVISITED

Our research proves that the mastering of these objectives is directly related to your success.

CHAPTER 6
Blending the Language

Chapter Objective:
To move from basic to more advanced knowledge and application of the language by examining compatibility and blending of the different styles.

Chapter Contents:
- Introduction
- Blending the Language: Style Combinations
- High D blending
- High I blending
- High S blending
- High C blending
- Objective Revisited

"I didn't say that I didn't say it. I said that I didn't say that I said it. I want to make that perfectly clear."
–George Romney

INTRODUCTION

PEOPLE GENERALLY MAKE THE MISTAKE OF ASSUMING THAT OTHERS INTERACT AND THINK IN THE SAME WAY THEY DO.

One of the biggest challenges to effective interaction is to recognize that people may have a behavioral style different from our own. Much interaction breaks down immediately because of a lack of awareness of behavioral differences. People do not all communicate alike. Effective communicators will first:

1. **Learn their own behavioral style.**
2. **Recognize others' behavioral style.**
3. **Cognitively adapt their behavior for greater communication.**

One of the most important skills to acquire is the ability to interact effectively with people at all levels of the organization. According to Zig Ziglar in *Top Performance,* over 80% of the people who move up in corporations are promoted because of their people skills, NOT technical ability.

Most people already adapt their behavior to the environment. The DISC language provides the knowledge to be able to adapt more quickly to the person by observing behavioral cues.

BLENDING THE LANGUAGE: STYLE COMBINATIONS

Understanding how the different styles "blend" will allow for a more thorough understanding of the DISC language and its powerful impact on interpersonal relationships and work interactions.

The DISC model interprets NEEDS behavior, or HOW we act. Most relational problems, either work, social, or personal, are based on conflicting beliefs (values). DISC does not measure an individual's values. Many people who have conflicting behavioral styles (DISC) have had long, successful relationships. Why? Understanding and adapting.

Note: An individual whose highest plotting point in Graph II is the "D" factor is referred to as a High D in this chapter (likewise with the I, S, and C factors). Please remember, "how" a person acts is determined by the intensity of all four factors, high and low.

Behavioral Style Match (BSM)

This rating, either good or fair, indicates how well the styles will initially blend and how much a person must adapt in order to effectively communicate. It is followed by a graphic visual showing the "comfort zone" and the "discomfort zone" of the interaction.

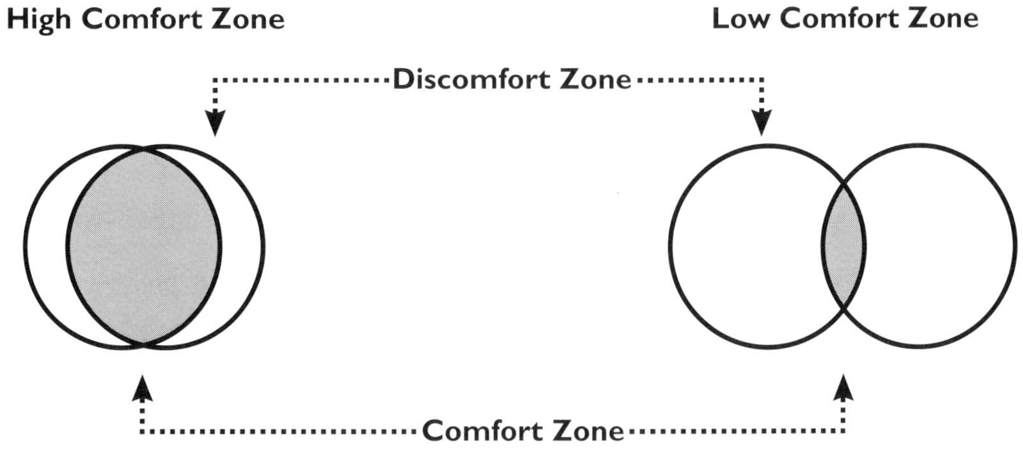

BLENDING THE LANGUAGE:

FIRST IMPRESSIONS & SOCIAL INTERACTIONS
How Your Style May Initially React with Various Styles

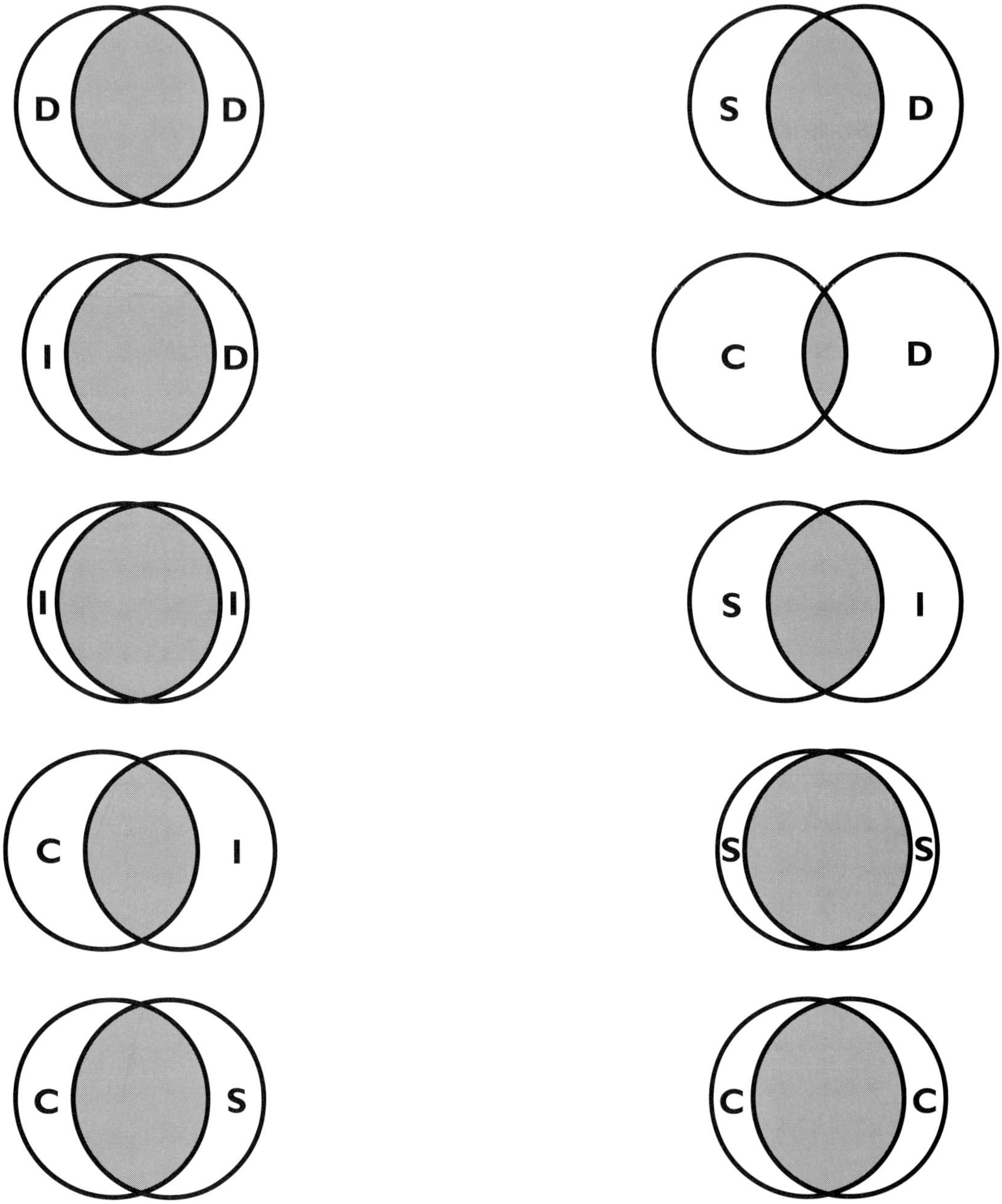

HIGH D BLENDING

High D – High D
High D communicating with a High D

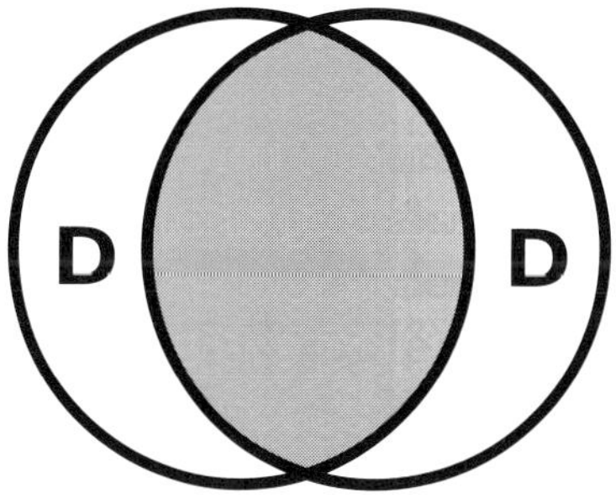

BSM: Good

High D's are competitive, direct and self-reliant. Two High D's will understand each other's drive for action. Both need a challenge and both need to direct. Expect the discussion between the two to be lively, as both are unafraid of conflict. If a vision and purpose is clearly painted, the High D's can work together well to get it done. Both are high-risk takers and may need to slow down in order to look at the facts. Because of their tendency to be task-oriented, each will need to heighten their awareness of the other and cognitively take time to listen before acting.

High D is looking for: RESULTS/EFFICIENCY

High D-High I
High D communicating with a High I

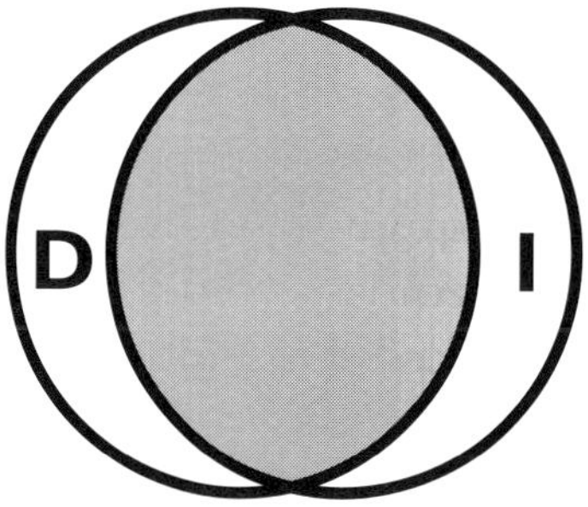

BSM: Good

The High D and High I both share a sense of urgency, risk-taking and desire to change their environment and the world, for better or worse (depending on their values). Both extroverted, they differ in the way they approach people. The High I will use verbal ability to win others to their argument, whereas the High D will be very direct and to the point. Working well together, the High D will need to add a little fun to the task and slow down just a bit, knowing that interaction and fun are motivating to the High I. The High D must allow the High I to verbalize and also must allow a bit more time for the decisions to be made.

High I is looking for: The EXPERIENCE

HIGH D BLENDING

High D-High S
High D communicating with a High S

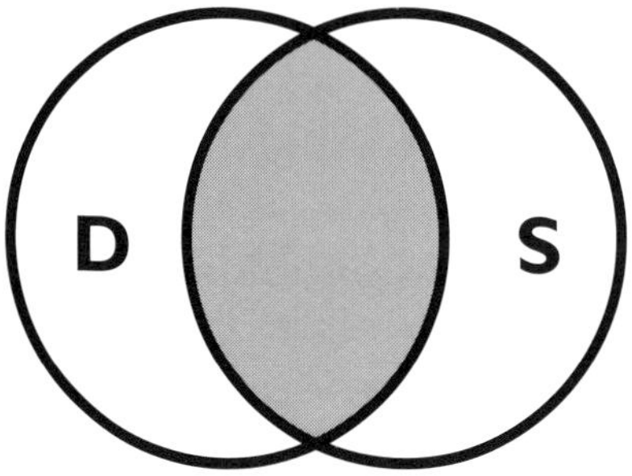

BSM: Fair

The High D will have a tendency to overpower the High S because of the High D's sense of urgency and high risk. The High D will need to slow down significantly, making sure the High S has the time to process the information given. The High S is a moderately low risk taker, requiring time to think. Desiring harmony, the High S may have a tendency to "go along", even though disagreeing with the High D. Non-emotional by nature, the High S will not show emotion. Lack of emotional display must not be confused with agreement. The High D must work hard to develop a trust relationship that allows the High S the comfort to verbalize concerns. This means the High D will need to work hard at listening.

High S is looking for: SECURITY

High D-High C
High D communicating with a High C

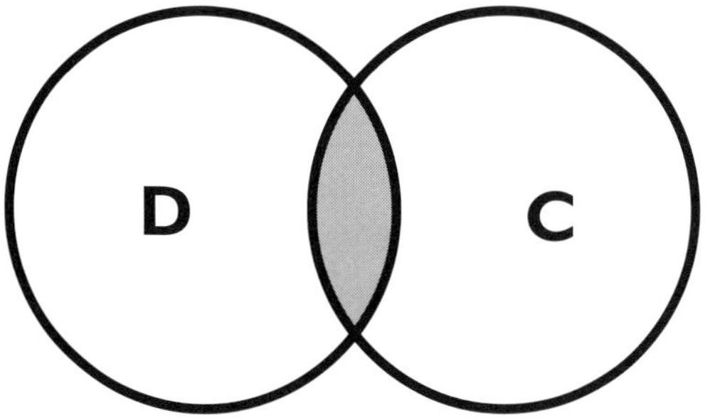

BSM: Fair

Fast mover to a slow mover. High risk to low risk. Little need for data compared to a great need for data. Quick decision maker to a slow decision maker. The High D will need to adapt extremely to increase the communication with the High C. The greatest challenge for the High D is to slow down and get the facts. The High D needs to give more information than normal but not talk personally with the High C or be too pushy. Both the High D and High C share a need to use time wisely and to control their environment.

High C is looking for: INFORMATION

HIGH I BLENDING

High I-High D
High I communicating with a High D

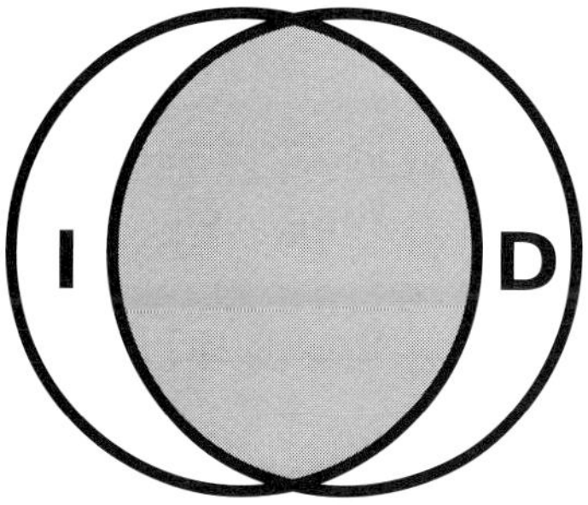

BSM: Good

High I's tend to be very verbal in their efforts to persuade someone to their point of view. A good behavioral match, as both styles are extroverted and see the big picture. The High I will need to be more direct with the High D and not beat around the bush in the discussion. Also, the High I will need to allow the High D to carry the conversation and work on asking more questions instead of telling the answers. The boldness and directness of the High D may be somewhat intimidating to the High I, causing the High I to give ground when ground should not be given. Being aware of the fact that the High D likes a battle, the High I can maintain their position without fear of loss.

High D is looking for: RESULTS/EFFICIENCY

High I-High I
High I communicating with a High I

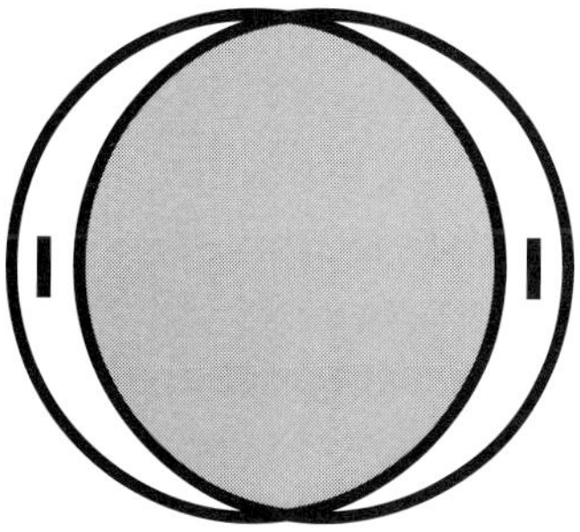

BSM: Good

High I's have creative, high-risk ideas but often need other styles to help keep their feet on the ground. Two High I's together will have a tremendous amount of fun. Make sure that the task completion and accomplishment is there, as the people-focus can easily cause them to get off track. Set strict schedules and deadlines, as the time management could be a possible problem.

High I is looking for: The EXPERIENCE

HIGH I BLENDING

High I-High S
High I communicating with a High S

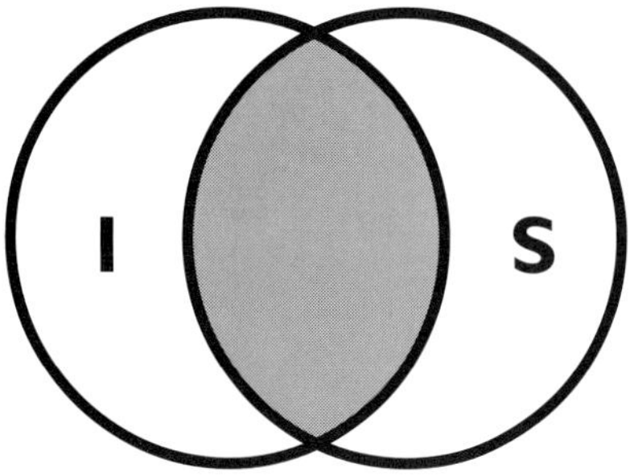

BSM: Fair

The High I will definitely enjoy a commonality with the High S in the area of people orientation. Both styles share the need for warmth and interaction on a personal level. The High I will need to tone down their approach, as it will be viewed by the High S as overly enthusiastic or perhaps insincere and pushy. The High I also has a greater sense of urgency and a higher risk factor than that of the High S. So the command for the High I is to tone down, slow down and encourage the High S to interact. Again, don't assume that the non-emotional nature of the High S is an indication of agreement. You will probably not know what the High S is thinking unless you are told. Therefore, the High I must talk less and ask more questions hoping to build a trust relationship.

High S is looking for: SECURITY

High I-High C
High I communicating with a High C

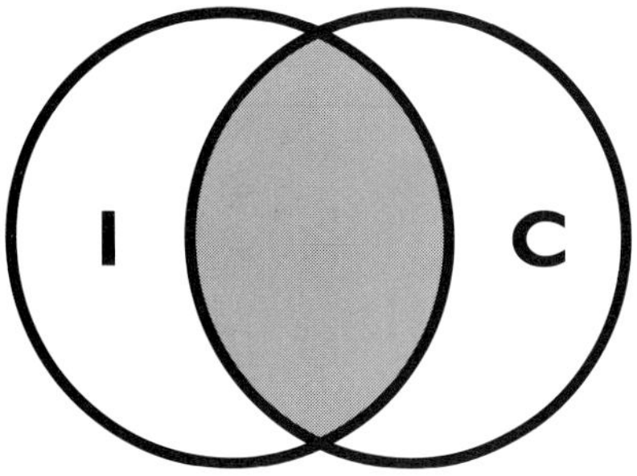

BSM: Fair

The High I will have few, if any, behavioral commonalties with the High C. This behavioral match is the toughest of all for the High I. Extrovert to an introvert. Feeling style to a data-oriented style. High risk to a low risk. Indirect style to a direct style. A trusting style to an un-trusting style. The High C is the challenge for the High I. However, if both can capitalize on their behavioral strengths, this can be an incredible team. The High I will have to slow down, keep a tight rein on emotions and provide the necessary data to the High C. Personal talk is not allowed as the private life of the High C is exactly that—private. The High I will need to reduce gestures and definitely not touch the High C.

High C is looking for: INFORMATION

HIGH S BLENDING

High S-High D
High S communicating with a High D

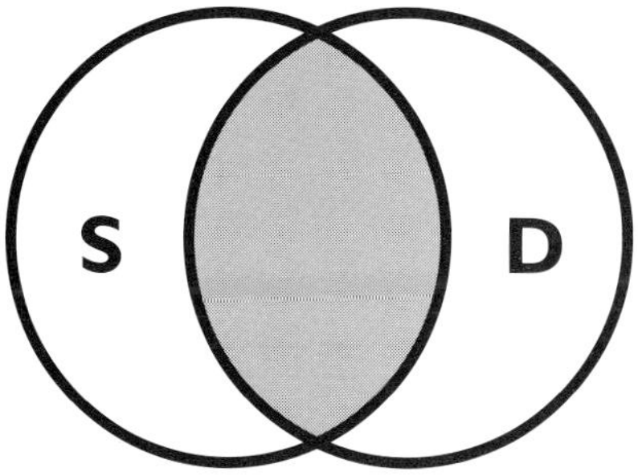

BSM: Fair

Slow pace dealing with a faster pace. People orientation compared to talk orientation. Slow decision maker to a fast decision maker. The High S will need to adapt to communicate effectively with the High D. The basic adaptation will be to pick up the pace, cover only the high points and be more direct with the High D. The High D will usually like and respect someone who is direct and straightforward. The High S will have to make sure not to be overpowered by the High D. The tendency of the High S will be to go along for the sake of harmony and peace. Going along is fine, as long as the High S agrees on the direction the High D is going. It will be difficult, but the High S must stand up to the High D. The best approach is to utilize a questioning method, forcing the High D to defend their position.

High D is looking for: RESULTS/EFFICIENCY

High S-High I
High S communicating with a High I

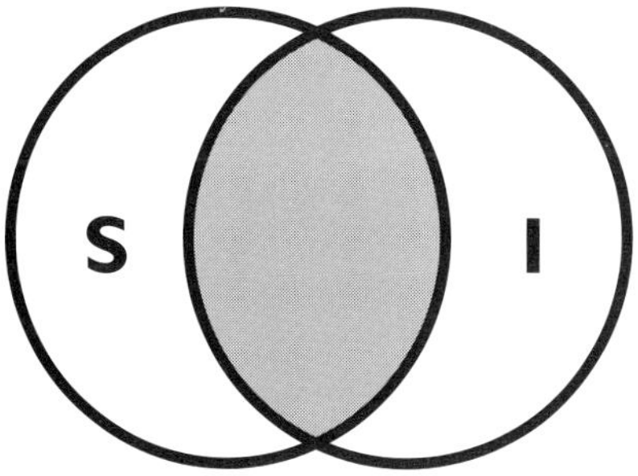

BSM: Good

Both of these styles share a need for warmth and interaction, as well as a need to verbalize. Both styles are also very people oriented and are concerned about the effect of their behavior on others. The High S is relatively low risk, compared to the high-risk nature of the High I. The High S will tend to be a much slower decision maker that the High I, as well as being more methodical and systematic. The High S should loosen up with the High I to allow for more freedom and fun and at the same time, provide opportunities for the High I to verbalize. Find ways to support the ideas of the High I and encourage creativity and innovation. A good behavioral match, mostly because of their people focus, the High S and High I should interact well.

High I is looking for: The EXPERIENCE

HIGH S BLENDING

High S-High S
High S communicating with a High S

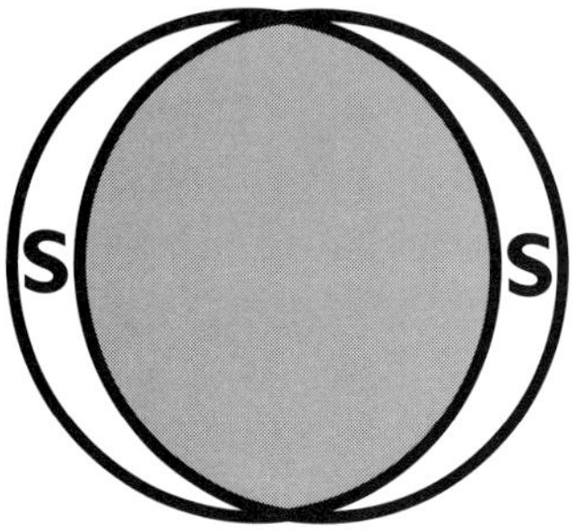

BSM: Good

An excellent behavioral match, two High S's will get along great with each other. Both will have a high task and high people orientation. Both will also have a strong need for closure. Their risk factor may be too low, which could cause them not to achieve their entire potential. Decision-making could also be too slow or too late; but in terms of compatibility, a High S –High S match very well.

High S is looking for: SECURITY

High S-High C
High S communicating with a High C

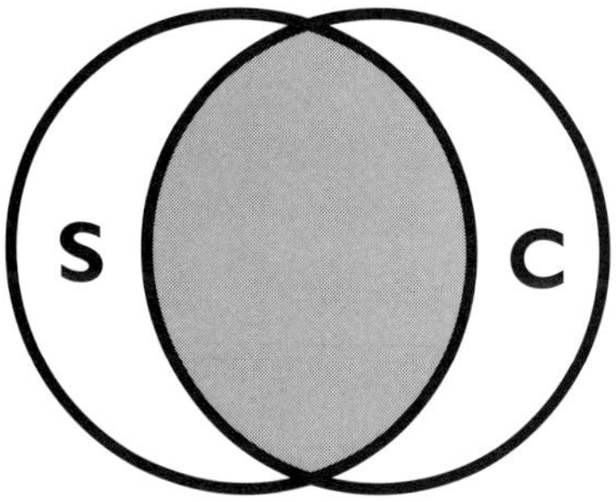

BSM: Good

The High S and the High C both share a need for a low risk, cooperative environment whether on the job or at home. Both tend to have methods and procedures they follow. The main difference between the High S and the High C is that the C is more focused on data and the S is more people oriented. When dealing with change, the High S will need enough information to feel comfortable with the situation, while the High C will need adequate data in order to prove the change is for the better.

High C is looking for: INFORMATION

HIGH C BLENDING

High C-High D
High C communicating with a High D

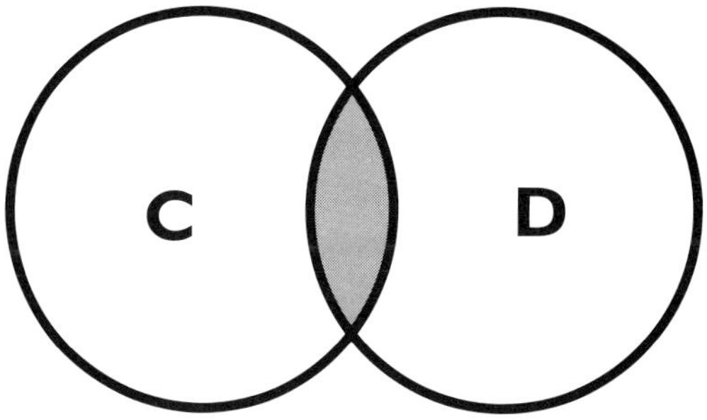

BSM: Fair

Both the High C and the High D are task oriented. The area of potential conflict lies in the arena of speed and risk orientation. The low risk of the High C vs. the high risk of the High D. Slow decision-making requiring a great deal of data as opposed to fast decision making requiring little data. Both are alike in that they have high expectations of each other, but this may cause the C to be too critical and the D to be too demanding (depending on their values). However, awareness of their behavioral differences can give birth to a fantastic team.

High D is looking for: RESULTS/EFFICIENCY

High C-High I
High C communicating with a High I

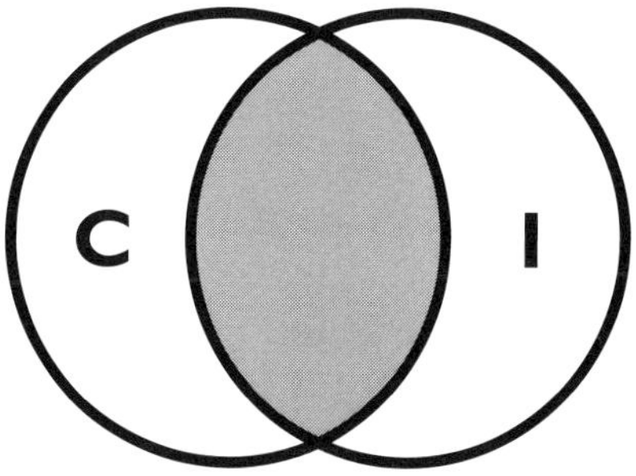

BSM: Fair

The High C – High I relationship is, behaviorally, the most difficult. Introverted to extroverted. Pessimistic to optimistic. Slow decision maker to fast decision maker. Low risk to high risk. Point after point seems to cause the High C and High I to clash. The High C will have to really loosen up and become more like a High I. By becoming more people focused, more fun and excited, the High C can adapt to create a winning communication with the High I. The High C must pick up the pace, using questions as a means to direct the High I to the desired conclusion. Move methodically to the desired goal allowing the High I to verbalize along the way.

High I is looking for: The EXPERIENCE

HIGH C BLENDING

High C-High S
High C communicating with a High S

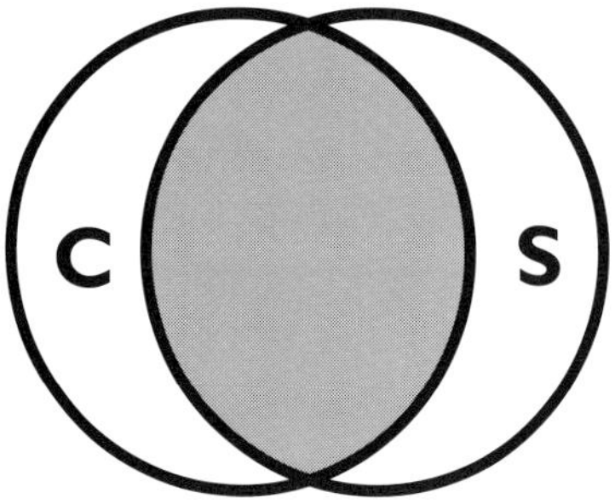

BSM: Good

The High C and the High S both share a need for a low risk, cooperative environment whether on the job or at home. Both tend to have methods and procedures that they follow. The main difference between the High S and the High C is that the C is more focused on data and S is more people oriented. When dealing with change, the High S will need enough information to feel comfortable with the situation, while the High C will need adequate data in order to prove the change is for the better.

High S is looking for: SECURITY

High C-High C
High C communicating with a High C

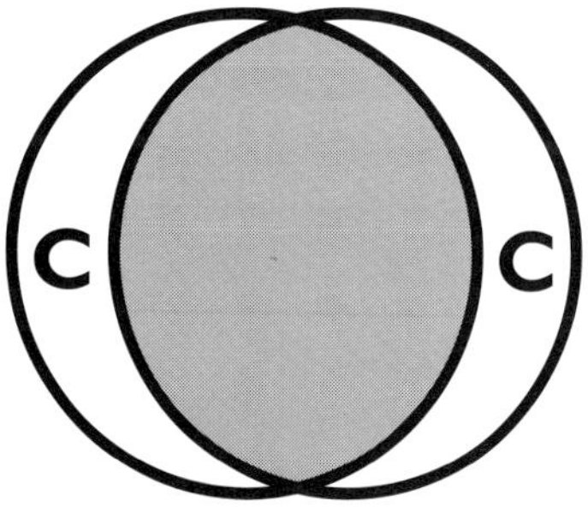

BSM: Good

Two High C's tend to have great relationships at home and on the job because they both share the strong tendency of needing procedure and order. Also, they have a need to gather data and thoroughly examine the facts before making a decision. Both low risk, slow decision makers and task oriented, the High C's tend to get along very well. However, one area of frustration could appear due to their perfectionist tendencies. Overall, an excellent behavioral match.

High C is looking for: INFORMATION

OBJECTIVES REVISITED

Importance of Blending:

- People do not all communicate alike.
- BSM indicates how styles initially blend.
- Interacting with people at all levels is an important skill to acquire.
- The STYLE INSIGHTS INSTRUMENT can make blending styles immediate.

Authors' Note:

Any behavioral styles can learn to work well together. Usually in training, when the individuals are made aware of behavioral differences and understand that the differences are not right or wrong, more of a behavioral tolerance and appreciation is developed. Breakdowns in relationships most often are a result of conflict in the area of values. Although this chapter defines need-related conflicts, these can and are overcome often, mostly through training on the DISC language. By being aware of possible communication problems, the student of the DISC language can immediately adapt their behavior for better communication.

CHAPTER 7

Reading the Job: Using the Work Environment Analysis

Chapter Objective:
To use the Work Environment Analysis to explore the behavioral demands of a job, providing the employee and manager with valuable information used to meet those demands.

Chapter Contents:
- Introduction
- Who should use the Work Environment?
- Uses
- Master Job Graph
- Using the Software Report
- How to Use Menu Options
- Objectives Revisited

"Put your personnel work FIRST because it is most important."
-General Robert Wood

INTRODUCTION

The Work Environment Instrument was developed to provide a systematic and comprehensive way of exploring the behavior demanded by various jobs. Most jobs have a job description or a list of duties and responsibilities. A job description rarely tells us anything more than what the person is to do in the job; it leaves out how he is to do it and when it must be done. Work Environment identifies all the human factors that are absent in job descriptions.

If we were to take the duties and responsibilities of any position and identify the amount of time spent completing each duty and responsibility in a given week, we could compile the amount of time spent on the various activities. By analyzing the activity and the behavior required for its successful completion, we could determine the amount of time spent dealing with the various human factors. We could then discover the dominant human factors that are present in the position.

Management by Objectives is a system for identifying and prioritizing duties and responsibilities of a position. Using this system to identify and prioritize, we discover that a manager and subordinate rarely see the position in the same light. For example: if you were to ask the manager and the subordinate to look at the duties of the job, list those duties, and prioritize those duties in order of importance, you would discover that they would not agree in most cases, either upon the duties or the priority of those duties. As often as managers and subordinates disagree on what are the top 1 to 3 priorities, they also differ many times on their perceptions of the behavior required to be successful in a position.

The combination of the Style Insights and Work Environment instruments allows us to analyze not only what behavior the person brings to the job, but also the behavior required to be successful in that job. This system allows us to analyze both the behavior of the person and the behavior required by the job. It also helps the person decide whether or not he or she is willing to pay the price for success.

INTRODUCTION

When a person is hired to do a job that requires the same behavior he/she brings to the job, several things happen: One, the individual can immediately focus energy on completion of the job itself. Two, he/she will enjoy doing the job because of the natural match with his instinctive behavior. By contrast, those people who bring different behavior to the job than what the job demands must first focus energy on adjusting their behavior to the job. After expending this energy to bring about the behavioral change, they can then use what energy is left to perform the duties of the job. Some jobs can be so stressful in forcing individuals to be something they are not, there is little energy left for the completion of the job.

An example of this type of conflict would be a person who is very aggressive and outgoing, has a tremendous sense of urgency, and likes to follow his/her own rules and regulations who is placed in a position that requires attaining high quality, following many rules, following the system to perfection, and starting and finishing one activity at a time. The person described would be under stress in the completion of the required tasks and would only stay with the job if he/she could not find another one, which met his/her natural behavioral instincts.

Anytime two people have different perceptions of the same job, the result will be a poor evaluation or substandard performance. For example: Several years ago a manager giving a performance evaluation to a subordinate made the parting comment, "You'd better shape up or you will be fired!" The subordinate responded, "What do I have to do to shape up?" The manager responded with, "All I know is that you'd better shape up or you will be fired!"

This example is an indication that many managers lack the skills to assist their employees in meeting the behavioral demands of the job. This particular position was a certified one; and the person had met all the educational qualifications for the job, but by the manager's perception was not meeting the behavioral qualifications of the job.

WHO SHOULD USE THE WORK ENVIRONMENT?

Both managers and their subordinates participate in this system. The manager's responsibility is to develop the Master Job Graph or Job Report. This will allow a comparison of all people performing that particular job to the Master Job Report.

To establish a Master Job Graph, more than one person should respond to the Work Environment Instrument. Three or four people who know and understand the job should participate. If all participants see the job in the same light, then a report may be generated from that particular graph. If there are differing viewpoints, then have the managers negotiate each statement and respond to another Work Environment Instrument. Using the negotiated Work Environment Instrument, a Master Job Graph may be generated.

All present employees should respond to the Work Environment Instrument as they perceive their job. By running the software program with their perceptions as compared to the Master Job Graph, we can determine all areas where they see the job differently. It is also very helpful to have new employees respond to a Work Environment Instrument for the same purpose. Again, we can make comparisons by using all of the menus available on the software. Sometimes it helps to have prospective employees fill out the Work Environment Instrument with regard to an "ideal job". This gives an indication of the type of behavior that the person would LIKE to be using on the job.

WORK ENVIRONMENT USES

The Work Environment System may be used for the following:

- Master Job Graph description
- Job applicants
- Revitalizing and redirecting the present staff
- Stress evaluation
- Performance evaluation

The software designed to work in conjunction with the Work Environment Instrument contains the following menu:

1. Job only.
2. (Jane's) perception of the job.

Comparison reports can be generated from the print menu, which can be two perceptions of the job or a candidate vs. the job.

By using one or more of the menus available on the software, a report may be generated showing side by side all the pertinent information with regard to the four dimensions of behavior:

Problems (D)

People (I)

Pace (S)

Procedures (C)

MASTER JOB GRAPH

Establishing a Master Job Graph is just as important as writing a job description. Each business should establish the Master Job Graph for its own jobs and not use an example from another company. Ownership and commitment to the type of behavior required is essential to the successful application of the Work Environment System. If a job description is available, have all those participating in the exercise read it. After reading the job description, have at least four people respond to the Work Environment Instrument. Remind each person to keep his focus on the job, itself, and the behavior required as he reads each statement. Do not let personal bias, such as "how I like to do the job" or "how the job has been done in the past", influence the response to the instrument.

After each person has completed the Work Environment Instrument, score each instrument and run a report so that each person's perceptions can be better understood. Negotiate until all agree on the graph points and then run the new Master Job Report.

JOB APPLICANTS

When hiring new employees, it is much easier to learn what the applicant perceives the job to be by using the Work Environment Instrument. First, the applicant completes the instrument, imagining what his "ideal job" would be. Then the applicant responds to a second Work Environment Instrument, completing the instrument as he "perceives the successful functioning of the job" for which he is applying. This procedure will allow comparison of the applicant's ideal job with the behavior needed in the job.

REVITALIZING AND REDIRECTING PRESENT STAFF

Low productivity is often caused by a lack of understanding of the behavior the job requires. This may be addressed by developing a Master Job Graph and having all employees who perform that job respond to a Work Environment Instrument. This will identify any area in which the employee has misdirected his energy.

WORK ENVIRONMENT USES

STRESS EVALUATION

An employee whose behavior fits the job requirements experiences less stress and is more productive. The Work Environment can be significant in examining the behavioral and environmental indicators. For example, would a High D or High I feel uncomfortable in a High C job? Probably! Not only would they feel uncomfortable, but they may take more time off work for "illness", be more accident-prone on the job, and have a lower productivity rate than the quality-conscious High C in the same job.

If you find a High D in a High C job, does it mean he/she should be fired? NO!! It does mean there should be some discussion between managers and employees regarding job roles. Perhaps there can be adjustments in the manner in which the job is completed, or perhaps there are some modifications of the job, which could be made so a person with High D behavior would function more effectively.

PERFORMANCE EVALUATION

Managers evaluate performance based on their perceptions. Subordinates tend to perform jobs based on their perceptions. Performance evaluation provides a valuable opportunity to use the Work Environment as a comparison of each person's perception of a job. If perceptions are different, the result is often poor evaluation and/or low productivity. By letting the instrument raise the critical issues, decisions can remain focused on the job. Performance evaluations can be done on a positive basis with new energy focused on the new action plan developed from the resulting dialogue.

USING THE SOFTWARE REPORT

The reports were written to provide you with a list of statements pertaining to the four dimensions of motivated behavior required by various jobs. Since the software can be used on any job, you may discover that some of the statements will not apply to a specific job. Remove any statement that does not apply.

The key factors are:

1. Position overview.
2. How the job deals with problems and challenges.
3. How the job addresses people, contacts, and interaction.
4. How the job deals with change or consistency.
5. How the job needs compliance to procedures or quality control.

The position overview page should be used to get a general feel for the position. This page is generated by looking at all four factors. The following pages look only at one factor at a time without regard for the other three factors.

It is very important to look at the position from both a four-factor and single-factor approach. If we look at the position of one factor at a time, we can draw an incorrect understanding of the position.

Look at the following graph using only the "D" factor.

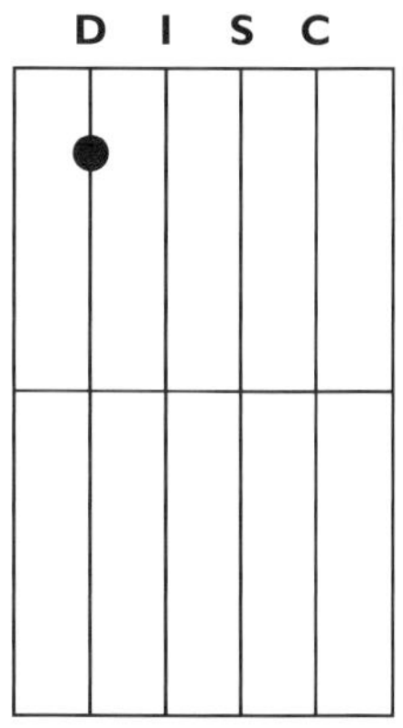

USING THE SOFTWARE REPORT

Looking only at the "D" factor, we can make these statements about the position:

Wide scope of authority
Demanding attitude
Change agent

Now let's look at another graph with the "D" factor in the same position, but let's add just the "C" factor into the picture.

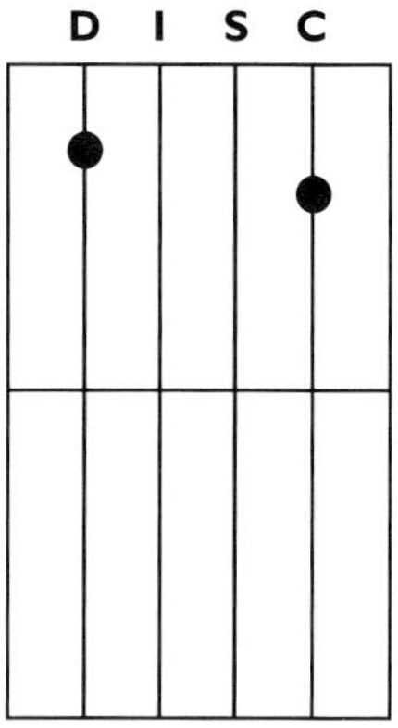

When the "C" factor comes into the picture, we must look very closely at the wide scope of authority because the "C" factor requires that quality, accuracy, data, and calculating risk become factors. Also we could not say change agent because past policies and procedures must be taken into consideration.

Use the position overview page to give you a general feel for the type and kind of behavioral skills the position will need. Look at the rest of the report to get specific information on each factor.

Some key issues for discussion are:

1. Authority and responsibility.
2. Degree of interaction with others.
3. Adherence to policy and procedures.
4. Adaptability to change.
5. Communication: listening, instructing, delegating.
6. Motivation: directive and leadership skills.
7. Cooperation with team members.
8. "Task" compared with "idea" orientation.

HOW TO USE THE PRINT MENU OPTIONS

1. Job Only

The most practical use of the job only perception is to produce the Master Job Report after you have determined the intensity of each factor using the Work Environment Instrument. This copy then becomes a file copy to compare with future reports.

GRAPHIC EXAMPLES

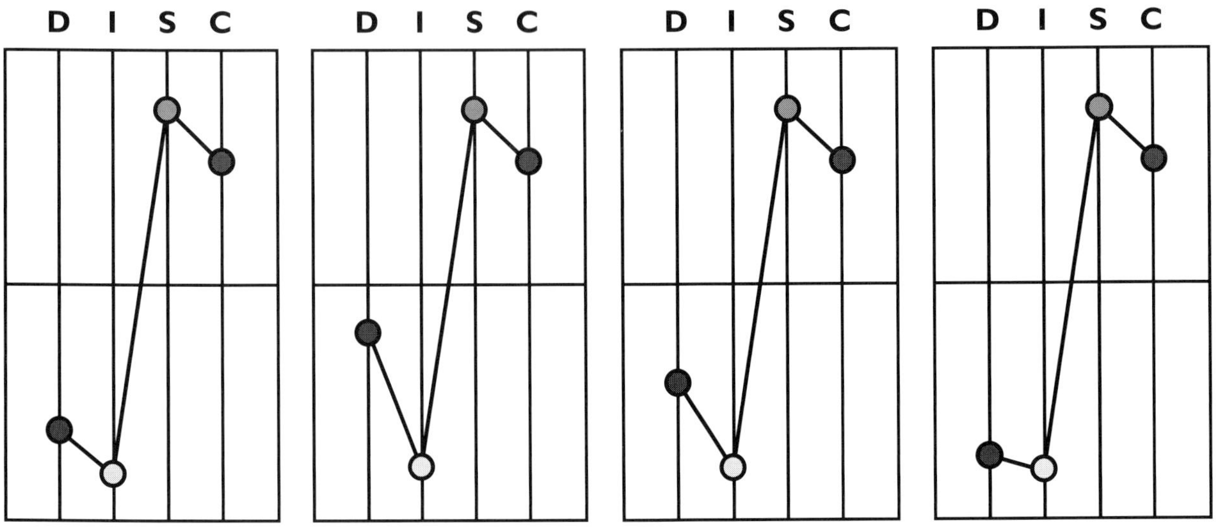

STEPS FOR ANALYSIS

1. Look over the D plot points on each graph.
2. If they differ only slightly, average the plot point. This then becomes the intensity of the D factor on the Master Job Graph.
3. If the plot points of the D factor are considerably different, look over the responses to the four Work Environment Instruments. Negotiate a new rating on the D questions.
4. Plot the new D factor intensity on the Master Job Graph.
5. Repeat this process for the I, S, and C factors.

HOW TO USE THE PRINT MENU OPTIONS

2. __________________'s perception of the job.

This report should be used with current employees and new employees in determining the intensity of perception of the job demands comparing each of the four factors. Both the employee and manager should review the report and discuss the shape of the graph generated from the Work Environment Instrument. This graph should be compared with the statements in the Work Environment report, and those items that are crucial to job success should be highlighted. Those of lesser or of no importance should be eliminated. If the job perception is significantly different or erroneous, run a report on _________'s perception compared to the Master Job Report. This will allow for a clear and objective manner in which to confirm job dimensions.

3. Job compared to ___________'s perception.

This report is especially useful when an individual's perception of the job varies significantly from the job demands or when evaluating new employees and obtaining their perception of the job. In the report, when there is agreement between the person's perception and the Master Job, only one column of items is printed. When there is significant difference, then two columns are printed. The job demands are printed on the left side of the page and the person's perception on the right.

See the examples below:
EXAMPLE A:

The job's demands and Jane's perceptions of the job are:

1. Rules and procedures.
2. Quality control.
3. Systematic approach to work.
4. Thinking before acting.
5. Analysis of facts and data.
6. Clarification or responsibility and authority.
7. Clean work area.
8. Disciplined use of time.
9. Balanced judgment.
10. Clarification of data.

Example A shows agreement between the person's perception and the job demands. The manager and employee should discuss and highlight those items that are most important and eliminate those that do not apply.

HOW TO USE THE PRINT MENU OPTIONS

EXAMPLE B:

The job's behavioral demands are:

1. Patience.
2. Ability to listen.
3. Working within the system.
4. Task-oriented concentration.
5. Follows through a task.
6. Limited change in work activities.
7. Team participation.
8. Security for self and others.
9. Job description in writing.
10. Consistent performance.

Jane's job expectations:

1. Juggling several balls at once.
2. Openness in communication.
3. Alertness and sensitivity to problems.
4. Ability to work on more than one project.
5. Flexibility.
6. Adaptability to change.
7. Support system to deal with details.
8. Questioning procedures.

Example B shows considerable difference between the two perceptions. Does this mean that Jane will not be successful or will fail? No, it does not. Intelligence modifies behavior, and, therefore, Jane would be able to adjust her perception to the job, especially when the job demands are presented clearly.

This discussion between Jane and the manager on this report should concentrate on the differences and similarities in perception and especially the source of the difference in perceptions. Sometimes the source is an unclear job description at the personnel office level. Other times the source of the difference is unclear communication from the manager or trainer. If the source can be identified, then perhaps misperceptions may be eliminated for future employees.

4. ________________'s perception compared to ____________'s perception.

This can be very important to analyze. Clarifying the differences in perception about the job will lead to increased productivity and better understanding of the job, as well as increased understanding of each other. If two perceptions are different on a given factor, you will see a side-by-side printout. If both perceptions are substantially the same, you will see only one set of statements.

HOW TO USE THE PRINT MENU OPTIONS

Dave's Perception
Many social interactions.

Comments:
Dave sees the job as requiring the following behavior:
1. Verbalizing.
2. High trust level.
3. Contacts with many people.
4. Optimistic outlook.

Bill's Perception
Many hours working alone.

Comments:
Bill sees limited contact with people suggesting the following behavior:
1. Low verbalizing.
2. Analytical.
3. Lower trust levels.
4. Pessimistic outlook.

Discuss the differences and analyze the requirements as dictated by the job. Don't discuss who is right and who is wrong. Let the JOB do the talking. Develop Master Job Graphs for future use.

Some statements may indicate only a slight difference in perception. Have both respondents give examples of this perception to see how this slight difference in perception can actually affect performance. Many disagreements start only with a slight difference in perception that becomes magnified when applied to specific functions of the job.

5. Job compared to ________'s basic style.
This report allows you to compare the behavioral tools a person brings to the job with those required by the job. A difference does not mean that the person cannot do the job IF he is willing to pay the price for success. People with versatility can adapt themselves to many different job requirements. Understanding the requirements of the job will allow the development of good coping skills. Life is full of activities that place stress on everyone's natural style. Understanding and coping are essential for positive mental and physical health.

HOW TO USE THE PRINT MENU OPTIONS

What happens if a person's basic style is totally different from the behavior required by the job? In the short run, nothing. In the long run, the company may experience these types of problems from this person:

Stress related disorders
Family problems
Low productivity
Conflict
Absenteeism
Turnover

When you place a "square peg" (person) in a "round hole" (job) you can expect these problems.

Job Requirements
Complete authority to carry out the job.

Comments:
The job is calling for the type of behavior:
1. Decisiveness.
2. Results.
3. Set precedent.
4. Take high risks.
5. Do it now.

Basic Style
Clarification of authority and responsibility.

Comments:
This person is comfortable in an environment where he can use his/her natural style as follows:
1. Do it right the first time.
2. Analyze before deciding.
3. Follow precedent.
4. Lower risk by investigation.
5. Patience.

The above example shows the stress that can be related to just one statement in the report. Keep in mind that experience and intelligence can assist this person in coping with this situation. The key to remember is: "How does this one factor affect the total productivity of the job and possibly the success of this company?" For example, managers who take a long time to make decisions often cause the productivity of others to be lowered while they are being kept waiting. By contrast, managers who decide too quickly often make bad decisions. Keeping the focus on the job always leads to better performance for the organization.

HOW TO USE THE PRINT MENU OPTIONS

6. Job compared to _____________'s motivated style.

The individual's response to environment or motivated style reflects the extent to which he modifies his basic style to meet the demands of the situation; that is, to survive or to succeed. Many times there may be a significant difference between the basic and motivated styles. This means that the person is making significant behavioral changes in order to survive or succeed in the work arena. It is important to determine whether this shift from basic to motivated style is a shift TOWARD or AWAY from job perception.

Job Requirements
Independent thinking.

Comments:
The job is calling for the following:
1. Results by doing it now.
2. Breaking or bending a few rules to get results.
3. Try new ways to get results.
4. Do it your way.
5. Go for it.
6. Don't ask questions, think...then act.

Response to the Job
Follow rules and procedures.

Comments:
This person is motivated to project the following behavior:
1. Do it right the first time.
2. Don't take risks for fear of making mistakes.
3. Always be prepared for meetings.
4. Quality over quantity.
5. Follow precedent.
6. Ask questions and get correct answers before acting.

If a person's basic style is close to that required by the job, but their response to the environment is being directed AWAY from the job, you may want to do an interaction analysis. Causes for this misdirected behavior may be:

Economic environment
Fear of being fired
Rejection of the boss's style
Emulation of the boss's style
Misunderstanding of behavior needed to be successful
Loss of self-confidence

OBJECTIVES REVISITED

Importance of the Work Environment Analysis:

- Defines all the human factors absent in job descriptions.
- Allows us to define the behavior the person brings to the job and define the behavior required to be successful in the job.
- Helps the manager and subordinate have the same perception of the job.
- Helps managers assist employees in meeting behavioral demands of the job.

Authors' Note:

The Work Environment Analysis is a very powerful tool that should be used in every work situation. The power of the instrument lies in its ability to get everyone on the "same sheet of music" related to the behavioral needs of the job. How many problems are caused by managers and employees who "see" the job differently? Also, the ability to compare people's perceptions of the job facilitates communication and understanding. The consultants who have effectively used this instrument report its valuable contribution to the work place and to human resources development.

CHAPTER 8
Selling with "Style"

Chapter Objective:
To teach you how to "blend" your sales style with your customer's buying style for easier sales.

Chapter Contents:
- Introduction
- Recognizing Behavioral Styles
- Buying Style Characteristics
- "C" Style
- "S" Style
- "I" Style
- "D" Style
- Blend Your Sales Style
- How to Build a Winning Sales Presentation
- Objectives Revisited

"Everyone is a salesperson. Everyone is selling something every day."
– Bill J. Bonnstetter

INTRODUCTION

Research conducted by Target Training International, Ltd. has conclusively proven the following statements to be true:

1. People tend to buy from salespeople who have behavioral styles similar to their own.
2. Salespeople tend to sell to customers who have a behavioral style similar to their own.
3. Salespeople who are aware of their own behavioral style and learn to "blend" with their customer's style are able to increase their sales.

The "Ford" or the "Pontiac"

A Pontiac salesperson, with a High S behavioral style, was showing a new vehicle to a couple. Knowing the DISC language, the salesperson realized both the husband and the wife had High C behavioral styles. The couple expressed immediately that their desire was to buy a Ford, but merely wanted some information on a comparable Pontiac model. The salesperson did not "push" them in any way, but offered them a variety of information they requested. Knowing that they were going to the Ford dealership up the street, the Pontiac salesperson recommended them to a Ford salesperson who was a High D, and did NOT know the DISC language.

Why? The salesperson was hoping the High D would be "pushy" with the couple, and they would then come back and buy the Pontiac. The High D salesperson was "pushy" and tried to close the deal immediately. After a few days of gathering more information, the couple came back and bought the Pontiac.

NOTE: You may feel like the couple was manipulated. The point of including this true story is: Whether we like it or not, people buy from people they like! They liked the laid-back, slow-paced Pontiac salesperson and did not like the fast-paced, quick-closing Ford salesperson. The salesperson was more important than the brand of vehicle.

INTRODUCTION

How many sales do we lose because of not "behaviorally" treating the customer properly?

PEOPLE BUY FROM PEOPLE THEY LIKE!
The problem is: What do they like?

Some buyers:

Like you to be direct.
Like to have fun.
Like new products.
Like proven products.
Like a lot of data.
Like to be touched.
Like personal talk.
Like time to think.
Like to negotiate.
Like showy products.
Like traditional products.
...and some DON'T!

If you, the salesperson, don't understand behavioral styles and do not have a good knowledge of the DISC language, you are saying goodbye to your valuable sales dollars. The single, best way for a sales manager to increase sales dollars and customer satisfaction is to train the sales team on the DISC language.

There are three steps to selling with "style":

1. Know your own behavioral style.
2. Know your customer's behavioral style.
3. Blend your sales style to eliminate tension in the sales process.

RECOGNIZING BEHAVIORAL STYLES

Method #1

This method, if used properly, can show you your own behavioral style and that of your customer.

If you know someone who knows your potential buyer, ask him/her the following questions to help you prepare for the sales call.

1. Is the person extroverted or introverted?
The High D and the High I factors are extroverted.
The High S and the High C factors are introverted.

2. Is the person people- or task-oriented?
The High I and the High S factors are people-oriented.
The High D and the High C factors are task-oriented.

Example: Lee Trevino

1. Extroverted or introverted?
Lee Trevino is definitely extroverted, indicating he is a High D or a High I.

2. People- or task-oriented?
Lee Trevino is people-oriented, indicating he is a High I behaviorally.

Using this method to understand your customer's primary style, simply ask the same questions in your mind as you observe the customer.

RECOGNIZING BEHAVIORAL STYLES

Method #2

This is the most accurate method of knowing your own and other's behavioral styles without using the Style Insight Instrument. Each of the four factors, has an emotion associated with it. By observing the emotions of the four factors we can plot the entire graph.

Step 1: Plotting the "D" factor

The High D emotion is anger. A High D will be quick to anger and tend to have a short fuse. A low D will be slow to anger and tend to have a long fuse.

Example conversation: (Person B trying to know the style of Person A)

Person A: *People just bug me sometimes.*

Person B: *Really? Do you have somewhat of a "short fuse" or can you take a lot before you get angry?*

Person A: *Oh, I can take a lot, but when I blow — watch out!*

Based on Person A's response we can plot the "D" factor below the energy line because Person A claims to have a long fuse. If Person A claims to have a short fuse, we can plot the "D" factor above the energy line.

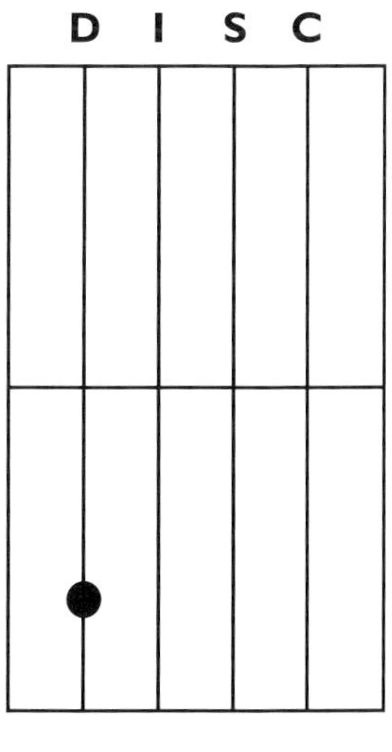

Step 2: Plotting the "I" factor

The High I emotions are optimism and trust. A High I will tend to be optimistic, have a positive outlook, and be very trusting of others. A Low I will be pessimistic and skeptical with a tendency to distrust others.

Example conversation: (Person B trying to know the style of Person A)

Person B: *I'm excited about my job. They like my work and said there was a future for me.*

Person A: *Really? That's great! I think you'll do just fine there. I'm glad they're taking care of you.*

Based on Person A's response we can plot the "I" factor above the energy line because Person A is showing optimism. If Person A had said something to the effect of "Yeah, right! I'd make sure I got that in writing," this would have indicated a Low I below the energy line. Based on the first two emotions, we know the approximate plotting point of the "D" and the "I" factor, as seen in the graph below.

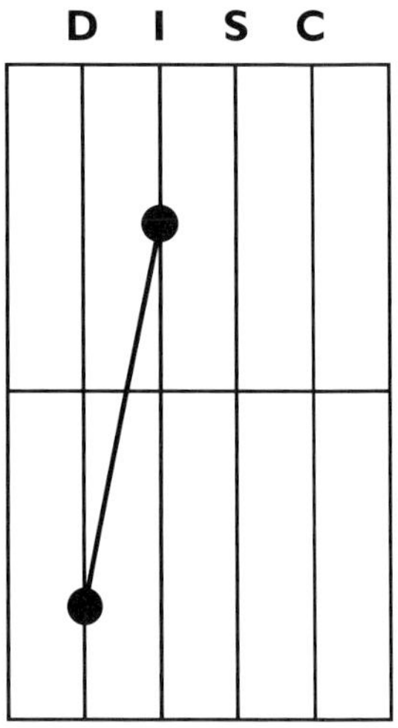

RECOGNIZING BEHAVIORAL STYLES

Step 3: Plotting the "S" factor
The High S emotion is non-emotional. The High S feels emotion, but hides it. A Low S will tend to show whatever emotion he/she is feeling. This particular factor is mostly observable. However, certain questions can reveal that you are talking to a High S.

Questions to ask a third party who knows your potential buyer:

1. Does the potential buyer like new products or traditional products?
New products are the Low S.
Traditional products are the High S.

2. How does the potential buyer maintain his work area?
Neatly organized is the Low S.
A little on the sloppy side is the High S.

3. Does the potential buyer show emotion?
Hard to read is the High S.
Easy to read is the Low S.

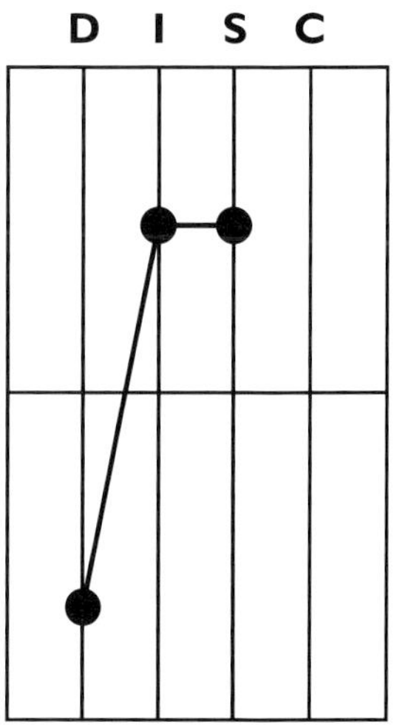

Step 4: Plotting the "C" factor

The High C emotion is fear. A High C will tend to respect rules and go "by the book." A Low C will tend to exhibit no fear, and not to follow rules and procedures or go "by the book." The higher the "C" factor, the more the person will tend to be a better, safer driver.

Example conversation: (Person B trying to know the style of Person A)

> **Person B:** *Have you gotten many speeding tickets?*
>
> **Person A:** *Heck, no! I never get caught. I know where all the cops hang out.*

Based on Person A's response, we can plot the "C" factor below the energy line because Person A tends to break the rules of the road. Had Person A said he/she was a great driver, or if you noticed him/her driving safely while riding with him/her, you would have plotted the "C" factor above the energy line.

Based on the emotions of the four factors, we now plot the entire graph of Person A as follows:

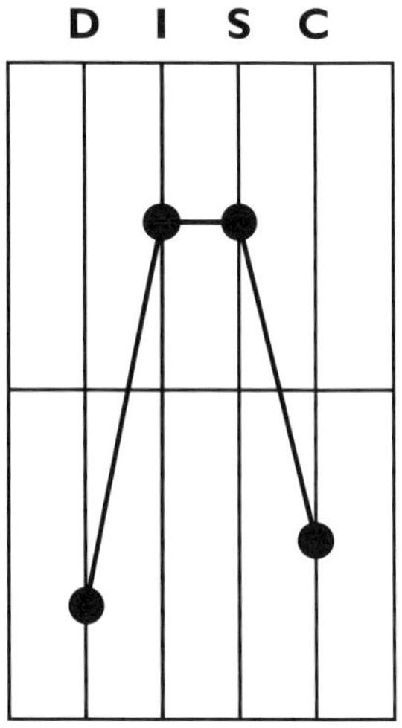

Behaviorally, Person A is a Low D and Low C with a High I and a High S. Utilizing Method #1 of extroverted or introverted, we notice that Person A is outgoing and friendly. Therefore, we know his/her highest point is the "I" factor.

RECOGNIZING BEHAVIORAL STYLES

Method #2 is very effective in reading the entire graph. It can also be used to identify the behavioral style of a person whom you haven't met by simply talking to someone who does know that person.

Recognizing the Behavioral Style
Actual phone conversation, using Method #2 of reading a person's style.
(Jim's thoughts are in parenthesis.)

Fred: *Jim, why don't you call Mike tomorrow?*

Jim: *Fine! I'll call in the morning! By the way, about Mike, is he optimistic and trusting?*

Fred: *Oh, definitely! And he is very patient with people.*

Jim: *(High I, Low D)*

One simple question gave the caller very valuable information about the potential buyer before the sales call even started. This salesperson now planned his presentation for the High I buyer, realizing also that the "D" factor was below the midline. People who know your potential buyer can give you excellent clues about behavioral style.

Using Method #1 and/or Method #2 should allow you with practice to readily identify the behavioral style of your customers. Then, by understanding the characteristics of the four buying styles you can "blend" your style for increased sales.

HIGH C BUYING STYLE CHARACTERISTICS

Percentage of U.S. Population: 24%

Type of products they tend to buy: Proven products

TYPICAL CHARACTERISTICS

- May be suspicious of you and your products.
- Does not make changes to new suppliers readily.
- Usually not too talkative.
- Is not an "innovator." Will not readily try out new and innovative technology.

TYPE OF SALES PRESENTATION REQUIRED

- Needs a lot of "proof," background information and proven results before making a purchase.
- Needs time to absorb details and digest facts before going to the next step.
- Highly suspicious of new and unproven products--use testimonials or plenty of research information to back up your presentation.
- Make sure testimonials are from others with a "C" behavioral style.
- Don't Rush! Don't waste time with small talk. Get right to the point with plenty of facts and figures. Answer all of their questions.

HIGH C BUYING STYLE CHARACTERISTICS

STATEMENTS THAT MOTIVATE A HIGH C

- There has been a great amount of input into this idea, which ensures its quality.
- Once you've taken the time to examine the facts, you'll see this is right for you.
- You're in a position to examine the facts, interpret them and draw your own conclusions.
- With something as important as this, let's set up several sessions where we can examine all possible alternatives.
- I brought along all the information you'll need in order to thoroughly investigate this product and determine if it's right for you.
- Others have found this to be the perfect solution to their problem. With your emphasis on standards, you will probably do it better.
- You can see that our warranty eliminates any risk on your part. We stand behind the product 100%.
- This is a proven product, having been on the market for years, so you know you have something you can rely on.

DRIVING FORCES FOR SELLING A HIGH C

- Set an environment where they will like and trust you.
- Present ideas in a non-threatening manner.
- Find ways to minimize risk.
- Do not hard sell!
- Give a complete proposal—explain details.

HIGH C BUYING STYLE CHARACTERISTICS

DRIVING FORCES IN SELLING A HIGH C

- Emphasize losses caused by delay.
- Stress security if they buy now, or loss of security if they wait.
- Do not over-promise.
- Sales presentation must be consistent with sales material.

HINDERING FACTORS IN SELLING A HIGH C

- Getting personal about family, if you don't know him or her.
- Touching or patting on back when you first meet.
- Loud, emotional sales presentation.
- Being shallow with answers to questions.

TYPICAL QUESTIONS ASKED BY THE HIGH C STYLE

1. Is it a proven product?
2. What else can you tell me about the product?
3. I don't have to decide now, do I?
4. What happens if it doesn't work?
5. Are you sure it lives up to all of your claims?
6. What is the warranty?
7. Is this the best on the market?

HIGH C BUYING STYLE CHARACTERISTICS

TYPICAL QUESTIONS ASKED BY THE HIGH C STYLE

8. This isn't a new method, is it?

9. What are your qualifications?

10. Who are you?

11. How long has your company been in business?

12. Will you be able to meet my exact specifications?

13. What is everyone else using?

CLOSES TO USE WITH A HIGH C

The "Puppy Dog" – Try before you buy
By allowing the High C to use the product first and test it out, they begin to sell themselves, as well as experience the immediate benefits of the product.

The "Think About It" Deposit
Invariably, the High C buyer will not make the decision on the first presentation. A gently suggested deposit to hold the vehicle while the "C" has time to think about it is really a commitment. Even if the High C has the information where they feel comfortable, they will probably not make an immediate decision. Here's how it works:

SALESPERSON: *Mrs. Smith, you've invested a lot of your valuable time finding the right vehicle. I respect the fact that you need to think about it, but I want to make sure the car is still here when you decide to invest. You could help me out by placing a small deposit to hold the vehicle while you think about it. Of course, if you should decide not to purchase this vehicle, we'll gladly refund your deposit. I've also put together a packet of information for you.*

PEOPLE BUY FROM PEOPLE THEY LIKE!

HIGH S BUYING STYLE CHARACTERISTICS

Percentage of U.S. population: 23%

Type of products they tend to buy: Traditional products

TYPICAL CHARACTERISTICS

- May be somewhat shy individual, but wants to be your friend.
- Not as suspicious as the "C", but still very slow to make changes.
- Needs to trust thc salesperson.
- Not an "innovator." Likes a traditional way of doing things.
- Family-oriented.

TYPE OF SALES PRESENTATION REQUIRED

- Take it slow and easy. If you go too fast, you'll lose the sale.
- Provide plenty of proof and statistics.
- Earn their trust and friendship; visit about family and hobbies.
- May require additional visits for reassurances before the sale is made.
- Use facts and figures. Make repeat visits.
  Make sure you answer all their questions.

HIGH S BUYING STYLE CHARACTERISTICS

STATEMENTS THAT MOTIVATE A HIGH S

- I feel you are open to a number of possibilities, and I want to recommend this plan of action.
- Make some calls to others who have made the same type of change. I have a list that will help you.
- By accepting this plan, you are investing in a great deal of security for you and your family.
- Here is a comprehensive packet of information that will provide you with all the information needed to make a wise decision.
- We'll make sure we take the time to investigate all the possibilities before we go ahead.
- We've been a leader in the industry for ____ years, so we're going to be here when you need us.
- You can see that our warranty eliminates any risk on your part. We stand behind the product 100%.
- This is a proven product, having been on the market for ____ years, so you know you have something you can rely on.

DRIVING FORCES FOR SELLING A HIGH S

- Be sincere by using a quiet manner, simple explanations and explain details.
- Involve the family in decisions if they receive benefits.
- The "S" will make emotional decisions if family is involved.
- Do not hard sell!
- Give them time to think.

HIGH S BUYING STYLE CHARACTERISTICS

DRIVING FORCES FOR SELLING A HIGH S

- Give assurances that their decision is right.
- Stress security if they buy now, or loss of security if they wait.
- Full explanations.
- Show how your program will do the complete job, so they don't have to buy anything later.

HINDERING FACTORS IN SELLING A HIGH S

- Going too fast!
- Getting too friendly on the first meeting.
- Loud, emotional sales presentation.
- Being shallow with answers to questions, or not having answers.
- Hard selling or trying to close too fast.
- Bad mouthing current suppliers; they're probably friends.

TYPICAL QUESTIONS ASKED BY THE HIGH S STYLE

1. I always buy from another supplier; what's your price?
2. I buy from someone else and the service is good. Why should I switch to you?
3. This is a proven product, isn't it?
4. What happens if it doesn't work?

HIGH S BUYING STYLE CHARACTERISTICS

TYPICAL QUESTIONS ASKED BY THE HIGH S STYLE

5. What does the warranty cover?
6. How long has this model been out? What's the track record?
7. Why don't you call me in a week? I'd like to think this over.
8. Will this do the job itself, or are there other things I'll need to buy with it?
9. There's no rush, is there?
10. What is everyone else using?

CLOSES THAT WORK WELL WITH A HIGH S

The "Puppy Dog" – Try before you buy
By allowing the High S to use the product first and test it out, they begin to sell themselves, as well as experience the immediate benefits of the product. Usually, the family of the "S" will develop an attachment to the product also.

The "Think About It" Deposit
Invariably, the High S buyer will not make the decision on the first presentation. A gently suggested deposit to hold the vehicle while the "S" has time to think about it is really a commitment. Even if the "S" has the information where they feel comfortable, they will probably not make an immediate decision. Here's how it works:

SALESPERSON: *Mrs. Smith, you've invested a lot of your valuable time finding the right vehicle. I respect the fact that you need to think about it, but I want to make sure that when you decide to invest that it is still here. You could help me out by placing a small deposit to hold the vehicle while you think about it. Of course, if you should decide not to purchase this vehicle, we'll gladly refund your deposit.*

PEOPLE BUY FROM PEOPLE THEY LIKE!

HIGH I BUYING STYLE CHARACTERISTICS

Percentage of U.S. Population: 26%

Type of products they tend to buy: Showy products

TYPICAL CHARACTERISTICS

- A friendly people-oriented person who would rather talk and socialize than do detail work.
- Will be glad to see you; will trade jokes and personal stories.
- Likes to try out new, innovative and showy products.

TYPE OF SALES PRESENTATION REQUIRED

- Spare the details; the "I" will not want to hear them. Will be a very quick buyer, usually on the first visit. BEWARE! Your competition can steal them away just as easy. So give plenty of follow-up service.
- Present new, innovative and showy products. The "I" likes to try new things.
- Allow time for socializing, perhaps over lunch.
- Have fun in the presentation. Tell stories.
  It's okay to touch the High I (upper forearm or back).
- Eliminate a lot of details. Just hit the high points.

HIGH I BUYING STYLE CHARACTERISTICS

STATEMENTS THAT MOTIVATE A HIGH I

- It's the type of program that will utilize your ability to work with a new and innovative program.
- This product allows you and your company to lead the way into the future.
- This program puts you on the "cutting edge" of technology in your industry.
- Yes, we have several companies that are looking at it, but most settle for the way things have always been. We felt you were more into moving into the future with the latest technology.
- In fact, we'd like to showcase your business as one who is moving into the future with this latest advancement.

DRIVING FORCES FOR SELLING A HIGH I

- Provide recognition of their accomplishments.
- Let them talk for a while.
- Use their own words to direct the conversation back to business.
- Use testimonials and drop names!
- Provide friendly environment.
- Don't dwell on details.
- Support their dreams.
- Summarize major selling points.
- Don't get them lost in the facts.

HIGH I BUYING STYLE CHARACTERISTICS

DRIVING FORCES FOR SELLING A HIGH I

- Be enthusiastic. Have fun!
- Close quickly, even on the first call.
- Give them choices of packages: three investments from large to economy.

HINDERING FACTORS IN SELLING A HIGH I

- Letting them talk so much that you lose the sale, or can't sell. Use their words and questions to keep them on track.

TYPICAL QUESTIONS ASKED BY THE HIGH I STYLE

1. Can you lower the price a little?
2. Are there any benefits for purchasing the product? Incentives? Like a free trip?
3. Would you mind if I told my neighbor about your product?
4. Have you had coffee yet? Let's talk over a cup of coffee. You bring the doughnuts.
5. What are your payment plans?
6. If I buy, who pays for the delivery?
7. Who else is doing this in my industry?

HIGH I BUYING STYLE CHARACTERISTICS

CLOSES THAT WORK WELL WITH A HIGH I

The "Alternative of Choice"
Give the "I" a choice of two options. By selecting either one, he indicates that he is going ahead with the purchase.

Example: *You like both models I showed you, which one best meets your needs?*

PEOPLE BUY FROM PEOPLE THEY LIKE!

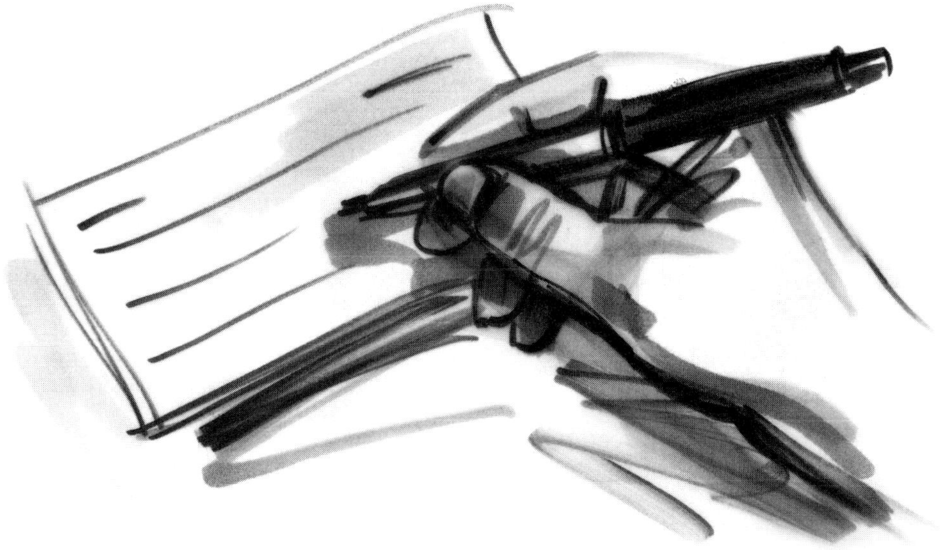

HIGH D BUYING STYLE CHARACTERISTICS

Percentage of U.S. population: 27%

Type of products they tend to buy: New Products

TYPICAL CHARACTERISTICS

- An entrepreneur with many interests. Often has several jobs or activities going on at once.
- Highly interested in new products and innovation.
- Usually has a fairly high ego factor.
- Does not like to waste time.

TYPE OF SALES PRESENTATION REQUIRED

- Don't waste time. The "D" buyer doesn't want a lot of facts and figures. Just hit the high points and get to the "bottom line."
- You and your product must appear credible.
- Can be difficult to switch from present trusted suppliers, but once switched, will remain very loyal as long as you provide service.
- Does not want to see many testimonials, research, data, etc.
- Will be impressed with an efficient, businesslike approach.
- Will take interest in new products.
- Be concise and businesslike. Don't waste time with idle talk. Get to the point quickly, solve problems fast and make the sale.

HIGH D BUYING STYLE CHARACTERISTICS

STATEMENTS THAT MOTIVATE A HIGH D

- You'll want to try this out. You're the type of person who can make this work.
- This program will put you in the driver's seat. It will increase your current efficiency by ___%. This is totally new—there is nothing like it on the market.
- You can easily see the advantages of using this method.
- This puts you on the cutting edge of your industry, a leader in your field.
- This provides you with an opportunity to get credit for what you do. It's something you can call your own.

DRIVING FORCES FOR SELLING A HIGH D

- Prepare your sales presentation for efficiency. Omit minor details.
- Flatter the ego. Concentrate on the immediate sale.
- Start with business--they will let you know if they want to chat.
- Ask questions so they can tell you about their operation.
- Stress opportunities for prestige, challenge and efficiency.
- Give direct answers.
- Emphasize results and the bottom line.
- Be efficient.
- Ask for the High D's opinion.

HIGH D BUYING STYLE CHARACTERISTICS

HINDERING FACTORS IN SELLING A HIGH D

- Being indecisive.
- Not answering objections directly.
- Explaining too many details.
- Don't give opinions, give options.
- Focus on the "D." Do not work with three or four customers at once.

TYPICAL QUESTIONS ASKED BY THE HIGH D STYLE

1. What does it cost?
2. Is this the top of the line model?
3. Can I change it?
4. Is it new?
5. What is the warranty?
6. Are you sure you know what you're talking about?
7. Who else is using this model?
8. Can I get it now?
9. What are my payment options?
10. How much will it increase my efficiency?

HIGH D BUYING STYLE CHARACTERISTICS

CLOSES THAT WORK WELL WITH A HIGH D

The "Alternative of Choice"
Give the High D a choice of two options. By selecting either one, they are indicating that they are going ahead with the purchase.

Example: *You liked both models I showed you, which one best meets your needs?*

The "Take Away"
This close was developed to challenge the strong ego of the "D" profile. The close can backfire, but also can be very effective if done properly. Once the "D" has an eye on the product they want and is struggling with the money issue, the salesperson says:

SALESPERSON: *You know, Sue, I thought this was the right product for you, but maybe I made a mistake. Maybe we should look at your budget range. Let's look at this model.*

Those who have successfully used this close, state that the "D" will bounce back and buy the one he/she was struggling with. By taking it away for a monetary reason, it sends a subtle message, which causes them to want to prove to you and themselves that they CAN afford it. Be careful when using this close. It is very effective, but must be sincere in its delivery. We present this close because it is a "behavioral close," but you need to examine it and decide for yourself if it is a close you would like to use.

PEOPLE BUY FROM PEOPLE THEY LIKE!

We now have looked at the buying characteristics of all four styles. By "blending" your style with theirs, you will increase your sales. Guaranteed.

BLEND YOUR SALES STYLE

As you've seen, all customers are not alike. Each requires a different type of approach, and responds to you in different ways. By "blending" your sales style with theirs, your sales presentations will attain maximum success. In order to do this, you must compare the strong and weak points of your own style with those of your different prospects and adjust yours accordingly. The following five reference pages give you the information you need for each style of salesperson.

BASIC PATTERNS AND APPROACHES

Learn to interpret patterns and the most common acts that go along with them. This will enable you to establish instant rapport that allows people to feel at ease with you. After the initial period you can relax and make minor adjustments.

STYLE TENDENCIES	*Greater*			*Lesser*
Tendency to Use Logic:	**S**	**C**	**D**	**I**
Tendency to Trust:	**I**	**S**	**D**	**C**
Tendency to Buy Quickly:	**D**	**I**	**S**	**C**
Tendency to Be Loyal:	**S**	**C**	**D**	**I**

D Behavioral Selling Skills D

Dominant/Driver/Choleric (Using DISC Model) Dominant

Step A: Know Yourself: "D" Salesperson

- Results oriented
- Wants to close fast
- Argumentative
- May try to overpower the person
- Likes to win
- May not follow up properly
- May be unprepared
- Can handle several customers at once

Step B: Read the Person You are Speaking With:

Extroverted:	**Introverted:**
Friendly - I	Cooperative - S
Direct - D	Analytical - C

Behavioral Style Match (BSM):

1 - Excellent	3 - Fair
2 - Good	4 - Poor

Step C: Use This Chart When You Are Selling To:

"D" BSM - 2

"D" is looking for: RESULTS

- **Be direct**
- **Give alternatives**
- **Make sure you let them win (make sure you win, too)**
- **Disagree with facts**
- **Enjoy the "combat" (good match)**
- **Don't try to build a friendship**
- **Do not dictate to them**
- **Move quickly; they decide fast**
- **Do not try to overpower them**

"S" BSM - 3

"S" is looking for: SECURITY

- **Slow down presentation**
- **Build trust**
- **People focus**
- **Give them the facts they need**
- **Logical presentation**
- **Get "little" agreements**
- **Listen carefully**
- **Show sincerity in presentation**
- **Don't control or dominate**
- **Do not close fast**

"I" BSM - 2

"I" is looking for: THE "EXPERIENCE"

- **Be personal, friendly**
- **Slow down, take time**
- **Joke around and have fun**
- **Allow them to talk**
- **Provide recognition**
- **Don't talk down to them**
- **Talk about people**
- **Follow up often**

"C" BSM - 4

"C" is looking for: INFORMATION

- **Give them the data**
- **Do not touch**
- **Be patient, slow**
- **Use flyers with data**
- **Give more info then you'd like**
- **Keep control**
- **Do not talk personally**
- **Do not be pushy**

I Behavioral Selling Skills I

Influencer/Expressive/Sanguine (Using DISC Model) Influencer

Step A: Know Yourself: "I" Salesperson
- Social
- People-oriented lack of attention to detail
- May over-promise
- May be "too talkative"
- May close too slowly, or not at all
- Enthusiastic
- Wordy, non-logical presentation

Step B: Read the Person You are Speaking With:

Extroverted:	**Introverted:**
Friendly - I	Cooperative - S
Direct - D	Analytical - C

Behavioral Style Match (BSM):

1 - Excellent	3 - Fair
2 - Good	4 - Poor

Step C: Use This Chart When You Are Selling To:

"D" BSM - 2

"D" is looking for: RESULTS
- **Do not touch**
- **Stay business-like**
- **Be direct and to the point**
- **Do not over-promise**
- **Do not joke**
- **Let them win (you win also)**
- **Confidently close, not allowing them to overpower you**

"S" BSM - 3

"S" is looking for: SECURITY
- **Give them the facts**
- **Slow down**
- **Be friendly, personal and earn their trust**
- **Provide assurances of your promises**
- **Get "little" agreements**
- **Let them talk; you ask questions**
- **Take necessary time before closing**
- **Follow up after the sale**

"I" BSM - 2

"I" is looking for: THE "EXPERIENCE"
- **Have fun**
- **Don't waste too much time talking**
- **Make sure you close**
- **Give them the recognition**
- **Let them talk more than you**

"C" BSM - 4

"C" is looking for: INFORMATION
- **Keep your distance**
- **Do not touch**
- **Give them the facts, figures, and proof**
- **Do not waste time**
- **Do not be personal**
- **Be friendly and direct**
- **Answer all questions, then close**
- **Be concerned with details**

S Behavioral Selling Skills S

Steadiness/Amiable/Phlegmatic (Using DISC Model) Steadiness

Step A: Know Yourself: "S" Salesperson

- Natural salesperson, personable
- Steady and dependable
- Easily discouraged, low confidence
- Great on follow-through (may over service)
- May give away $$$ under pressure
- More enthusiasm may be needed
- May over use facts
- May wait too long to close

Step B: Read the Person You are Speaking With:

Extroverted:	**Introverted:**
Friendly - I	Cooperative - S
Direct - D	Analytical - C

Behavioral Style Match (BSM):

1 - Excellent	3 - Fair
2 - Good	4 - Poor

Step C: Use This Chart When You Are Selling To:

"D" BSM - 3

"D" is looking for: RESULTS

- **Be confident; don't be intimitated**
- **Close sooner than normal**
- **Disagree with facts, not person**
- **Do not be overpowered by them**
- **Let them win (you win, too)**
- **Move faster than normal**
- **Come on as strong as "D" is, but friendly**

"S" BSM - 1

"S" is looking for: SECURITY

- **Give them the facts**
- **Provide the assurances they need**
- **Be yourself**
- **Close when you feel you have their trust**
- **Assure them of the right decision**
- **Introduce them to managers, service managers, etc.**
- **Follow up after sale**

"I" BSM - 2

"I" is looking for: THE "EXPERIENCE"

- **Allow them to talk, but keep focus**
- **Minimal product knowledge**
- **Provide follow-up**
- **Give recognition**
- **Listen to their stories**
- **Have fun with them**
- **"Jump" to close when ready**

"C" BSM - 1

"C" is looking for: INFORMATION

- **Answer questions with facts**
- **Do not be too personal**
- **Be direct and friendly**
- **Do not touch**
- **Give them their space**
- **Do not fear their skeptical nature**
- **Follow through on details**
- **Give information, then close**

C Behavioral Selling Skills C

Compliant/Analytical/Melancholic (Using DISC Model) Compliance

Step A: Know Yourself: "C" Salesperson

- Knows data
- May over use data, over-evaluate
- Needs more enthusiasm
- May have trouble selling products below their own standards
- Well organized
- Good service
- Analysis paralysis

Step B: Read the Person You are Speaking With:

Extroverted:	Introverted:
Friendly - I	Cooperative - S
Direct - D	Analytical - C

Behavioral Style Match (BSM):

1 - Excellent	3 - Fair
2 - Good	4 - Poor

Step C: Use This Chart When You Are Selling To:

"D" BSM - 4

"D" is looking for: RESULTS

- **Touch upon high points of facts and figures**
- **Do not "over-data"**
- **Move quickly**
- **Be brief, to the point**
- **Satisfy their strong ego**
- **Allow them to "win" (you win, too)**

"S" BSM - 1

"S" is looking for: SECURITY

- **Move slowly**
- **Provide facts and figures**
- **Do not over-control, be too pushy**
- **Provide assurances**
- **Develop trust**
- **Focus on reliability and service**
- **Personal talk allowed**

"I" BSM - 4

"I" is looking for: THE "EXPERIENCE"

- **People focus, friendly and fun**
- **Listen to them as they talk**
- **Ask questions**
- **Show excitement about products**
- **Close earlier than normal**

"C" BSM - 1

"C" is looking for: INFORMATION

- **Give data**
- **Remain in control**
- **Examine positives and negatives**
- **Close earlier than you would expect**
- **Follow through on promises**
- **Provide evidence**

Behavioral Selling Skills: Body Language

Salesperson "Do's"

- Relax position, lean back in chair
- Maintain friendly eye contact
- Nod your head in agreement
- Pause before answering a question or objection
- Sit closer to "I" and "S", sit across from "D" and "C"
- If standing: Move around, gesture, open arms
- Give more space to "D" and "C"
- Use forearm or back touch with "I" and "S"
- Raise or lower your voice for effect
- Frown thoughtfully

Salesperson "Don'ts"

- Close your arms in front of you
- Perch on your chair
- Touch "D" or "C"
- Jingle coins or doodle with things
- Twist ear or stroke chin
- Tug nose
- Sit across from the "I" or "S"
- Ignore any female prospect

Buyer's Eye Language: Emotionally-charged person blinks more

Seating Positions and DISC

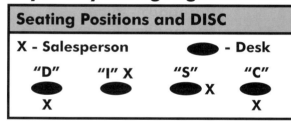

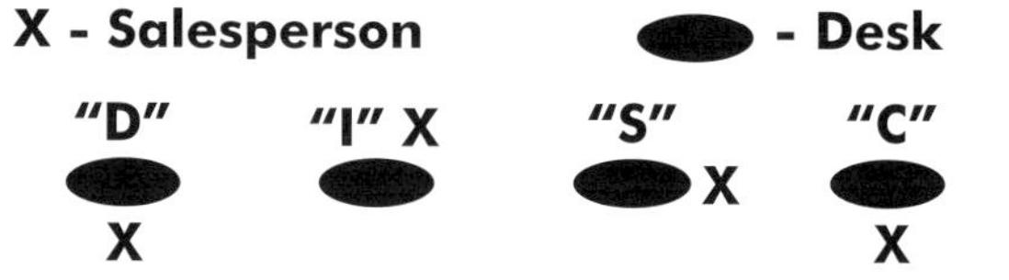

Impacting/Influential Communication

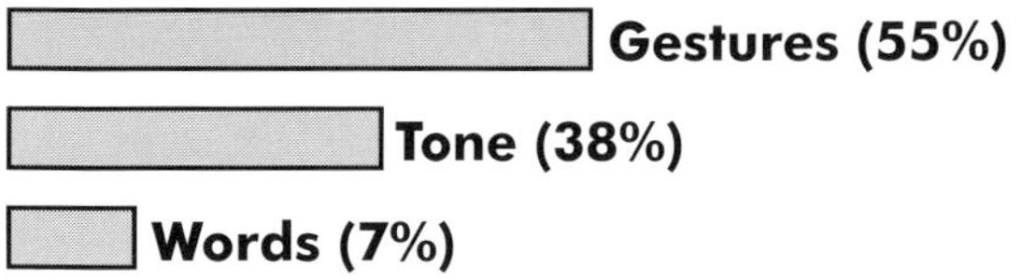

Buying Signals

- Bites lip/furrows brow
- Calls friend for advice
- Rubs chin
- Handles contract
- Scratches head
- Taps with pen
- Half closes eyes

Smiles:
Real smile reaches eyes. False smile reaches lips only.

"I'm defensive."
- Arms crossed
- Face drawn
- Body rigid and tight
- Leaning back

"I disagree."
- Set jaw
- Shaking head from side to side
- Narrowed eyes

"I'm losing interest."
- Broken eye contact
- Slouching in chair
- Checking watch
- Changing posture
- Turning away body 45° to 90°
- Sighing

"You are too close."
- Body Block
- Physical retreat
- Leg swinging or tapping
- Crossed legs away from you
- Broken eye contact

HOW TO BUILD A WINNING SALES PRESENTATION

Building A Winning Sales Presentation

Step 1: Evaluate

The first step in preparing your sales presentation is to list all the reasons your prospect will want to buy your products or services. Put yourself in place of the prospect and list all the reasons for their making a purchase.

1. ______________________________

2. ______________________________

3. ______________________________

4. ______________________________

5. ______________________________

Rewrite the buying motives in order of their strength for each buying style.

Buying Style: ____

1. ______________________________

2. ______________________________

3. ______________________________

Buying Style: ____

1. ______________________________

2. ______________________________

3. ______________________________

HOW TO BUILD A WINNING SALES PRESENTATION

Buying Style: ____

1. ____________________

2. ____________________

3. ____________________

Buying Style: ____

1. ____________________

2. ____________________

3. ____________________

List the characteristics of customers you like best.

1. ____________________

2. ____________________

3. ____________________

4. ____________________

5. ____________________

HOW TO BUILD A WINNING SALES PRESENTATION

What style would these customers tend to fall into?

____

____

____

____

____

List the characteristics of customers you don't like to sell or service.

1. ______________________________
2. ______________________________
3. ______________________________
4. ______________________________
5. ______________________________

What type would these customers tend to fall into?

____

____

____

HOW TO BUILD A WINNING SALES PRESENTATION

Step 2: Analyzing your Products or Service
Start by listing all the features that come to mind about your products or services and list them. Add any additional features contained in your company literature. Then take each feature and select the value or benefit each style will derive from the purchase.

1. Feature: ______________________________

Benefit for D's: ______________________________

____

Benefit for I's: ______________________________

____

Benefit for S's: ______________________________

____

Benefit for C's: ______________________________

____

2. Feature: ______________________________

Benefit for D's: ______________________________

____

Benefit for I's: ______________________________

____

HOW TO BUILD A WINNING SALES PRESENTATION

Benefit for S's: ______________________________

____

Benefit for C's: ______________________________

____

3. Feature: ______________________________

Benefit for D's: ______________________________

____

Benefit for I's: ______________________________

____

Benefit for S's: ______________________________

____

Benefit for C's: ______________________________

____

HOW TO BUILD A WINNING SALES PRESENTATION

Step 3: Demonstrations

List all the demonstrations that you can use to emphasize the benefits of your product or service. (Remember that your prospect will absorb your sales presentation through all five of their senses: see, hear, smell, feel and taste. Try to incorporate as many of these senses as possible into your sales presentation and note the buying style that will be most influenced by each demonstration.

1. ______________________________ Buying style: ______

____

2. ______________________________ Buying style: ______

____

3. ______________________________ Buying style: ______

____

4. ______________________________ Buying style: ______

____

5. ______________________________ Buying style: ______

____

HOW TO BUILD A WINNING SALES PRESENTATION

Step 4: Objections

List all the possible objections to using your products or services. Try to incorporate the answers to the more common objections into your sales talk. The best way to overcome objections is to pre-answer them in your presentation. In trying to answer objections before they are raised, it is best to understand the buying style of your prospect and understand the reasoning behind the objection. By understanding the reasoning you can welcome the objections and answer them to your prospect's satisfaction. Each objection should be followed with a trial close just to make sure you have answered them to your prospect's satisfaction.

Objection Analysis

Objection: ______________________________

Answer for buying style D: ______________________________

____

____

Answer for buying style I: ______________________________

____

____

Answer for buying style S: ______________________________

____

____

Answer for buying style C: ______________________________

____

____

HOW TO BUILD A WINNING SALES PRESENTATION

Step 5: Model Sales Presentation for Buying Style
Developing a trust relationship with a style.

Climate: ______________________________

Time: ______________________________

Pace of presentation: ______________________________

What type of information would you provide? ______________________________

____

What does this style want to know about your product? ______________________________

____

List the emotional and rational factors that will appeal to this type of buyer.

____

What type of support does this buyer need to support his problem solving?

____

What does this type of buyer need to know to make a decision today?

____

What objections can you anticipate from this type of buyer?

1. ______________________________

2. ______________________________

3. ______________________________

HOW TO BUILD A WINNING SALES PRESENTATION

Presentation For:

Pre-approach: ______________________________

____

Opening Statement: ______________________________

____

Outline the order in which you want to present your benefits and make special notations beside the points that will be real "hot buttons".

____

____

____

____

____

What closes will work best with this type of buyer?

1. ______________________________

2. ______________________________

3. ______________________________

4. ______________________________

5. ______________________________

Practice, practice, practice...

OBJECTIVES REVISITED

Importance of Selling with "Style":
Understanding behavioral styles will help you gain valuable sales dollars.
There will be less tension in the sales process.

AUTHOR'S NOTE:
All styles have their strong points. By blending your style with that of your customer, you are strengthening the points that will be impressive to your individual customers. Also, keep in mind that the study of human behavior is not an exact science. The principles we have presented are guidelines only and must be modified accordingly. A person's observable behavior is the sum of all four factors: D, I, S, and C. Those who have studied and applied "blending" continue to report amazing success stories of increased sales and customer satisfaction. By learning the DISC language and applying it to your sales program, you will find it to be the most valuable sales training in which you have ever invested.

"People buy what they need from people who understand what they want."
–William T. Brooks,
Author of *The New Science of Selling and Persuasion.*

CHAPTER 9
Application of the Language

Chapter Objective:
To provide easy to follow flow charts to assist you in the implementation of the language into an organization with the goal of creating more effective communications and relationships.

Chapter Contents:
- Introduction
- Benchmarking the Job
- Benchmarking Performers for Behavior
- Benchmarking Performers for Values
- Team Development Process
- Strategic Planning Process
- Sales Force Training Process
- Family Communication Process
- Objectives Revisited

"Unless you're the lead dog in the pack, the view never changes."
–Warren Claxton

INTRODUCTION

Research by Target Training International, Ltd. has clearly validated that when a salesperson "blends" his/her behavioral style to the customer, sales increase. Why? Again, research shows that people tend to buy from people with similar behavior to their own. Therefore, if I am a salesperson and I "blend" my style with yours, I have a greater chance of getting you to purchase my product.

Wait! What if I don't have a product? What if the only thing I have to "sell" is an idea, a plan, my skills and abilities, my company, my vision, my method, or my budgetary needs?

Can the DISC language increase the effectiveness of everybody who interacts with anybody? YES! YES! YES! The reason sales go up is NOT because the product is better. Sales go up because the communication and understanding is better. Every organization lists communication as an area needing improvement. Knowledge and application of the DISC language has a direct impact on communication. Who should learn the DISC language? Anybody who wants to move ahead in life, where getting ahead requires working with people. Profit, nonprofit organizations and even sports teams should be using the language.

The DISC language is a language of increased communication. Where does it fit in training? FIRST, always FIRST!

BENCHMARKING THE JOB*

The major benefit of benchmarking the job with the Work Environment Instrument is that we can compare present and future staff against the job and identify stress-related activities.

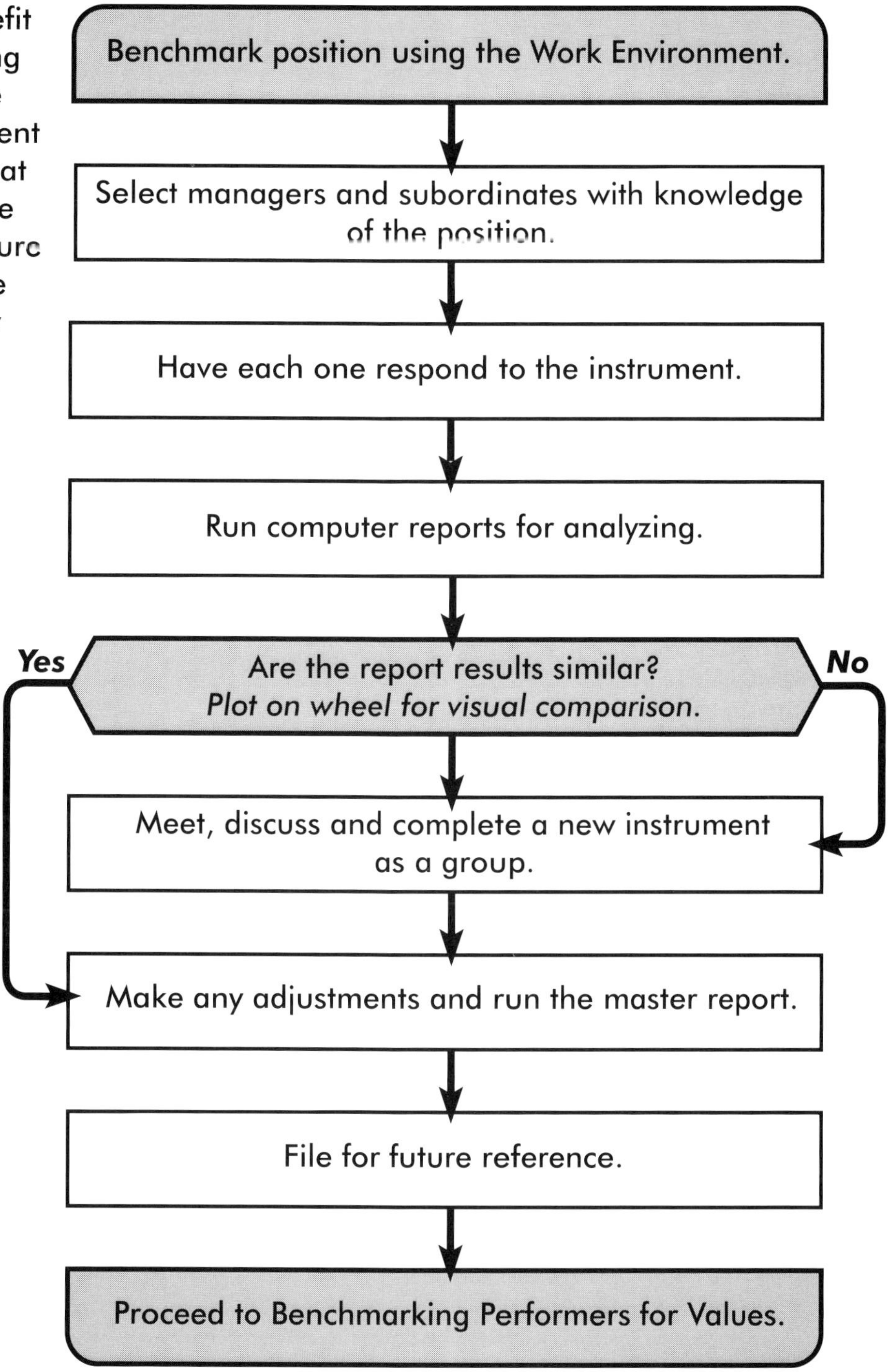

* Work Environment Instrument

BENCHMARKING PERFORMERS FOR BEHAVIOR*

The major benefit for benchmarking behavior helps us identify if superior performance is directly related to behavioral matching in the job.

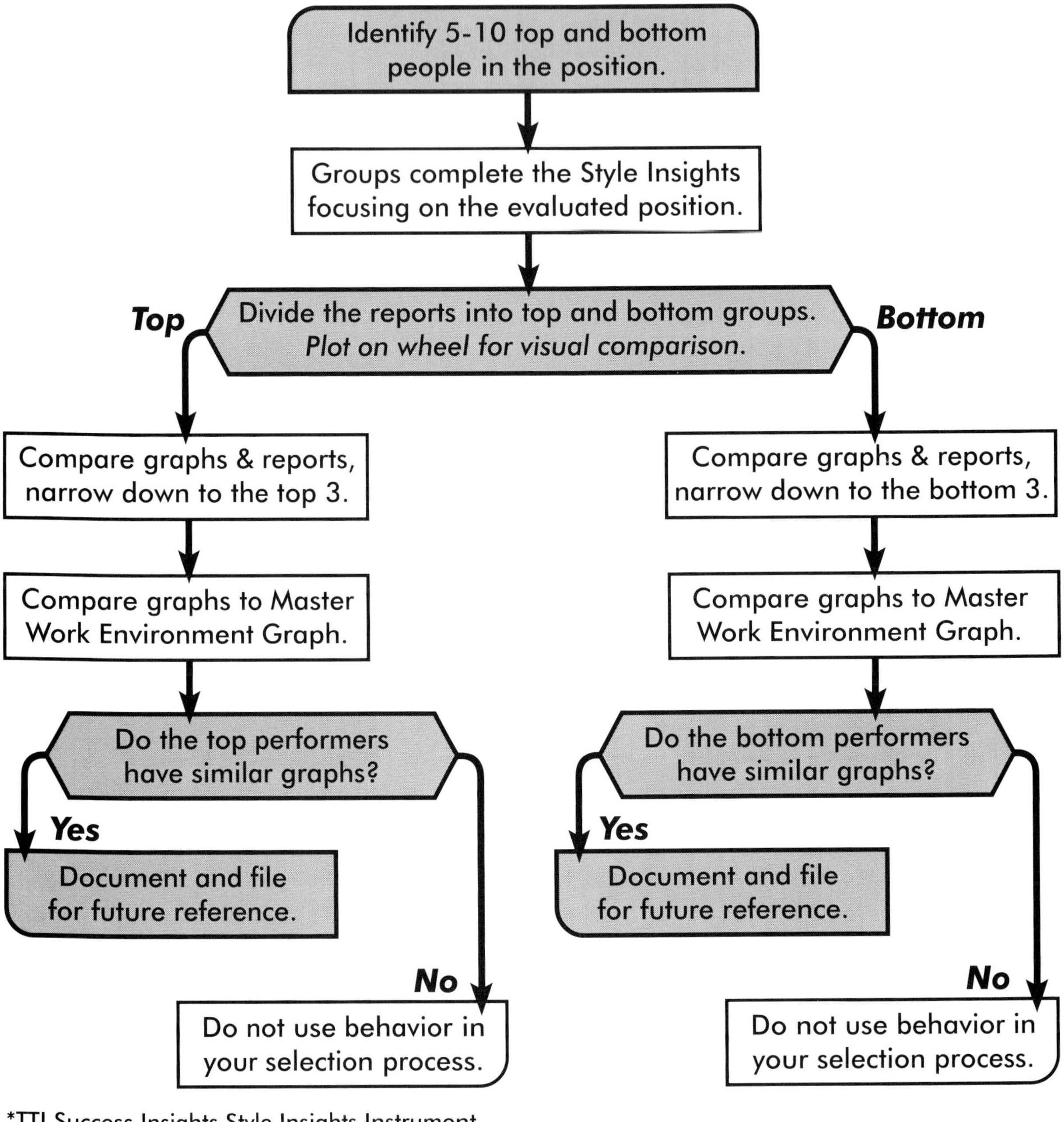

*TTI Success Insights Style Insights Instrument

BENCHMARKING PERFORMERS FOR VALUES*

The major benefit for benchmarking performers is to identify if superior performance is related to the rewards/culture of the job.

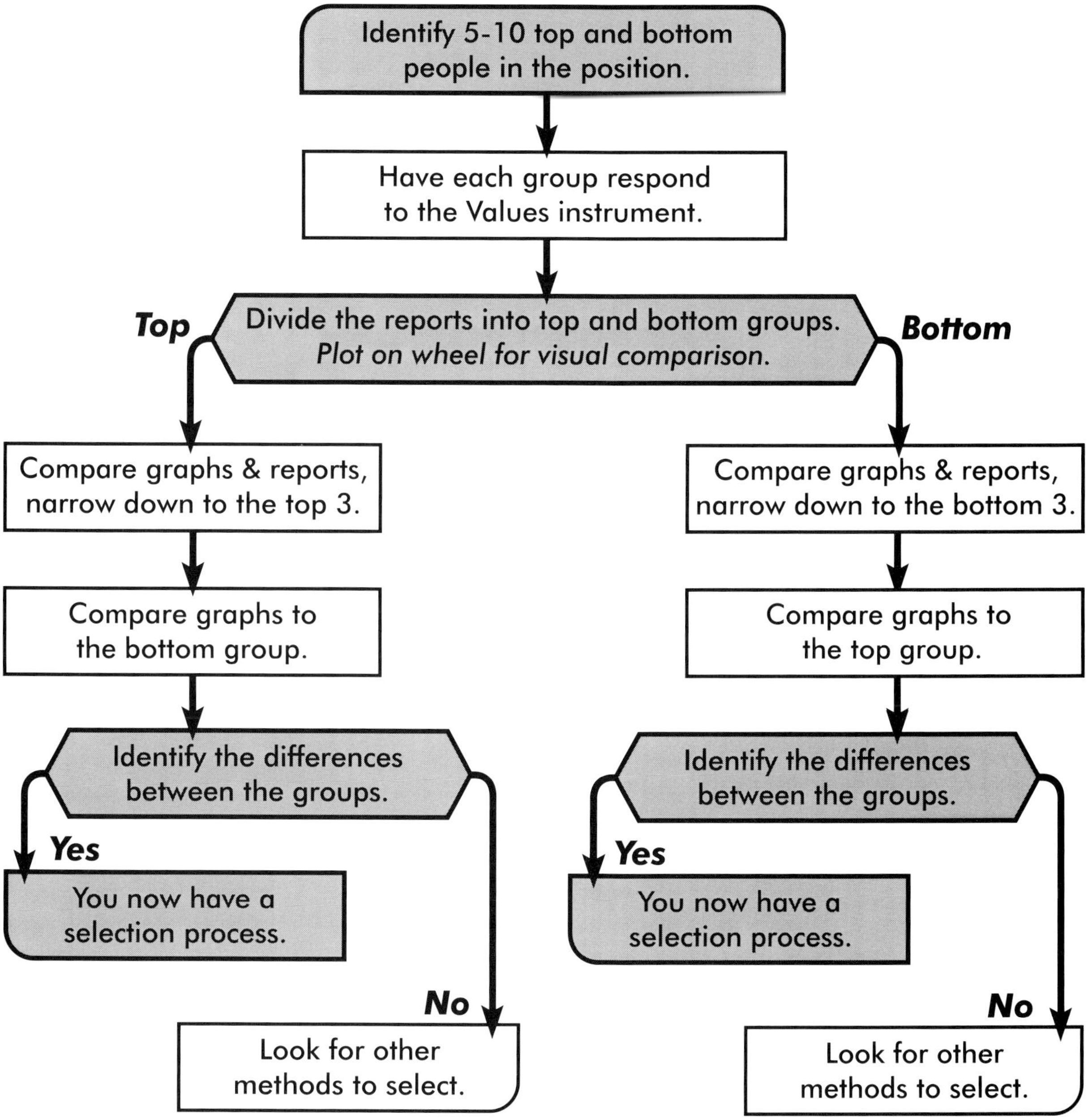

*TTI Success Insights Motivation Insights Instrument

TEAM DEVELOPMENT PROCESS

Suggested TTI Reports:
- TTI Success Insights Management-Staff or Team Building
- Personal Interests, Attitudes & Values

Using the reports you can accomplish actual team interaction and increase the longevity of the team experience.

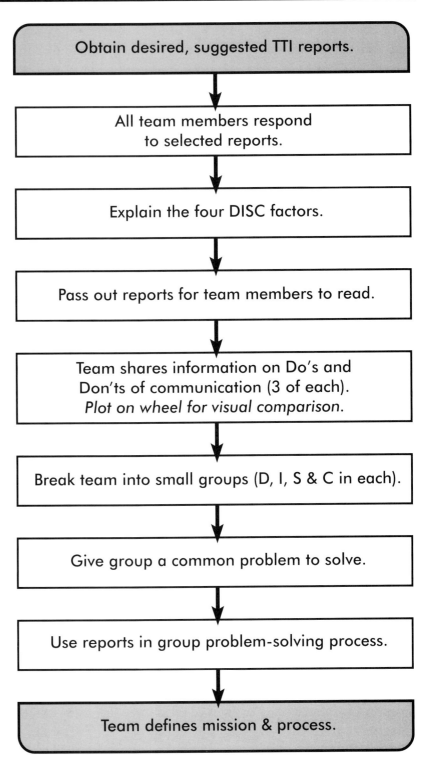

Obtain desired, suggested TTI reports.

↓

All team members respond to selected reports.

↓

Explain the four DISC factors.

↓

Pass out reports for team members to read.

↓

Team shares information on Do's and Don'ts of communication (3 of each). *Plot on wheel for visual comparison.*

↓

Break team into small groups (D, I, S & C in each).

↓

Give group a common problem to solve.

↓

Use reports in group problem-solving process.

↓

Team defines mission & process.

STRATEGIC PLANNING PROCESS

The major benefit for using DISC and Values is to speed up the process and also eliminate potential bias from the leadership team.

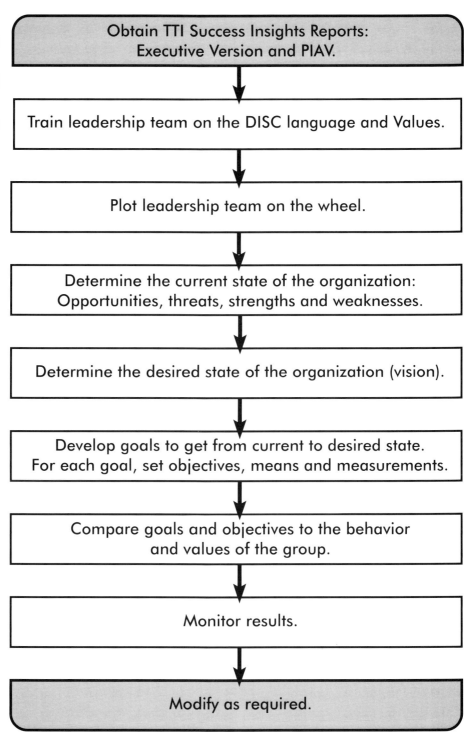

Obtain TTI Success Insights Reports: Executive Version and PIAV.

↓

Train leadership team on the DISC language and Values.

↓

Plot leadership team on the wheel.

↓

Determine the current state of the organization: Opportunities, threats, strengths and weaknesses.

↓

Determine the desired state of the organization (vision).

↓

Develop goals to get from current to desired state. For each goal, set objectives, means and measurements.

↓

Compare goals and objectives to the behavior and values of the group.

↓

Monitor results.

↓

Modify as required.

SALES FORCE TRAINING PROCESS

The major benefit is in people-reading and tailoring the sales presentation to meet the buyer's buying system.

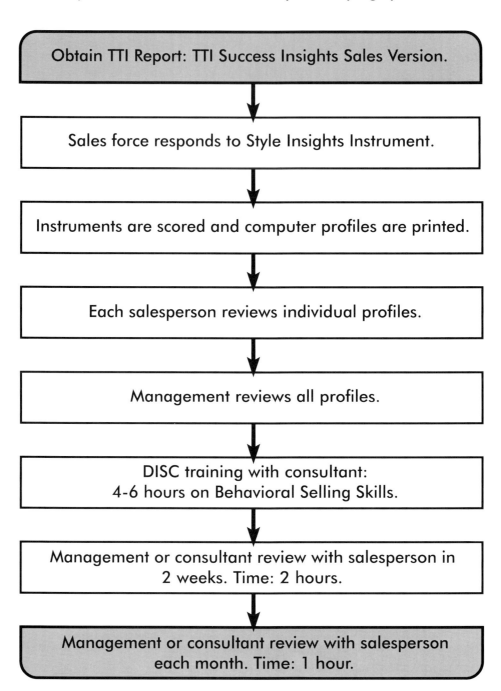

Obtain TTI Report: TTI Success Insights Sales Version.

Sales force responds to Style Insights Instrument.

Instruments are scored and computer profiles are printed.

Each salesperson reviews individual profiles.

Management reviews all profiles.

DISC training with consultant:
4-6 hours on Behavioral Selling Skills.

Management or consultant review with salesperson in 2 weeks. Time: 2 hours.

Management or consultant review with salesperson each month. Time: 1 hour.

FAMILY COMMUNICATION PROCESS

The major benefit to this process is so that all family members can see the value of being different.

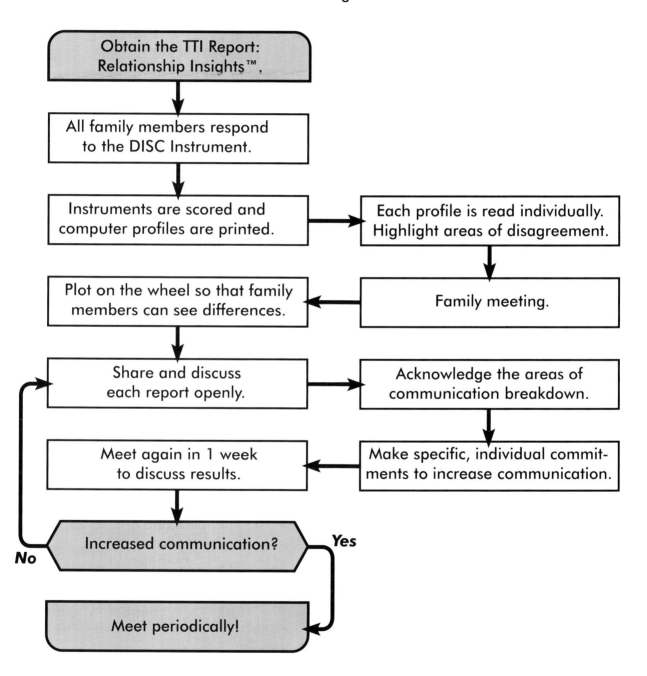

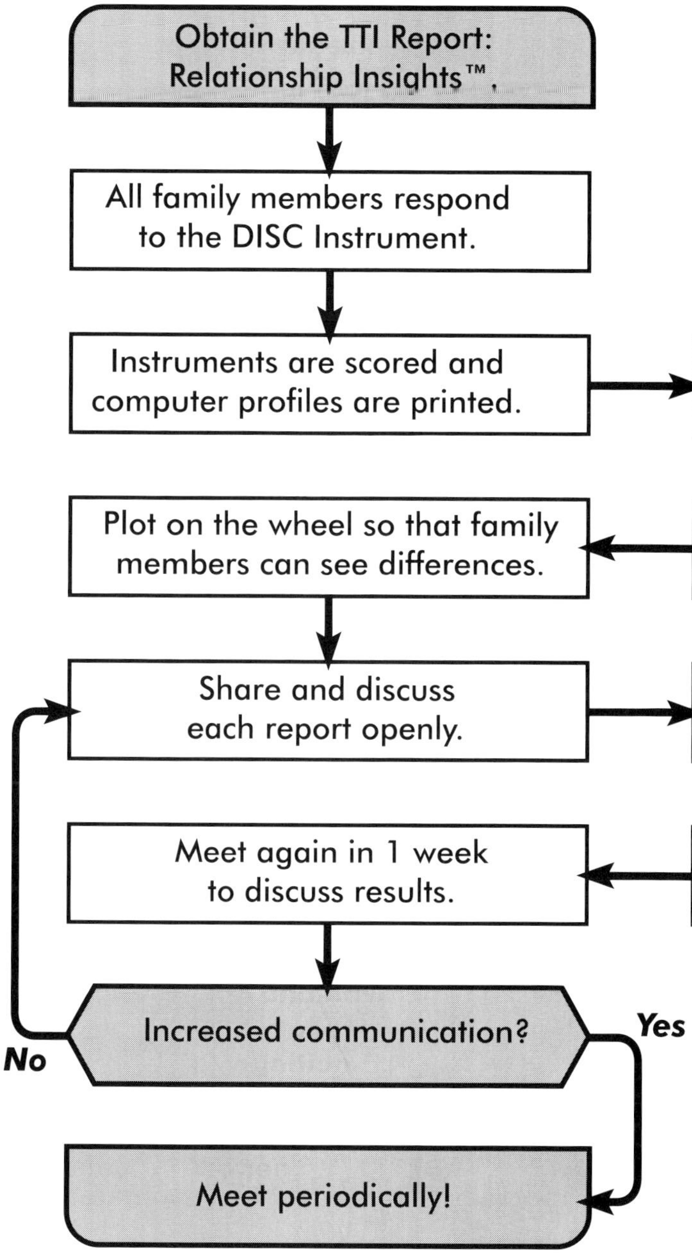

OBJECTIVES REVISITED

To present a visual flowchart of the proper usage of any of TTI's assessments.

CHAPTER 10
Questions & Answers

Chapter Objective:
To provide answers to the most common questions the authors are regularly asked and to clarify any questions you may be asking yourself at this point.

Chapter Contents:
Questions & Answers

"My greatest strength as a consultant is to be ignorant and ask a few questions."
–Peter Drucker

QUESTIONS & ANSWERS

1. Aren't there 16 classical styles that make up 95% of the population?

Yes, there are 16 classical styles. Some companies have incorrectly stated that these 16 classical styles make up 95% of the population. Research conducted by TTI has shown these 16 styles only comprise 65% of the population. The other 35% of the population are forced to "fit" into one of the 16 styles. Graph II literally has over 19,000 different combinations that are possible. TTI computerized reports generate 384 different reports, giving a much more accurate analysis.

2. Why don't you use Graph III?

Research by TTI has proven conclusively that when there is a disparity between Graph I and Graph II, Graph III does not give accurate information regarding behavior, and therefore is not valid. Graph I is the work environment and Graph II is the primary behavioral style. How can we logically average the two together and get a Graph III? The only way we can use Graph III is if Graph I and II are similar, in which case Graph III is still unnecessary because it will then mirror Graphs I and II. Consultants still using Graph III need to update their material.

3. Aren't you labeling people?

Yes, behaviorally we are. We are taking similarities seen in people as early as 400 B.C. and putting them into a useful observable language. DISC is a relationship language. If I know some of your needs and adapt my behavior to meet them, I can encourage better communication. On first meeting people, we immediately begin to form impressions of them and make value judgments. Many of the traits we judge as good or bad are merely behavioral traits. DISC, when properly used, is a language that actually decreases labeling and increases understanding of ourselves and others.

QUESTIONS & ANSWERS

4. Which style is the best?

There is no best style. Each style brings different strengths to the table. A highly successful team needs all four styles actively participating. Some managers have intentionally hired styles similar to their own. The result is a team that is weak in many of the areas that the neglected style would be strong in. Surveys of successful CEO's have shown the presence of all four styles.

5. Are you using the language of DISC to manipulate people?

That is not the goal of this manual. The DISC language should be used to promote better communication and relationships. It is a powerful language that is neither good nor bad until it is utilized by someone. An individual with a strong set of values will use the language for the good of others. However, some people will try to use the language in win/lose scenarios.

6. Do opposites attract?

Two rules seem to apply; "birds of a feather flock together" and "opposites attract". One person informed the authors that "birds of a feather flock together" applies to business, and "opposites attract" applies to relationships—especially marriage. We'll let you decide.

7. Which is the worst behavioral match?

The High I and the High C is probably the most difficult style combination due to the emotion of the "I" compared to the introversion of the "C," high risk vs. low risk, quick decision maker vs. slow decision maker. The High I – High C behavioral match can be quite conflictive, if they do not understand each other. However, many people with an "I" style are happily married to High C's and have been for many years. Most relationships stand or fall based on VALUES, not on behavioral style (DISC).

QUESTIONS & ANSWERS

8. What if my profile has a High I and a High C?

This is called me/me conflict. Relax, you don't have a split personality. You do have inner conflict. At a party you may be outgoing, fun and a little crazy. After the party you punish yourself and say "What a jerk I was." You may battle between making a quick decision and a desire for more data. You may vacillate between making a decision and not making a decision. There is nothing wrong with you. DISC measures the behavior of normal people. Awareness of your natural style allows you to modify your behavior when necessary.

9. Does the DISC model indicate abnormal behavior?

No, the Style Insights is not a clinical instrument. However, it is used by many clinicians to assist people in the understanding of normal behavior. Three unique patterns can occur which indicate possible problems. These are discussed in Chapter 6. The psychology behind the instrument is based on Marston's book, *The Emotions of Normal People*.

10. Why is the DISC language neutral?

If a High D person is good or bad, it has nothing to do with the fact that a person is a High D. A person's behavioral style is just that—a person's behavioral style. DISC measures HOW people act, not WHY (values). Some people have argued that when people are in a "survival" mode, the bad side of behavior comes out. In some cases that may be true, but again it is based on values. A High D who notices a fire may save himself and his things, or he may go in the building and risk his life to save others. This book is the first to state the DISC language as being neutral. History records men and women who faced death with a smile and a song, not the negative side of behavior. Why? Their values did not allow them to mistreat others even though they were mistreated. DISC is a neutral language.

QUESTIONS & ANSWERS

11. I thought the "blank factor" indicated fakeability?

No, the blanks in the instrument are descriptors that did not meet the standard necessary to be clearly called a D,I,S, or C descriptor. They are included in the instrument to make sure the instrument is scored properly. Some consultants train that the blanks indicate "fakeability." This position has not been statistically validated.

12. Is the Style Insights Instrument a personality test?

Emphatically, No! Personality extends far beyond the scope of the DISC instrumentation. Personality consists basically of everything we are. The DISC model measures "how" we act. It is the language of observable behavior and emotions. We therefore refer to the Style Insights Instrument as a "Behavior Analysis Instrument."

13. What about the Myers Briggs Type Indicator or the Wilson Learning Systems model?

Both, along with many others, are models based on Jungian psychology. The problem occurs in the classifying of all behavior into sixteen styles. According to recent research, this represents only 54% of the population. The other 46% are "fit" into the closest style. Statistically and behaviorally this causes questions as to overall accuracy and validity. Also, the DISC language has been validated by TTI as a "universal language," accurate worldwide as opposed to just the continental U.S. The Style Insights Instrument with the TTI computerized reports is the most accurate behavioral tool on the market today.

14. Graph I and Graph II disparity, what does it indicate?

When Graph I is significantly different from Graph II, it indicates the person is having to alter their behavior to meet the demands of the environment. What is the effect of altering the behavior? Research by Judy Suiter and Dr. David Warburton indicate increases in job dissatisfaction, health problems and stress all related to Graph I and Graph II disparity.

15. Can I change my NATURAL behavior? (Graph II)

Graph II is "you." Your Graph II behavior will only change as a result of a significant emotional event. Why would you want to change a part of you that is distinctly "you"? You will be most energized when you are exhibiting Graph II behavior, because it is part of your basic design. The wisest approach for effectiveness and success is to learn your behavioral style and then learn to adapt to others' styles. You can easily learn to change Graph I by adapting to the environment, but Graph II cannot be changed. Graph II rarely changes unless a person goes through a major life change.

16. How long does it take to effectively learn the language?

You can learn the basics quite easily and begin to "read" other people's behavioral style. DISC is literally a "language." However, it is a language of observation. Once you learn the basics of the language, you must make a conscious choice to use it daily. Write letters with DISC in mind. Communicate. Review and use just as you would any other language. We have seen excellent success in as little as five hours of training. This book, if reviewed often enough, will give you all you need to know in order to use the language "effectively." The authors have a combined total of thousands of hours using and applying the language and we are still learning.

17. How much of our behavior is needs-motivated behavior?

Over 80% of our behavior is needs motivated.

QUESTIONS & ANSWERS

18. What is the population breakdown of the four styles?

The population breakdown is as follows:

***D* - 27%**

***I* - 26%**

***S* - 23%**

C - 24%

CHAPTER 11
Validity

Chapter Objective:
To prove to distributors and their clients that TTI only sells time-tested, valid and proven assessments.

Chapter Contents:
- Information from the Experts
- Construct Validity
- Predictive Validity
- Face Validity
- Research
- Objectives Revisited

"First we will be the best, and then we will be the first!"
–Grant Tinker
American TV executive

COLLEGE OF DuPAGE

Health, Social and
Behavioral Sciences Division

425 Fawell Blvd.
Glen Ellyn, Illinois 60137-6599
www.cod.edu

630 942-2495
FAX 630 858-5409

July 30, 2004
Mr. Bill J. Bonnstetter, CEO
TTI Performance Systems, Ltd.
16020 N. 77th St.
Scottsdale, AZ 85260

Dear Bill:

Nearly twenty years ago, when I was a professor at Wheaton College, we conducted a series of construct reliability studies using the ***Style Analysis*** instrument. At that time the samples for the various studies ranged from a few hundred participants to a few thousand. Twenty years have passed. In those twenty years enormous growth has occurred for the TTI organization. Thousands of consultants now use the TTI products in the marketplace. TTI has now sold millions reports based on the suite of instruments on your web site. The research has changed as well.

Robust statistical analyses conducted in a series of research projects by Dr. Peter Klassen, principal of Documenting Excellence, provide a new level of statistical documentation. TTI continues in the vanguard of leadership in the personal assessment arena. Dr. Klassen has over the past three years conducted a repeated series of construct reliability, and factor analytic examinations of the Style Analysis and Values data. Numbers of participant data have increased to over 120,000 people. Dr. Klassen is not a distributor of TTI products, but an independent expert in statistical analysis. This makes his input objective and without product or company bias. The results of his investigations have confirmed high statistical reliability of TTI instruments. Nevertheless, suggestions were offered to make subtle changes in the existing instrumentation and to increase the already high statistical numbers.

TTI has carefully responded to the suggestions for change. The results are report products that provide a new level of accuracy for their participants and readers. With each change suggested, additional statistical analyses were conducted to re-validate the changes. These products with new levels of reliability, and population data based on 21st Century respondents, bring new insight to the marketplace. They have also received new names: ***Style Insights*** and ***Motivation Insights***. In my observation, TTI's three-year statistical investigations and resulting changes to instruments and report text files are second to none. You have a large database of respondents. The repeated statistical analyses made even after the most subtle of changes are admirable. The open nature by which TTI shares the resulting information with the greater assessment arena is un-matched. These items have positioned TTI as the assessment research benchmark as your competitors look on. The "TTI Challenge" remains un-touched by any organization.

Sincerely,

Russell J. Watson, Ed.D.

Russell J. Watson, Ed.D.
Professor – Psychology
Health, Social and Behavioral Sciences

NEW TTI INSTRUMENT RELIABILITY STUDIES

TTI continues the process of quality improvement in its assessments with this announcement of recently completed statistical studies. The following summary conclusions are excerpted from research completed on July 28, 2003, by Peter T. Klassen, Ph.D.

Style Insights™

(TTI's new DISC instrument referred to as Style Analysis 2 below.)

Summary Conclusion

Based on a series of examinations of scale and item reliabilities across multiple populations of respondents, revisions were developed and tested for TTI's Style Analysis™ that culminated in development of a revised instrument. The results of assessment of this revised edition indicate improved reliability for the two dimensions (adaptive, nature) of four parallel scales (D,I,S,C) ranging from .72 to .84. Each of the ninety-six items used to construct the scales contributes at a significant level to one or both the scales dimensions. Correlations between adaptive and natural scales indicate that these two dimensions of parallel scales are highly related, as one would expect, but also that the scales are sufficiently independent measures to justify separate interpretations and comparisons. Scores on the scales are distributed across all scale points, which supports making comparison between individuals and the self-reported behaviors in a population. Revision of the instrument included utilization of new population distributions that anchored comparisons in a population representative of the 21st century. Overall, the Style Analysis 2 is a strong, reliable instrument applicable across a variety of populations.

NEW TTI INSTRUMENT RELIABILITY STUDIES

Revised Scale Reliability

Scale reliabilities were calculated using Cronbach's Alpha. Cronbach's Alpha is considered the most appropriate statistical test for reliability, given the dichotomous responses used to construct the scales. For dichotomous data, this is equivalent to the Kuder-Richardson formula 20 (KR20) coefficient. These evaluations are a more rigorous approach than a traditional split-half statistic. Cronbach's Alpha ranges in value from 0 to 1. In general an Alpha equal to or greater than .6 is considered a minimum acceptable level, although some authorities argue for a stronger standard of at least .7. **These findings document the revised SA2 (Style Insights™) as an instrument with solid scale construction and reliability.**

New Style Insights™	Adaptive	Natural
Dominance-Challenge	.83	.84
Influence-Contact	.83	.81
Steadiness-Consistency	.78	.72
Compliance-Constraints	.73	.80

Motivation Insights™

(TTI's new Values instrument referred to as Personal Interests, Attitudes and Values 2 below.)

Summary Conclusion

Based on a series of examinations of scale and item reliabilities, revisions were developed and tested for TTI's Personal Interests, Attitudes and Values™ that culminated in development of a revised instrument. The results of assessment of this revised edition indicate high or improved reliability for the six scales with Cronbach's ranging .7 to .82. Each of the seventy-six items used to construct the scales contributes at a significant level to its assigned scale. Correlations among the six scales indicate that they are substantially independent in measurements. Scores on the scales are distributed across the scales leading to meaningful comparisons and interpretation. Overall, the Personal Interests, Attitudes and Values 2 is a strong, reliable instrument applicable across a variety of populations.

NEW TTI INSTRUMENT RELIABILITY STUDIES

Revised Scale Reliability
Scale reliabilities were calculated using Cronbach's Alpha. Cronbach's Alpha is considered the most appropriate statistical test for reliability, given the ranking of responses used to construct the scales. This statistic models internal consistency based on the average inter-item correlation. It is a more rigorous test than a traditional split-half statistic. Cronbach's Alpha ranges in value from 0 to 1. In general an Alpha equal to or greater than .6 is considered a minimum acceptable level, although some authorities argue for a stronger standard of at least .7. **These findings document the revised PIAV 2 (Motivation Insights™) as an instrument with solid scale construction and reliability.**

New Motivation Insights™ (PIAV 2)	
Theoretical	.77
Utilitarian	.80
Aesthetic	.82
Social	.82
Individualistic	.70
Traditional	.81

TTI is incorporating these new instruments into its product line to bring TTI Distributors and their Clients the most highly reliable assessments of their kind on the market today.

CONSTRUCT VALIDITY

The first thing a user should investigate with regard to any assessment is construct validity. Construct validity is theoretical with the simplest definition being, "Does it measure what you say it measures?" In our Four Factor Style Insights Instrument, we perform construct validity on a regular basis. Why? Because things change and words or phrases used change their meaning over time, such as "gay", which was once used to identify one of the Marston Four Factors in years past.

How do you know if a word or phrase has gone bad? The answer is simple—you do an item analysis or single factor analysis. Words that have a low correlation must be replaced.

Words that have almost identical connections between two factors also should not be used in an assessment. Introvert and extrovert are words that are very close. Both Dominant and Influencing are extroverted and Steadiness and Compliant are introverted.

In 1936, G. W. Allport and H.S. Odbert, *Trait-Names: A Psycho-Lexical Study, Princeton: Psychological Review Company,* identified over 17,000 English adjectives that described personal behavior. R. B. Cattell (1943), *The Description of Personality: Basic Traits Resolved Into Clusters, The Journal of Abnormal and Social Psychology, 36;* used the factor analysis method, which reduced Allport's and Odbert's work to a manageable list.

Words used on assessments must be consistent with what the author says they are measuring. Using the word trusting has met our construct validity criteria. Also, in literature, we point out that this is the exception to the rule.

Words such as *articulate, studious, strategic, deep, fast,* and *devout* are words that raise a suspicion on item analysis.

Paper assessments or computerized reports measuring behavior sometimes make the statement that the person is intelligent, honest, loves animals and is extremely fond of the outdoors. Behavioral assessments reporting that type of data are suspect from a construct validity standpoint. Behavior is how you do things, not what, why or a measure of your intelligence.

CONSTRUCT VALIDITY

In any Four Factor Model, the words or phrases used in the assessment should identify one of the four dimensions. The more words you used in an assessment, the lower the item analysis correlation. Thus, the lower the validity. However, this is a catch 22 because the marketplace has trouble understanding how we can produce reports that are so accurate with 24 questions.

In reality, we have 48 questions: you respond to 24 most and 24 least. Both the most and least choices are analyzed to develop each person's report.

Several years ago, we put 24 adjectives on a sheet of paper, six describing each of four dimensions. People were asked to nominate under one of the four groups the name of an individual that those six adjectives described. Those people were than assessed. The research proved people can be 82% accurate in putting people in the right category. Random would be 25% accurate only. However, identifying is not enough. You must be able to understand, appreciate and to know how to communicate with them.

The following are excerpts from *Concise Encyclopedia of Psychology,* edited by Raymond J. Corsini and Alan J. Auerbach:

> **...Testing and Legislation**
>
> During the spring and summer of 1964, while the Civil Rights Act of 1964 was being debated in the U.S. Senate, a case was brought before the Illinois Fair Employment Practices Commission in which it was alleged that a black job applicant was denied employment because he had failed a short psychological (IQ-type) test that was "culturally biased" against blacks. Although the commission dismissed this charge, the case drew widespread national press attention, particularly from business people who expressed the fear that governmental agencies would dictate selection procedures and hiring standards in private industry.
>
> To allay such fears, Senator John Tower of Texas introduced an amendment accepted by Congress that became part of the law. This amendment states: "notwithstanding any other provision of this (Act), it shall not be unlawful employment practice for an employer to give and act upon the results of any professionally developed ability test provided that such test, its administration or action upon the results is not designed, intended or used to discriminate because of race, color, religion, sex or national origin," (Civil Rights Act of 1964, Title VII, Section 703h). Many state legislatures in states where fair employment commissions or commissions against discrimination existed, followed the Senate's lead and incorporated a version of Paragraph 703h into their state laws.

Psychological tests used for employment selection, however, had an entirely predictable consequence, based on 50 years of data accumulated since World War I's Army Alpha: Blacks, and to some extent, other minorities (e.g., Latinos), earned lower scores than Whites, and at any cutoff score, a smaller proportion of Blacks than Whites qualified or "passed the test". In this context, the Equal Employment Opportunity Commission (EEOC) issued "Uniform Guidelines on Employee Selection Procedures".

The turning point came in the U.S. Supreme Court case of Griggs vs. Duke Power Company [401 U.S. 424, 3 FEP 175 (1971)]. The court ruled in favor of the plaintiff, Griggs, in a landmark decision in which a number of standards for test use were set. First, the initial burden was on the plaintiff to offer evidence that the selection procedure had adverse impact; and, second if the selection procedure did have an adverse impact, the defendant user had to assume the burden of demonstrating by appropriate means that performance on the test was related to performance on the job for which the test was used as a selection criterion. The court also indicated that "great deference" must be given to the EEOC Guidelines, which outlined standards of, and procedures for, test validation.

About 70,000 complaints of discrimination are filed with the EEOC annually. Of these 10% to 15% allege discrimination by unfair testing.

CONSTRUCT VALIDITY

Adverse Impact

In the historic March 8th U.S. Supreme Court decision regarding the Civil Rights Act of 1964, Justice Burger stated, "Nothing in the Act precludes the use of testing or measuring procedures; obviously they are useful". What Congress has forbidden is giving these devices and mechanisms controlling force unless they are demonstrably a reasonable measure of job performance. Congress has not commanded that the less qualified be preferred over the better qualified simply because of minority origins. Far from disparaging job qualifications as such, Congress has made such qualifications the controlling factor so that race, religion, nationality and sex become irrelevant. What Congress has commanded is that any tests used must measure the person for the job and not the person in abstract. Testing obviously will continue, as indeed it should.

Validation for purposes of EEO law is the technical process whereby the employer defends the use of a selection device, or standard, that demonstrates a very close relationship between performance against the standard and performance on the job.

No company can use any selection device or standard that has an adverse impact on the protected group. The protected group is usually a minority person, female, or person over the age of forty, but it can be anyone.

The EEO legislation was aimed at employers who administered tests that are not job-related or are discriminated against the protected group. For example, giving a math test to keep someone from being hired as a police officer was deemed not job related and therefore, illegal.

The EEOC, an agency of the federal government, issued the Uniform Guidelines on Employee Selection Procedures in 1966. These guidelines were issued to serve as a guide for applying the four-fifths rule. A selection for any race, sex or ethnic group which is less than four-fifths (4/5) or 80 percent of the rate for the group with the highest rate will generally be regarded by the federal enforcement agencies as evidence of adverse impact.

Smaller differences in selection rate may nevertheless constitute adverse impact where they are significant in both statistical and practical terms or where a user's actions have discouraged applicants disproportionately on grounds of race, sex or ethnic group.

CONSTRUCT VALIDITY

Greater differences in selection rate may not constitute adverse impact where the differences are based on small numbers and are not statistically significant, or where special recruiting or other programs cause the pool, minority or female candidates to be atypical of the normal pool of applicants from that group.

Where the user's evidence concerning the impact of a selection procedure indicates adverse impact but is based upon numbers which are too small to be reliable, evidence concerning the impact of the procedure over a longer period of time and/or evidence concerning the impact which the selection procedure had when used in the same manner in similar circumstances elsewhere may be considered in determining adverse impact. Where the user has not maintained data on adverse impact as required by the documentation section of applicable guidelines, the federal enforcement agencies may draw an inference of adverse impact of the selection process from the failure of the user to maintain such data if the user has an under-utilization of a group in the job category as compared to the group's representation in the relevant labor market or, in the case of jobs filled from within, the applicable workforce.

Consideration of user's equal employment opportunity posture: In carrying out their obligations, the federal enforcement agencies will consider the general posture of the user with respect to equal employment opportunity for the job or group of jobs in question. Where a user has adopted an affirmative action program, the federal enforcement agencies will consider the provisions of that program which includes the goals and timetables that the user has adopted. Also considered is the progress the user has made in carrying out that program and in meeting the goals and timetables. While such affirmative action programs may in design and execution be race, color, sex, or ethnic conscious, selection procedures under such programs should be based upon the ability or relative ability to do the work.

[Approved by the Officer of Management and Budget under control No. 3046-0017, (Pub.L96-511, 94 Stat. 2812 44 U.S.C. 3501 et. Seq.)]

PREDICTIVE VALIDITY

Since 1984, TTI has collected information on our behavioral instrument and values questionnaire. We meet or exceed the four-fifths rule. However, we have never released the statistics because our attorneys have advised us that the four-fifths rule does not apply to behavior or values. In fact, there are many scientists who claim that some or all of these types of issues are inherited.

The collected research of Bill J. Bonnstetter statistically demonstrates the following:

- People with a high Social value worldwide will run a company or department based on people issues.
- People with a low Social value will make decisions based on the bottom line.
- There is only a slight difference in the mean on each of the six values in the United States, Australia, South Africa, Ireland and the United Kingdom, which are all English-speaking countries.
- Top performing sales people in the United States and Germany have the same top three values, with the Utilitarian value being the strongest drive in both countries.
- There are more D's and I's percentage-wise in the United States' African-American population than in the Caucasian population. Statistics clearly demonstrated that more top managers and top sales people are behaviorally D's and I's.
- Behaviorally speaking, the same can be said for Finland.

Every company should do their own validation study to determine which questionnaires/instruments are worth their continued investment. Types of devices that companies need to be concerned about are those that assess ability, aptitudes, skills or knowledge. They are most likely to have adverse impact, whereas devices that assess personality traits, behavior or values are least likely to have adverse impact.

If knowledge always leads to success, every certified public accountant, lawyer, doctor and nurse would be successful. In each of those professions, behavior and values are the better indicator of success. Age, gender or nationality have nothing to do with successful people.

PREDICTIVE VALIDITY

In today's corporate environment, the proper use of test questionnaires and instruments as part of the selection process can make the difference between hiring the best or becoming noncompetitive.

Reading Levels
The reading level of any assessment can impact the result. The assessment could be valid; but if the reading level is too high, you may not get valid results from some people. Based on research, we have lowered the reading level to 5.9 on the Style Insights™ Instrument.

Instructions
The instructions can impact the usefulness of assessments. An assessment can be valid but not useful if the participant doesn't understand the instructions.

Emotions or Temperament
Dr. Jolande Jacobi provides us with a diagram that may help explain the differences between types and emotions in her book, The Psychology of C.G. Jung (1942). Jacobi looks at the brain and breaks it into two parts: conscious and unconscious. Stored in the unconscious according to Jacobi are:

1. **Forgotten material**
2. **Repressed material**
3. **Emotions**
4. **Irruptions**
5. **Part of the collective unconscious that can never be made conscious.**

In the conscious mind she placed sensation, feeling, intuition and thinking. Thus, she is positioning emotions as stronger than type as they are stored in the unconscious mind and provide a basis for the conscious mind to operate. Marston's anger and fear are very strong emotions and should carry more weight in evaluating how people act.

One should question assessments that have not compared their construct validity to other known assessments. TTI's behavioral assessment has been compared against other behavioral assessments in the marketplace. When vendors claim to be valid but offer nothing more than their opinion that they are better, one really needs to question their ethics. Our construct validity meets and exceeds industry standards.

PREDICTIVE VALIDITY

Emotions or Temperament

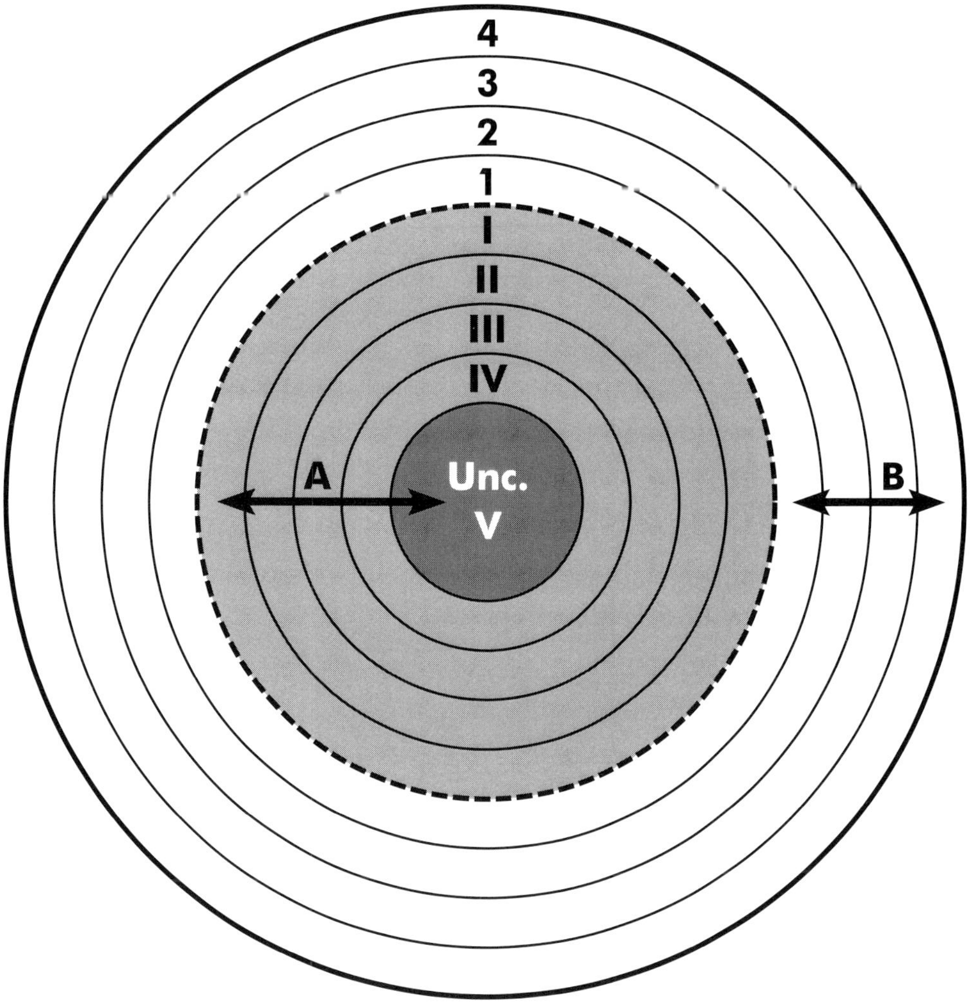

A. Unconcious

I. Forgotten material
II. Repressed material
III. Emotions
IV. Irruptions
V. That part of the collective unconcious that can never be made concious.

B. Concious

1. Sensation
2. Feeling
3. Intuition
4. Thinking

PREDICTIVE VALIDITY

Benchmarking

You cannot benchmark a personality contest. You cannot benchmark the performance of a team if the team's performance based on industry standards is a C-. Benchmarking only works when you truly have people who are performing at a superior level. Then, and only then, do you see a significant difference. If you do not see a significant difference in their behavior, then do not use behavior in your solution process.

Rule Out

Quite often it is easier to rule out people who cannot be superior performers. In looking at top performing sales people both in the U.S. and Germany, we validated that salespeople who were classified as Analyzers or Implementors had very little choice of becoming top performing salespeople.

Style Insights™

The Style Insights form and its various uses are all derived from the work of Dr. William Moulton Marston. There are at least fifty companies today using the Marston theory as the basis for examining behavior via a descriptive behavioral device. The Style Insights and its ancillary forms enable us to identify "patterns of behavior" in such a way as to make practical application of the Marston theory.

Reliability Estimates

Reliability estimates were obtained using the Spearman-Brown split-halves reliability coefficient. This coefficient indicates the degree of internal consistency of response to the instrument as a whole. The coefficients for each dimension are as follow:

Dominance	**r = .92**
Influence	**r = .89**
Steadiness	**r = .91**
Compliance	**r = .90**

It is evident from these reliability coefficients that there is an unusually high degree of internal consistency in response to the Style Insights Instrument as a whole and to each of the related dimensions.

PREDICTIVE VALIDITY

Strength of the correlation is indicated by the size of the coefficient. The coefficient can vary from +1.00 through 0 to −1.00. A coefficient near 0 tells us that there is no relationship between the variables. The closer a coefficient is to + or −1.00 the stronger the relationship.

Correlation Examples:
+/- 1.0 = Perfect correlation (extremely rare)
+/- .80 to .99 = Unusually high correlation
+/- .70 to .79 = Very high correlation
+/- .60 to .69 = High correlation
+/- .30 to .59 = Moderately high correlation
+/- .20 to .29 = Very low correlation
+/- .00 to .19 = No correlation

The study duplicates, in part, a study by Dr. Russell J. Watson, Wheaton College, "A Statistical Comparison Between the TTI Style Analysis and the Performax Personal Profile System," 1989.

Included in Watson's research is a reliability check for internal consistency of the Style Analysis using the Spearman-Brown split-halves and the Kuder-Richardson formula 21 reliability coefficients. The mean coefficients for each dimension were as follows:

Dominance	**r = .91**
Influence	**r = .90**
Steadiness	**r = .92**
Compliance	**r = .89**

Graph I represents the "most like" behavior, displaying the intensity of the four factors which allows interpretation of the behavior an individual believes must be projected to achieve success in a given environment.

The "least" choices are plotted on Graph II. This graph demonstrates the real self...or, the intensity of each factor...while the individual is under pressure and unable to mask behavior. The "least" graph is very important as it represents the real person, allowing conclusions to be drawn on how to best understand, manage and communicate with this person.

PREDICTIVE VALIDITY

Based on the individual's responses to the 24 "most" words, over 20,000 different graphs can be plotted, and over 20,000 different graphs can be plotted for the "least" responses. The magnitude of those numbers makes it impractical to write an evaluation of each potential graph, so, for evaluation purposes, these possible graphs are condensed into one of 384 graphs. The computer-generated reports are based on evaluating the 384 graphs from both the "most" and the "least" responses.

Current research indicates that 64% of the population will fall into 16 basic graphs. The remaining 36% of the population is distributed across the remaining 368 graphs. This is why it is so difficult to compare the Style Insights to other psychological instruments. As a result of this, the Style Insights Instrument is far more sophisticated than instruments that only measure one factor against another in each question. This leads to a discussion of face validity.

FACE VALIDITY

Dr. Russell J. Watson, Wheaton College, did a study of face validity. The participants were asked to evaluate the "perceived accuracy" of their own computer-generated reports. The perceived accuracy of the reports was 88.49% with a standard deviation of 6.43%. The perceived accuracy of the reports according to the key dimensions were as follows:

Primary Dominance 91%

Primary Influence 94%

Primary Steadiness 85%

Primary Compliance 82%

This study confirms what behavioral researchers have discovered...that different styles see the world in different ways.

The purpose of the Style Insights Instrument was to make the theories of Marston and Jung understandable and useful in people's lives. The theory of four to eight basic types can be looked at in many ways. To assist users of the Style Insights and the accompanying software, we have completed the data in several different ways to assist in a broad range of applications.

FACE VALIDITY

Style Insights™ Instrument

The Style Insights, while based primarily on William Marston's book *Emotions of Normal People* also uses the works of Carl Gustav Jung. Jung's work starts from the assumption that there are three pairs of functions that are expressed differently in each person:

extroversion-introversion

perception-intuition

thinking-feeling

In each case a person shows a preference of one of the two possibilities, which then results in eight possible combinations or types. Marston's system is in complete mathematical harmony with the works of Jung.

Isabel Briggs Myers added a further pair of functions judging-perceiving and developed the Myers-Briggs type indicator. This test places people into sixteen types.

Conclusion

The Style Insights Instrument has compared favorably against other Marston-based instruments. The researchers concluded that the Style Insights Instrument displayed a high degree of similarity to the compared instruments and is an assessment tool that shows much evidence of constructive validity. The instrument was developed in the late 1960s and has never been challenged in court. It is widely used by business and government including several agencies in the United States. Marston-based instruments similar to the Style Insights have been administered to over 30 million people worldwide and have earned the respect of many professionals based on its accuracy and validity.

Practical Research

Every company wants to know: "Will this assessment work for me?" Most companies will not allow us to use their name in the study, but in the next section we will discuss some of our research done over the last 20 years that has solved problems for our clients.

Groundbreaking Research on What is Inside Top Sales Performers in the United States and Europe

By Bill J. Bonnstetter, President and CEO
Target Training International, Ltd.

Research studies of top salespeople in both the United States and Europe confirm that top sales performance can be predicted. These findings confirm that top performing salespeople are similar in very specific ways. This research carries significant implications for people who are considering sales as a career, are currently selling or are accountable for sales performance. The net conclusion of the research shows that top salespeople around the world place a high value on efficiency, utility and economics.

The most successful organizations in the world already know that hiring the right sales people has the potential of becoming one of the most powerful secret weapons in their arsenal of competitive strategies. What they may not know is that hiring the right salespeople can be as simple as following a recipe based on recent findings from an international study I conducted with Frank Scheelen of Institut for Managementhberatung and Bildungsmarketing.

As global competition and increased customer demands require organizations to improve in key performance areas such as customer service, quality, reducing costs and customization, aggressive organizations must be ever vigilant in the identification, acquisition, development and integration of innovative technology. The type of innovative technology is now available to select top performers.

As a result of our 20 years of research, development and distribution of assessment tools to measure performance, we have been telling organizations that it is what's on the inside, not the outside, that counts, especially in sales performance. What we are fighting is the myth that hiring good looking and intelligent sounding people correlates to sales performance.

Much of the research conducted in the past on top salespeople has been focused on behavior. Behavioral research has been popular because, like looking good and sounding good, behavior can be observed. Little, if any significant study has been focused on what goes on inside a top salesperson. Our groundbreaking research in the United States and Europe now confirms that attitudes far outweigh looking good, sounding good or behavior in distinguishing top salespeople.

RESEARCH

Two of our most significant assumptions were confirmed by the two studies:

1. Top performing salespeople around the world are similar; and
2. Attitudes or values are more important than behavior in sales performance (Refer to Study One and Study Two in the following pages)

In both studies, only top performing salespeople responded. In the United States study and a separate German study, top salespeople responded to two assessments. One was based on internationally validated DISC behavioral model and the other was based on the Personal Interests, Attitudes and Values model.

The DISC assessment identifies eight basic patterns that define how people tend to behave. **Listed below are brief descriptions of the eight behavior patterns:**

1. **Conductor – direct and results-oriented**
2. **Persuader – optimistic and flexible**
3. **Promoter – verbal and trusting**
4. **Relater – cooperative team player**
5. **Supporter – accommodating and persistent**
6. **Coordinator – cautious and self-disciplined**
7. **Analyzer – precise and detail-oriented**
8. **Implementor – creative and indecisive**

The PIAV assessment measures six distinct attitudes that provide the context for motivation or why people act the way they do. **Listed below are the six attitudes with a brief description of the focus of each:**

1. **Utilitarian/Economic – a focus on practicality, efficiency**
2. **Theoretical – a focus on education, learning and truth**
3. **Aesthetic – a focus on beauty, harmony and balance**
4. **Individualistic – a focus on controlling one's own destiny or the destiny of others**
5. **Social – putting others before self**
7. **Traditional/Regulatory – a focus on a system for living**

RESEARCH

The results of the United States DISC behavior study of top salespeople in 178 firms are illustrated with pie charts. As you can see on the next page, top sales performers tended to be spread across four behavioral patterns. In the German study, top sales performers tended to be spread across three of the same behavioral patterns. In view of these results, it is reasonable to conclude that salespeople with most, if not all, behavioral patterns can be top performers.

However, when it comes to what is on the inside of top performing salespeople, both United States studies as well as the German study confirm it is hands-down, a Utilitarian attitude. The implications for the global sales community, whether they are salespeople or those who must hire, manage, develop and motivate them, are clear. The most important selection criteria when hiring salespeople is a high Utilitarian attitude. Once salespeople with a high Utilitarian attitude are hired, the job satisfaction and motivation buttons that need to be pushed are efficiency, practicality and economics.

Studies of attitudes also reveal that when a person's highest attitude is fulfilled, they will begin to be motivated towards their second highest attitude. For instance, a top performing salesperson whose highest attitude is Utilitarian and second highest attitude is Aesthetic will begin to be motivated by beauty and harmony only after they have made as much money as they want through the most efficient and practical methods. This provides important insight into incentives. Income and other financially related incentives will yield the best effects with high Utilitarian salespeople, unless the salesperson is completely satisfied in those areas. Although financial rewards are always a safe bet, incentives should ultimately be tailored to each salesperson's motivations.

RESEARCH STUDIES

Tops Sales Leaders USA vs. Germany
Study One: Top Sales Leaders, USA
N = 178

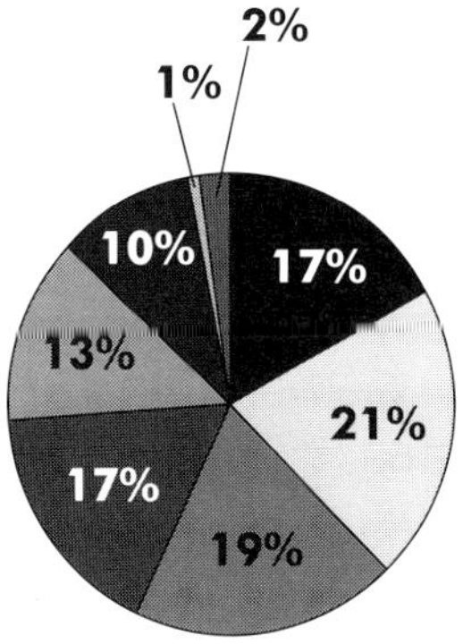

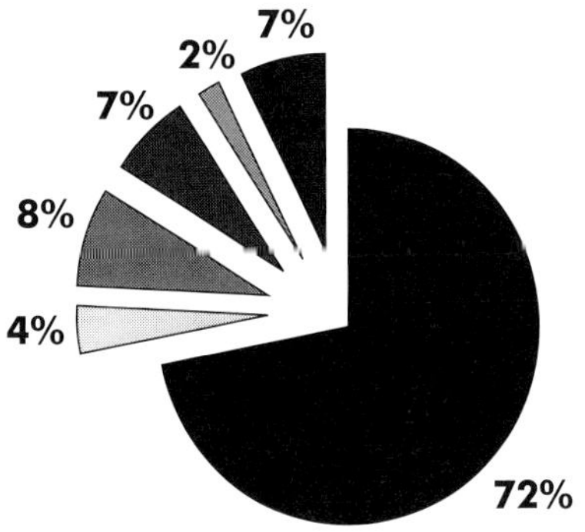

Behavior - Top Sales Leaders: USA

■ Conductor - 17% ▨ Supporter - 13%
▢ Persuader - 21% ■ Coordinator - 10%
▨ Promoter - 19% ▨ Analyzer - 1%
■ Relater - 17% ▨ Implementor - 2%

Attitudes - Top Sales Leaders: USA

■ Utilitarian - 72% ■ Social - 7%
▢ Theoretical - 4% ▨ Aesthetic - 2%
▨ Traditional - 8% ■ Individualistic - 7%

Study Two: Top Sales Leaders, Germany
N = 492

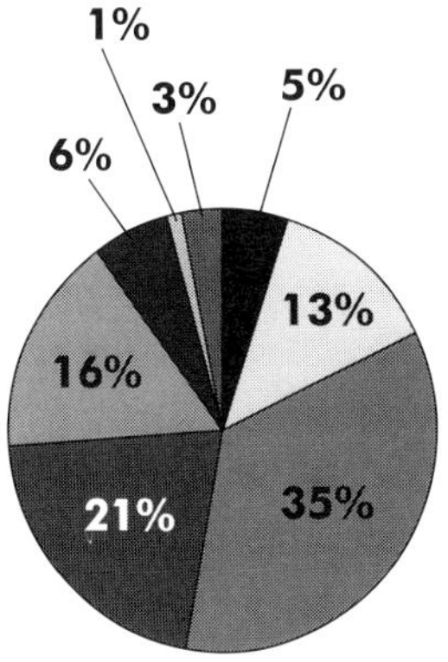

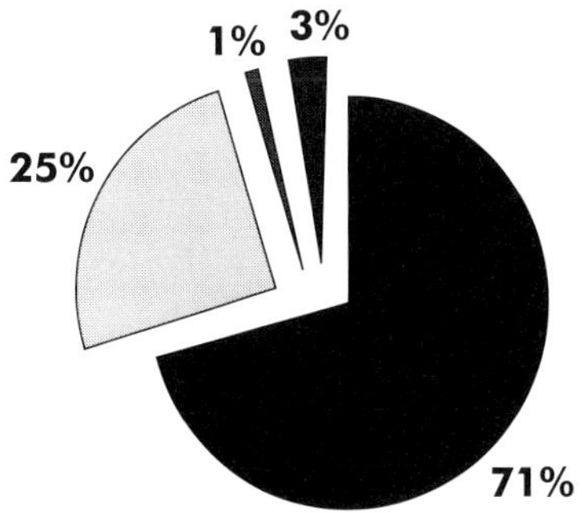

Behavior - Top Sales Leaders: Germany

■ Conductor - 5% ▨ Supporter - 16%
▢ Persuader - 13% ■ Coordinator - 6%
▨ Promoter - 35% ▨ Analyzer - 1%
■ Relater - 21% ▨ Implementor - 3%

Attitudes - Top Sales Leaders: Germany

■ Utilitarian - 71% ■ Social - 1%
▢ Theoretical - 25% ▢ Aesthetic - 0%
▢ Traditional - 0% ■ Individualistic - 3%

THE SUCCESS INSIGHTS WHEEL

Germany: N = 492

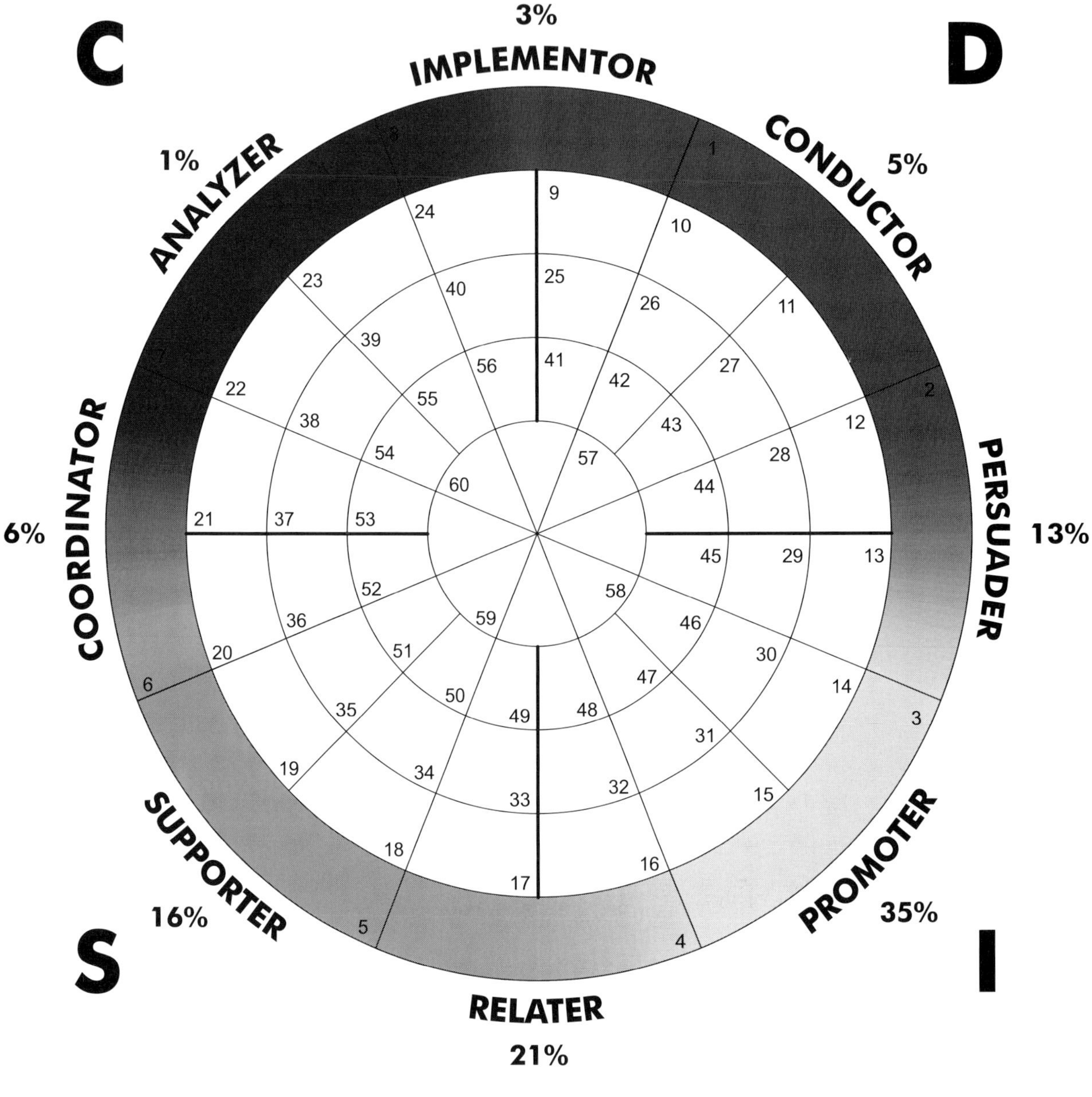

THE SUCCESS INSIGHTS WHEEL

USA: N = 178

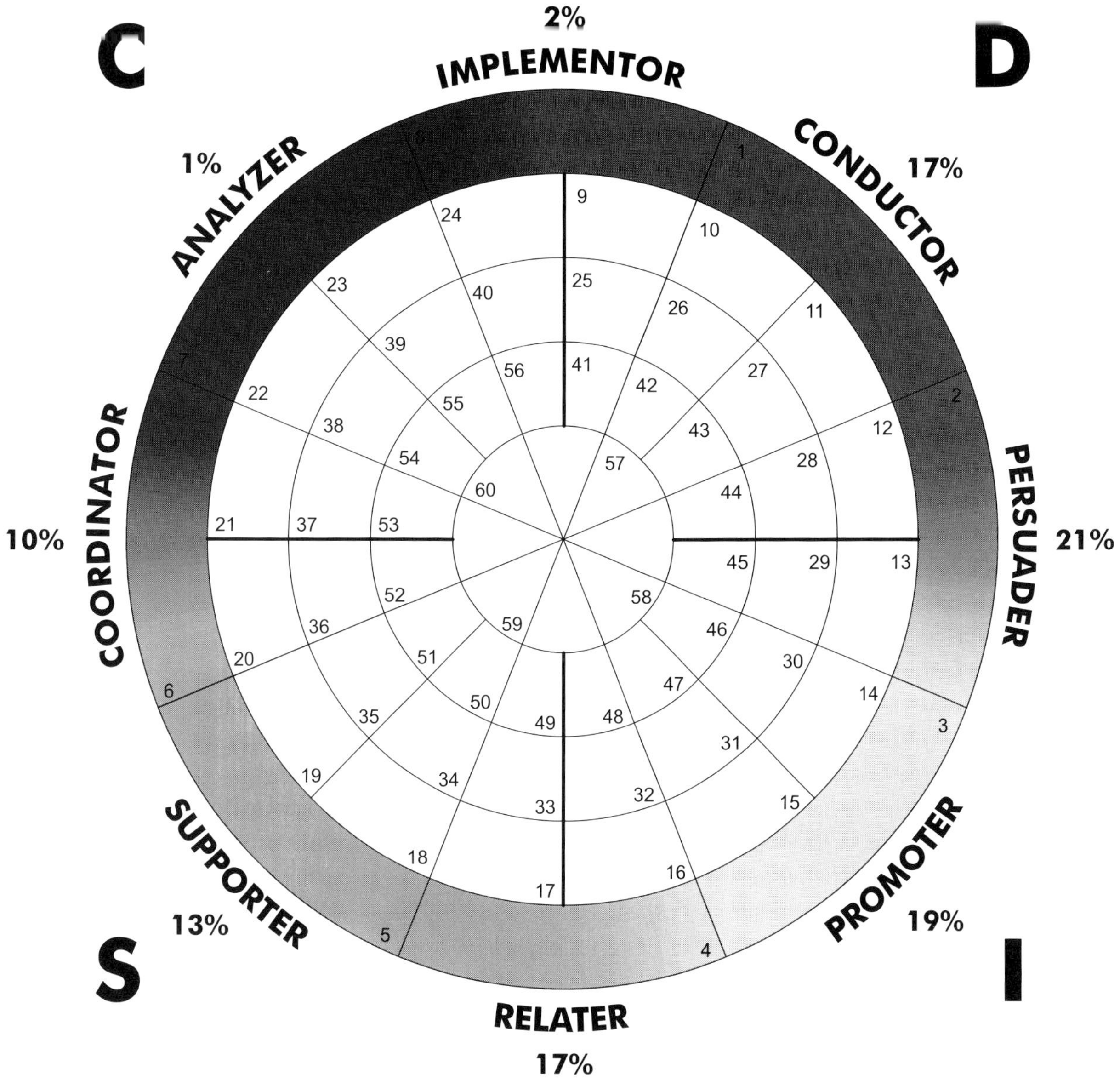

RESEARCH

STATISTICS RELATING TO DRIVER ANALYSIS SYSTEM EFFECTIVENESS:

Company Name	1988	1989	1990	1991	1992	1993
West's Best Freight % of turnover		180%	37% 65% reduction in accidents 80% reduction in workman's comp. claims			
Barr-Nunn Transport % of turnover		108%	70%	43% 50% reduction in accidents 50% reduction in workman's comp. claims		
		1993 1st Place - ITCC "Safest Fleet"				
D.M. Bowman, Inc. % of turnover		130%	67% 50% reduction in accidents 65% reduction in workman's comp. claims			
Eagle Transport % of turnover		180%	160%	87% 60% reduction in accidents 50% reduction in workman's comp. claims	50%	
Marten Transport % of turnover	120%	90%	70%	60%	47%	45%

RESEARCH

DISCOVERING THE PERSON AT WORK

- **Face Validity**
- **Construct Validity**
- **Predictive Validity**

David Maddrell Warburton, Ph.D.
Department of Psychology
University of Reading
Reading RG6 2AL
UK

Judy Suiter,
Competitive Edge, Inc.
Atlanta, GA

Project Researcher, David Maddrell Warburton, Ph.D.
Dr. David Warburton's educational background includes: B.Sc. from Royal Veterinary College, University of London and Birkbeck College, University of London in Psychology. He received an A.M. in Psychology at Indiana University and his Ph.D. in Psychology and Physiology (with highest distinction) from Indiana University.

He has served as Lecturer and Reader at Reading University, Visiting Professor at Indiana University, Distinguished Lecturer at University of California, San Diego; Personal Professorship at Reading University and Fellow of the British Psychological Society and is a Chartered Psychologist (Founder Member).

Professor Warburton has also been Technical Advisor to the World Health Organization, Surgeon General of the U.S. on Smoking and Health, Food and Drug Administration of the U.S. on nicotine, to the UK Independent Scientific Committee on Smoking and Health, and New Zealand's government on toxic substances. He is Membre du Jury, Foundation de France pour la Recherche sur la Maladie D'Alzheimer. His list of positions and appointments are extensive and available on request.

RESEARCH PROJECT PHASE I – Discovering the Person At Work

General Introduction

As part of a program of profiling the behavioral style of managers using Style Analysis (Target Training International, Ltd., 1991), we have collected information which has enabled us to carry out four studies that provide confirmatory validations of the DISC system and the software.

Validity has been investigated in terms of:

- Face validity (Study One). Face validity refers to whether the test "looks valid" to the people who take it and to untrained colleagues.
- Construct validity (Study Two). Construct validity considers the relationship of the DISC model with related assessments of behavioral style.
- Predictive validity (Studies Three and Four). Predictive validity refers to the extent in which it could be said a person is likely to become dissatisfied with their work, to become sick, etc.

In the past validity testing has been regarded as not generalizable to different situations. However, this pessimism has arisen as the result of validation with samples which have been too small to yield stable estimates of the relation of the predictor and the criterion variables. It has been estimated that over half the validation samples have included no more than 50 people (Schmidt, Hunter, and Urry, 1976). With such small samples, the validation is not technically feasible.

STUDY ONE – NOMINATED GROUPS

The aim of this study was to make an evaluation of the face validity of the DISC profiles. Face validity is a highly desirable feature of any assessment, because it establishes appropriateness for application in practical situations for the person and their colleagues.

One previous approach, which has been adopted, is to ask individuals to assess the accuracy of their own report. The rationale behind the present study is that the measures of behavioral style should ideally be closely related to actual behavioral styles in daily work life as seen by their coworkers. Evidence of this sort increases face validity with the client company and acceptance of their predictive applicability to work situations.

RESEARCH

Subjects
The subjects were 91 middle managers from a variety of industries.

The majority of the volunteers were male (68%) with ages ranging between 28 and 62. Of these, 39% were between 28 and 36 and 6% were over 55. The majority were married (68%) with a further 2% cohabiting. 17% were single, 7.8% divorced, 4.3% separated and less than 1% widowed. Of the whole sample 53% had children, of which 26% had one child, 41% had two children and 33% had three or more.

The educational qualifications of the group were mixed, with 8% having no formal qualifications, 29% having high school graduation certificates at 16 years, 26% having high school graduation certificates at 18 years "A" levels, 10% having a college degree and 27% having a higher degree or professional qualification.

Procedure
Our methodology has been the use of "The Method of Nominated Groups." In this procedure, independent judges were asked to select one or more colleagues who were best described by sets of six adjectives taken from the Managing for Success Users Manual Revised Edition (Target Training International, Ltd., 1989). Altogether, there were four sets, one for each of the four primary behavior styles.

For Dominance, these adjectives were ambitious, forceful, decisive, strong-willed, independent and goal-oriented. For Influencing, these adjectives were magnetic, enthusiastic, friendly, demonstrative, political, and superficial. For Steadiness, the adjectives were patient, predictable, reliable, steady, relaxed and modest. And for Conforming, they were dependent, neat, conservative, perfectionist, careful and compliant.

The subjects were asked to name people who were close to them in their work, and who were best described by these words. These nominees filled in the DISC profile. All these assessments were made prior to exposure to the Managing for Success software, and the selected adjectives were not those used in the profiling in order to avoid response bias.

Analysis

1. Percentage Identification Success Rate (n=91)

Table 1: Identification Success Rate

D Style	I Style	S Style	C Style
86.3%	91.2%	71.0%	76.4%

Accuracy of Colleagues Identification—81.2%
(Chance—25%)

X2 = 16.63; p<0.0005, i.e., a highly significant goodness of fit for a predicted frequency of 100%.

2. Calculation of Accuracy of Judgment

The raw scores for the primary styles were transformed into percentages and the percentage disparity between the ratings for the Response to the Environment Style of the nominee and maximum (98%) was assessed.

Table 2: Mean Style Score of the Nominees

D Style	I Style	S Style	C Style
75.3%	88.5%	79.5%	86.1%

Accuracy of Colleagues Assessment—82.4%

Conclusions

It is clear from the data (n=91) analyzed that individuals who impress others as representing one behavioral style in their every day behavior answer the DISC in a similar manner (Predictive accuracy of over 81%).

From this data, there can be no doubt that the DISC responses give a very accurate picture of the person's habitual behavior patterns at work as seen by colleagues.

This finding establishes a high face validity of the DISC profiling.

RESEARCH

STUDY TWO - THE DISC CONSTRUCTS IN CONTEXT

A second approach to the criterion of validity is to examine the extent to which it fits with predictions made from other theories of behavior at work, construct validity. Construct validity is important because it makes the results from measures easier to interpret and relate to real life situations, like work.

Methods

A series of questionnaires were selected as representing various aspects of behavioral style. These were Type A B, Extroversion-Introversion, Stability-Neuroticism, Optimism-Pessimism. In addition, we included some questionnaires on substance use, alcohol consumption and cigarette smoking.

Some Significant Positive & Negative Correlates of DISC (N = 150)

	D	I	S	C
Type A	+	-	-	+
Extroversion	+	+	-	-
Optimism	+	+	-	-
Control Optimism	+			
Pessimism	-		+	+
Alcohol Use	+	+	-	-
Cigarette Use	+	+	-	-

D - DOMINANCE STYLE - Driving, Decisive

Positive
- Type A
- Extroversion
- Optimism
- Control Optimism
- Alcohol Use
- Cigarette Use

Negative
- Pessimism

I - INFLUENCING STYLE - Interacting

Positive
- Optimism
- Extroversion
- Alcohol Use
- Cigarette Use

Negative
- Type A
- Pessimism

S - STEADINESS STYLE - Stable

Positive
- Introversion
- Pessimism

Negative
- Type A
- Optimism
- Alcohol Use
- Cigarette Use

C - CONFORMING STYLE - Cautious, Careful

Positive
- Type A
- Introversion
- Pessimism

Negative
- Optimism
- Alcohol Use
- Cigarette Use

Conclusions

First, it is clear that each behavioral style has a unique pattern of associations. Second, each pattern is a coherent one, demonstrating internal consistency of the single DISC constructs. Thus, DISC constructs can be related meaningfully to other theories of behavioral styles, which have been applied to work.

RESEARCH

STUDY THREE - STYLE DISPARITY AS A PREDICTOR OF A STRESS RESPONSE

In this study the predictive validity of the Style Insights was tested by examining its validity as a predictor for stress responses. It was argued that an important aspect of job satisfaction was the match of the person to the demands of the job, with a good match giving high levels of job satisfaction. It is also believed that low levels of job satisfaction result in poorer physical and mental health, as well as high levels of absenteeism.

In this study we investigated the importance of a disparity between Adapted Style (Graph I) and Natural Style (Graph II) as a predictor of job dissatisfaction, weakened physical health, poorer mental health and absenteeism.

Methods

DISC profiling was done for 150 managers using the Style Insights. Occupational data was collected using the Occupational Stress Indicator.

The Occupational Stress Indicator is divided into seven questionnaires. The first questionnaire collects biographical information, and the other six make up the Indicator itself. The questionnaire order is important because completion of stress-related questionnaires can be seen by some individuals as threatening, and they become reticent.

Biographical data is requested first because it is simple to complete and settles individuals into the rhythm of answering questions. Next comes job satisfaction, and it is only the last sections that explicitly examine stressors and coping strategies. Most questions are brief, and respondents simply mark their answers, but other questions are deliberately verbose in order to slow down the rate of responding and help comprehension.

The four elements of the Occupational Stress Indicator occur in the different questionnaires in Table 1.

Table 1: The Content of the Occupational Stress Indicator

Element:	Questionnaire:
The Individual	• Biographical Data
	• General Behavior
	• How You Interpret Events Around You
Stressors	• Sources of Pressure in Your Job
Coping with stressors	• Interpretation of Events
Effects of stressors	• Coping Behaviors and Health

A brief rationale of each questionnaire is given below to explain why it is included and what it measures.

Biographical Data Questionnaire

The Biographical Questionnaire is divided into seven parts:

1. Family

This subsection records very basic biographical details. It helps to focus the attention of the respondents and gets them into the right frame of mind for questionnaire completion.

2. Education

Research indicates that there is a relationship between occupational stressors and duration of full-time education.

3. Commitment

This section establishes the extent in which individuals are committed to their current jobs.

4. Interests

This part assesses coping behaviors and the devotion of time to work-related activities.

5. Habits

There is a range of lifestyle behaviors that are related to stressors. Smoking and drinking were particularly interesting for our study.

6. Life History

There are fluctuations in stress responses that are due to the experience of "life events". These events can be positive (getting married) or negative (redundancy). Both types of events induce a stress response, indicating that the event was significant in the individual's life.

7. Work History

This part identifies some occupational characteristics, such as position in the organization hierarchy and how they fit in, etc.

THE OCCUPATIONAL STRESS INDICATOR

The six remaining questionnaires form the Occupational Stress Indicator. Each of these questionnaires is divided into a series of sub-scales that measure different dimensions of stressors and the stress response. The contents of each sub-scale are outlined, indicating the nature of the underlying theme.

Sources of Pressure in the Job

This section concerns a wide range of possible occupational stressors. The items contain both job- and home-related aspects, although on balance, it is the occupational theme that dominates.

The sub-scales assess six types of stressors:

1. Intrinsic Factors

These sources of stress originate in the fundamental nature of managerial work and encompass perceived ability to influence and are a general measure of outlook on life and organizational events.

2. The Managerial Role

This sub-scale measures how individuals perceive the expectations that others have of them, concerning those behaviors that managers are expected to exhibit in their job.

3. Relationships With Other People

The nature of management demands a high degree of contact with other people, both inside and outside the organization. Most important, however, are relationships with superiors.

4. Career and Achievement

By the process of selection and self-selection, those occupying management positions might be expected to be especially aware of their position in the management hierarchy. One of the principles on which organizations operate is that in trying to attain personal success by career advancement, individuals contribute to company success. The need to achieve personal and corporate success can be a major source of satisfaction or a major stressor, if blocked.

RESEARCH

THE OCCUPATIONAL STRESS INDICATOR

5. Organizational Structure and Climate
Managers are in an interesting position: they work within the organization structure and contribute to its design. In this sense, sources of organizational stress originate from structural design and process features of the organization, although company climate will embrace an individual's perceptions of both.

6. Work-Home Interface
One of the features that make managerial and professional work different from other jobs is that there is a hazy overlap between work and home. There is a two-way relationship, with stressors at work affecting home life and vice versa.

INTERPRETATION OF EVENTS

The importance of stressors is how individuals interpret events around them.

The more individuals feel that they have control over their life, the smaller their subsequent stress response. There are three sub-scales that measure different aspects of control:

1. Organizational Forces
This sub-scale measures the degree to which employees perceive the influence of intra-organizational pressures. In other words, within any company there will be a range of "invisible" influence systems. These systems may be unspoken and difficult to define, but still exert an important effect on behavior.

2. Management Processes
While the first sub-scale examined the influence being exerted within the company, this sub-scale measures three key aspects on which individuals generally express a need to exert influence: how their performance is appraised, how they get promoted, and who has the power.

3. Individual Influence
This sub-scale completes the picture by measuring perceived control at the level of the individual manager. This perceived control is a function of perceived ability to influence, and is a general measure of outlook on life and organizational events.

THE OCCUPATIONAL STRESS INDICATOR

Coping Strategies at Work

This straightforward questionnaire assesses sources of coping. There are six sub-scales:

1. Social Support

This sub-scale measures the degree to which individuals rely on others as a means of coping. It may not necessarily be in the form of talking, the mere existence of supportive relationships will be significant.

2. Task Strategies

The sub-scale measures the way the individual copes by work organization. This ranges from organization in the narrow sense of tasks, but may also entail reliance upon organizational processes in the wider sense.

3. Logic

Individuals can cope with stress by adopting an unemotional and rational approach to the situation. This may involve the suppression of any feelings that might be expressed but will also involve actively trying to be objective.

4. Work and Home Relationship

It has already been stated that the overlap between work and home lives is an extensive one. This sub-scale recognizes the dual role that this relationship can possess and examines its role in coping strategies. Again, this may take various forms, from the existence of certain qualities in home life to the activities of individuals when they are there.

5. Time

One of the major factors that managers have to negotiate with is time. "Time Management" is sold as a valuable managerial skill and coping strategy.

6. Involvement

This set of questions is difficult to label, but the underlying theme refers to the individual submerging or committing themselves to their work.

RESEARCH

THE OCCUPATIONAL STRESS INDICATOR

General Behavior

This questionnaire measures Type A behavior. Type A behavior is an overall style or manner of behavior that is characterized by excessive time consciousness, abruptness of speech and gesture, competitiveness, etc. Ironically, these actions are the very behaviors that personify the stereotype of the dynamic executive, and so are rewarded in companies. This behavior is said to be a significant and independent predictor of coronary heart disease and other stress-related ill health.

There are three sub-scales measuring different aspects of the Type A personality:

1. Attitude to Living

This sub-scale measures the underlying perspective that individuals have regarding their lives and work. It measures the basic components concerning confidence, commitment, etc., as well as addressing work priorities and degree of dedication.

2. Style of Behavior

While the first sub-scale measured the mental component of Type A behavior, this sub-scale measures the behavioral component, i.e., what individuals actually do, such as speed and abruptness of behavior.

3. Ambition

This sub-scale could well be included as part of the previous two. However, while a high need for achievement is manifest in both attitude and style of behavior, it is a separate quality in its own right.

THE OCCUPATIONAL STRESS INDICATOR

Feelings about the Job

This questionnaire measures job satisfaction. While the precise relationship with the stress response is complex, it is usual for those who are experiencing stress responses to have negative attitudes towards their work. While being considered as an outcome in its own right, job satisfaction can be regarded as related to work attitude.

Five sub-scales measure different critical aspect of work:

1. Satisfaction with Achievement, Value and Growth
This sub-scale represents a major component of job satisfaction that might be expected in a managerial group. It concerns the individual's perception of their current scope for advancement. Closely related to these aspects of work are perceptions of value in terms of income, praise and effort. Whether the job is seen as challenging, skills are also important.

2. Satisfaction with Job
Clearly, the nature of managerial work is wide and varied so the scope of this sub-scale is limitless. While the sub-scale explicitly mentions the type of scope of job tasks, etc., these are intended to be metaphors. In other words, when individuals express satisfaction or dissatisfaction with their job, they mean simply the "type of work".

3. Satisfaction with Organizational Structure
The nature of managerial work is such that the nature of the company and its characteristics has particular importance. It measures several important structural aspects of organizations.

4. Satisfaction with Organizational Processes
The background rationale for this sub-scale is similar to the previous one. However, the focus is not on structural characteristics, but rather on internal processes.

5. Satisfaction and Personal Relationships
Although this sub-scale contains three quite diverse items, they all have a high interpersonal content. The nature of managerial work demands a high degree of contact with people, so that the quality of relationships is relevant.

RESEARCH

THE OCCUPATIONAL STRESS INDICATOR

Current State of Health
This part asks eighteen questions referring to mental ill health and twelve on physical ill health:

Part A: Mental Health
The items measure overall mental ill health and tap a range of different aspects of it. The role of these questions is to give an insight into mental health, but not a clinical diagnosis.

Part B: Physical Health
All items relate to physical symptoms of the stress response.

RESULTS

As a first analysis of the data, the only information that was examined was the Primary Behavioral Style disparity. The DISC data from the Style Insights was transformed into percentages and the percentage difference on the Primary Style was used as the independent variable. The dependent variables were job satisfaction and the amount of mental ill health.

The association between the independent and dependent variables was examined with simple bivariate regression analyses. This showed that the assumption of linearity was invalid, and so a logarithmic transformation was used. As well as determination of the correlation coefficient, Pearson r, a coefficient of determination, r2, was calculated as a measure of the predictable variability, i.e., the percentage of overall variability in job satisfaction, mental health and absenteeism that is attributable to style disparity.

Job Satisfaction
The bivariate regression of job satisfaction on style disparity gave a significant correlation (Pearson r=0.39; p=0.001, n=150) or a coefficient of determination of 0.152, i.e., 15.2 percent of the variability in job satisfaction is directly predictable from the variability in style disparity.

THE OCCUPATIONAL STRESS INDICATOR

Mental Health

The bivariate regression of mental health on style disparity gave a significant correlation (Pearson r=0.38; p=0.001, n=150) or a coefficient of determination of 0.144, i.e., 14.4 percent of the variability in mental health is directly predictable from the variability in style disparity.

Physical Health

The bivariate regression of physical health on style disparity gave a significant correlation (Pearson r=0.23; p=0.01, n=150) or a coefficient of determination of 0.053, i.e., 5.3 percent of the variability in physical health is directly predictable from the variability in style disparity. It should be noted that the physical health scale is a psychosomatic scale with "mental health" items, such as inability to get to sleep or stay asleep, decrease in sexual interest, tendency to sweat or feelings of your heart beating hard, etc.

Absenteeism

The bivariate regression of absenteeism on style disparity gave a significant correlation (Pearson r=0.27; p=0.01, n=54) or a coefficient of determination of 0.073, i.e., 7.3 percent of the variability in absenteeism is directly predictable from the variability in style disparity.

Alcohol Use

The bivariate regression of alcohol use on style disparity gave a significant correlation (Pearson r=0.31; p=0.001, n=150) or a coefficient of determination of 0.096, i.e., 9.6 percent of the variability in alcohol use is directly predictable from the variability in style disparity.

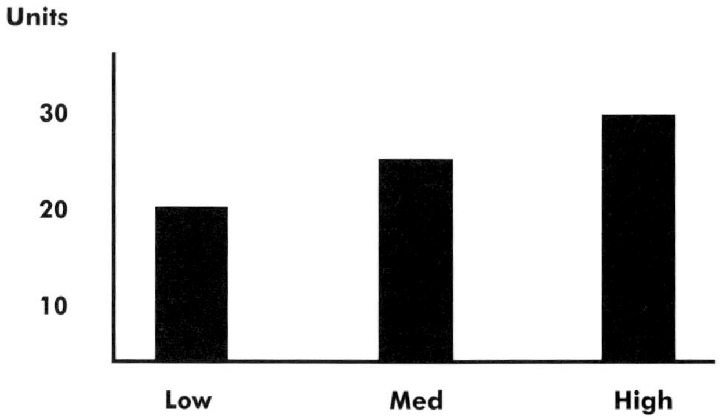

RESEARCH

THE OCCUPATIONAL STRESS INDICATOR

Cigarette Use

The bivariate regression of mental health on style disparity gave a significant correlation (Pearson r=0.29; p=0.1, n=36) or a coefficient of determination of 0.084, i.e., 8.4 percent of the variability in cigarette use is directly predictable from the variability in style disparity.

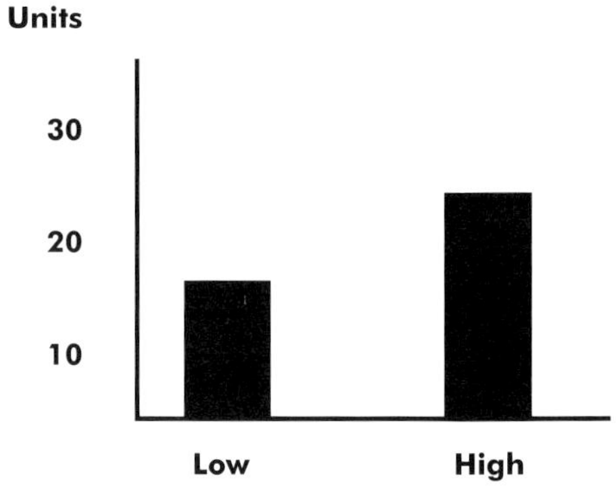

Conclusions

This analysis gives evidence for DISC disparity as a predictor of job satisfaction, mental health, physical health, alcohol use and absenteeism.

Although we examined style disparity on only one dimension, 15.2 percent of the variance for job satisfaction, 14.4 percent of the variance for mental health, 5.3 percent of the variance for physical health, 9.6 percent of the variance for alcohol use and 7.3 percent of the variance for absenteeism is attributable to variability in style disparity.

At this point, a note of caution must be sounded. By saying that style disparity is a predictor of job satisfaction, mental health, physical health, alcohol use and absenteeism, should not be taken to indicate that style disparity caused these effects. Correlation is a necessary, but NOT a sufficient condition for establishing causality.

In order to establish a causal relationship, it would be necessary to conduct an experiment and manipulate disparity. Of course, that happens when people switch jobs and reduce style disparity.

THE OCCUPATIONAL STRESS INDICATOR

However, research has established that there is a causal relationship between job fit and occupational dissatisfaction, mental health, physical health, alcohol use and absenteeism.

This body of evidence gives us confidence that DISC disparity is a predictor of problems at work and at home.

STUDY FOUR – DISC PROFILES AS MODERATORS OR STRESSORS

An important aspect of any instrument is its predictive validity. This refers to the degree to which a measuring instrument can estimate some behavior external to it, such as its ability to predict everyday aspects of work.

Occupational research has devoted a great deal of time to uncovering factors which moderate an employee's response to job characteristics. There have been three parallel lines of study. On the one hand, there are studies concerned with the moderating effects of extrinsic factors, such as a rural versus urban background. A second view has been a values approach e.g., an individual's espousal of or alienation from, some value e.g., the Protestant Work Ethic (Blood, 1969; Stone, 1976). On the other hand, there are those concerned with the importance of intrinsic job characteristics to individuals. The latter concept is variously described as "higher-order needs strength" (Hackman and Lawler, 1971; Brief and Aldag, 1975), or "self-actualization needs strength" (Sims and Szilagyi, 1976).

In a comparative study, Wanous (1974) contrasted needs strength, values and rural versus urban (extrinsic) factors as moderators. He found that needs strength was the strongest moderator, followed by values that showed intermediate effectiveness as a moderator, and least by the extrinsic difference.

In this study, we have examined higher order needs as represented by Natural Style as a predictor of stress responses and the interaction of Natural Style with job stressors as a moderator of responses.

RESEARCH

DISC PROFILES AS MODERATORS OR STRESSORS

Methods

In addition to the DISC profiling, occupational data was collected using the Occupational Stress Indicator (Cooper, Sloan and Williams, 1988). This instrument assesses six different aspects of work. Of relevance to this study were data on sources of pressure in their job, job satisfaction and their current state of mental health.

Results

An initial correlational analysis established that high pressure at work was associated with stress responses, both in terms of job satisfaction and mental health. However, Natural Style, per se, was not a predictor of either type of stress response.

The second analysis was designed to provide a test of the moderating effect of Natural Style on the relationship between perceived sources of pressure in the job and either job satisfaction or mental health. Thus, the independent variables were the sources of pressure, while the dependent variables were job satisfaction and state of mental health.

An analysis of covariance variant of moderated regression analysis was used. In this analysis, no prior decisions were made about the form of the need-stressor interaction (i.e., linear or nonlinear). The analysis fell into two parts:

First, three equal groups were formed for each DISC dimension to give high, medium and low need groups (each of 50 people). The choice of three groups was determined by the need to obtain sensitivity of analysis while retaining subgroups of sufficient size to achieve stable regression coefficients.

The second step involved separate regression analyses within each group. The presence of a moderator effect was detected by testing for parallelism of the separate group regression lines. Identical slopes implies equal predictability within each group, and so no moderator effect. A Bonferroni correction was applied for multiple tests.

This analysis has been completed for the 48 combinations of style and sources of pressure to determine which style would be most susceptible to each source of pressure.

RESEARCH

NATURAL STYLE AS A MODERATOR OF THE STRESS RESPONSE

JOB SATISFACTION

SOURCES	D	I	S	C
1. Intrinsic			-	
2. Managerial Role	+			
3. Personal Relations		-		-
4. Career/Achievement	-	-		
5. Corporate Structure		-		
6. Work/Home Interface			-	

Key: - exacerbation + amelioration

MENTAL HEALTH

SOURCES	D	I	S	C
1. Intrinsic			-	
2. Managerial Role	+		-	
3. Personal Relations		-		-
4. Career/Achievement	-	-		
5. Corporate Structure		-		
6. Work/Home Interface			-	

Key: - exacerbation + amelioration

RESEARCH

CONCLUSIONS & REFERENCES

First, the bivariate regression analysis showed a negative association between job pressure satisfaction with the job and a positive correlation with the amount of mental ill health.

The analysis of the data gives good evidence of interactions of Natural Style with specific sources of pressure in the job. For example, there was a negative effect of poor personal relationships on stress responses in the group, but the effect was magnified in High I individuals. In contrast, there was an overall negative effect of managerial role pressures on job satisfaction and mental health, but this effect was less in High D managers.

REFERENCES

Revell, A., Wesnes, K., and Warburton, D. M. Self-medication with alcohol as a coping strategy. In Titmar, H. *Advanced Concepts in Alcoholism*. Oxford: Pergamon, pp. 117-125, 1984.

Schmidt, F. L., Huter, J. E., and Urry, V. W. (1976) Statistical power in criterion-related validation studies. *Journal of Applied Psychology*, 61, pp. 473-485.

Warburton, D. M. Modern biochemical concepts of anxiety. *International Pharmacopsychiatry* 9: 189-205, 1975.

Warburton, D. M. Physiological aspects of information processing and stress. In Hamilton, V. H. and Warburton, D. M. (Eds.) *Human Stress and Cognition*. London: Wiley, pp. 33-65, 1979.

Warburton, D. M. Physiological aspects of anxiety and schizophrenia. In Hamilton, V. H. and Warburton, D. M. (Eds.) *Human Stress and Cognition*. London: Wiley, pp. 431-465, 1979.

Warburton, D. M. Stress and the processing of information. In Hamilton, V. H. and Warburton, D. M. (Eds.) *Human Stress and Cognition*. London: Wiley, pp. 469-475, 1979.

Warburton, D. M., Wesnes, K. and Revell, A. Personality factors in self-medication by smoking. In W. Janke (Eds.) *Response Variability to Psychotropic Drugs*. London: Pergamon, pp. 167-184.

CONCLUSIONS & REFERENCES

Warburton, D. M. and Wesnes, K. Mechanisms for habitual substance use: food, alcohol and cigarettes. In Gale, A. and Edwards, J. (Eds.) *Physiological Correlates of Human Behaviour*. Volume 1. London: Academic Press, pp. 227-297, 1983.

Warburton, D. M. The neuropsychobiology of stress response control. Wiepkema, P. R. and Van Adrichem, P. W. M. *The Biology of Stress in Farm Animals*. Dordrecht: Martinuus Nijhof, pp. 87-100, 1987.

Warburton, D. M. Stress and Distress in response to change. In Box, H. (Ed.) *Primate Responses to Environmental Change*. London: Chapman-Hall, pp. 337-356, 1990.

Warburton, D. M., Revell, A. D. and Thompson, D. H. Smokers of the future. *British Journal of Addiction*, 86: pp. 621-625, 1991.

Wesnes, K. and Warburton, D. M. Stress and drugs. In Hockey, G. R. J. (Ed.) *Stress and Fatigue in Human Performance*. London: Wiley, pp. 203-243, 1983.

Wesnes, K., Warburton, D. M. and Revell, A. Work and stress as motives for smoking. In Cumming, G. and Bonsignore, G. *Smoking and The Lung*. New York: Plenum, pp. 233-248, 1984.

Correlates of DISC with Behavioral Styles (n=150)

	D	I	S	C
Type A	+0.3897*	-0.2437	-0.2381	+0.2332
Extroversion	+0.2256	+0.4556*	-0.2296	-0.4442*
Optimism	+0.2955	+0.4249*	-0.2754	-0.2457
Control Optimism	+0.5484*	+0.1316	-0.0495	+0.0811
Pessimism	-0.2433	-0.3057*	+0.3547*	+0.4485*
Alcohol Use	+0.2718*	+0.4539*	-0.3216*	-0.3853*
Cigarette Use	+0.2923*	+0.4390*	-0.2426	-0.3514*

***P<0.01———————————————————————————p.0.01**

RESEARCH

MAINTENANCE WORKER'S SAFETY STUDY

Safety Analysis Project – Summary Report
XYZ Company* has established an effective safety program that has substantially reduced its rate of worker-related injuries. The program has focused on education and the formation of a structure that enhances the transmission of safety-related information and reinforces safety through a reward system. The effectiveness of this program could be enhanced by the development of a pre-employment assessment approach that utilizes valid predictors of work-related injury. The current research project commissioned by XYZ Company and conducted by Resource Analysis, Ltd. is part of the process of improving the ability of the railroad to meet its goal of reaching an ever increasingly higher level of safety performance.

The Safety Analysis Project (SAP) was initiated in July of 1993 and involved the assessment of maintenance workers throughout the XYZ Company system. Subjects were selected using a stratified random sample to ensure proportioned representation of workers from the entire system. Inclusion in the sample was determined by willingness to participate, the availability of supervisor ratings, and the availability of injury data. Confidentiality of results was maintained. A sample of 230 maintenance workers resulted from the selection process.

Sample:
The sample was composed of 230 males, ranging in age from 22 to 64 years, with a mean of 42.2 years. (SD = 9.38). The educational level of the sample averaged 11.2 years (SD = 4.38), with 56% completing high school, 8% having some post-high school education, and 36% having an eleventh grade education or less. The sample was very stable in terms of work history, with the mean number of years at XYZ Company being 17.2 years (SD = 6.36) and the median being 17.5 years. The vast majority of the sample (87%) had worked at the Company for over 10 years. The data also shows that for the majority of the subjects (60%), XYZ Company was their first and only job. An additional 23% had only one job prior to working at XYZ Company. The overall picture of the sample is of middle aged, high school or less educated individuals with highly stable work histories. The nature of the regions sampled suggests that the sample is very likely rural or small town in origin.

*Actual name of the company was not included to protect them. Research completed by Dr. Jim Hall.

MAINTENANCE WORKER'S SAFETY STUDY

Safety Analysis Assessment Battery

The Safety Analysis Assessment Battery consists of a series of instruments that have been widely used in industry and transportation. The battery included the DISC Style Insights; the Personal Interests, Attitudes and Values Instrument; the Safety Analysis Questionnaire; and the SRA Pictorial and Mechanical Reasoning Tests.

The DISC Style Insights is an instrument that assesses the individual's basic style of behavior (Basic DISC), the preferred behavioral style usually seen at home or when under a great deal of stress; the individual's behavioral response (Response DISC) to the environment' and the individual's view of the behavior required for response patterns is assessed along four dimensions; Drive (D) "how we deal with problems and challenges"; Influence (I) "How we influence and relate to others"; Steadiness (S) "how we respond to changes"; and Compliance (C) "how we react to rules and regulations."

The Personal Interests, Attitudes and Values Instrument is used to assess the interests, goals, and preferences that guide a person's functioning. This instrument assesses six basic values: **Theoretical** (Tv) "gaining of knowledge for its own sake"; **Utilitarian** (Uv) "interest in gaining money"; **Aesthetic** (Av) "primary interest in form, harmony and enjoying life for its own sake"; **Social** (Sv) "interest and caring about others as a primary concern"; **Individualistic** (Iv) "primary interest in power"; and **Traditional** (Rv) "strong need for order."

The Safety Analysis Questionnaire is a 34-item instrument that measures knowledge and beliefs about basic safety issues. This questionnaire has been widely validated in samples of factory workers and transportation workers. A high score (total possible equals 34) indicated understanding of safety-related issues, including rule following, personal responsibility, and knowledge of basic concepts in safe operations.

In addition to the style, values, and safety instruments, the SRA Pictorial and Mechanical Reasoning Tests were administered. These two tests have been used at other companies as part of their pre-employment assessment.

RESEARCH

MAINTENANCE WORKER'S SAFETY STUDY

The supervisor of each subject was asked to complete a ten item rating form. The supervisor rated the subject's knowledge of safety procedures, along with his view of the extent to which the subject used appropriate safety measures in the workers daily functioning.

Results

The purpose of this study is to develop pre-employment screening instruments that have the ability to predict which individuals would have an increased likelihood of experiencing on-the-job injuries. Therefore, number and type of injuries was used as the primary grouping variable. Subjects were divided into groups based on injury history. Individuals who had no record of any serious or chronic work-related injuries were categorized as "non-injured." Subjects who had experienced any serious or chronic injuries were classified as "injured." The injured subjects were categorized into single serious or chronic injury group, and multiple injury group. Analysis of this categorization revealed no significant differences on any measures between these two groups of injured subjects. Therefore, in this analysis, these two subgroups were merged into a single injured group, leading to comparisons based on two groups; "Non-injured" group and "Injured" group.

The "Non-injured" group was composed of 97 individuals averaging 39.71 years of age (SD = 9.40), with an average of 11.3 years of education (SD=4.81), and an average of 14.81 (SD=8.15) years of service at XYZ Company. The "Injured" group was made up of 133 subjects averaging 43.57 years of age (SD =7.58). These individuals had an average of 11.1 years of education (SD = 4.28), and an average of 18.88 years (SD=3.88) of service at XYZ Company. The "Non-injured" group was significantly younger than the "Injured" group (t=3.46, df=228, p=0.01). A significant difference (t=3.21, df=228,p=0.01) was found on total number of years at XYZ Company. A review of the data suggest that these differences may have been accounted for by the existence of a small number of outliers in the "Non-injured" sample who were significantly younger and had been at XYZ Company less than 5 years. No significant differences were found on any of the other demographic variables assessed.

MAINTENANCE WORKER'S SAFETY STUDY

It was assumed that the two groups would differ on measures of behavioral style, values, and knowledge of safety. The hypotheses were based on the assumption that these factors should all influence injury history. **The following exploratory hypotheses were tested:**

1. **There would be a significant difference on basic style, response style, and work style between the Injured group and the Non-injured group. The specific pattern was not hypothesized.**

2. **There would be a significant difference on each of the values scales between the Injured and the Non-injured group.**

3. **The non-injured group would score significantly higher on the Safety Analysis, suggesting a relationship between knowledge and behavior.**

4. **Supervisors would rate the non-injured subjects as more knowledgeable about safety as measured by overall ratings.**

5. **Scores on Pictorial and Mechanical Reasoning Tests would not be significantly different for the two groups.**

Data analysis consisted of subjecting the data to multi-variant analysis of covariance (MANCOVA). This analysis was chosen to allow for the effects of the significant differences found on age and total number of years at XYZ Company to be statistically controlled. Scheffe's test, a robust post hoc test of significance of differences, was applied to determine the source of significant MANCOVAs. The p=0.05 level of significance was accepted as an appropriate alpha level.

MANCOVA analysis of style variables revealed a significant main effect for group (Wilks Lamba = .891, Rao's R=2.02, p=0.02, df=13,215). Post hoc Scheffe's tests showed significant differences for Basic D; Basic S; Response D, Response S, and Response C. Table A shows the means and standard deviate for these variables.

RESEARCH

MAINTENANCE WORKER'S SAFETY STUDY

Table A:
Means and Standard Deviations of Significant Style Differences

Injured		Non-injured
Basic D	7.25 (SD=3.53)	8.28 (SD=3.95)
Basic S	3.91 (SD=2.40)	3.27 (SD=1.88)
Response D	3.80 (SD=2.69)	2.88 (SD=2.51)
Response S	6.74 (SD=2.85)	7.58 (SD=2.68)
Response C	4.85 (SD=2.07)	5.44 (SD=2.15)

The Scheffe's probability levels for differences between the two groups are shown in Table B.

Table B:
Scheffe's Post hoc Analysis of Differences

Variable	p Level
Basic D	0.05
Basic S	0.005
Response D	0.004
Response S	0.03
Response C	0.02

MANCOVA analysis of the Personal Interests, Attitudes and Values data revealed no significant main effect. Exploratory analysis of the individual values suggested a difference between the groups on Social values (Injured M=44.95, SD=9.35; Non-injured M=47.0, SD=10.82 t=2.05, df=228 p=0.05), but not on any of the other value scales.

No significant difference was found for the groups on the Safety Analysis. The means and standard deviations for the two groups were: injured, M=24.22, (SD=3.71), and non-injured, M=24.15 (SD=3.10).

MAINTENANCE WORKER'S SAFETY STUDY

Analysis of the supervisor's ratings showed no group differences, either on individual items or total score (Injured 32.60 SD-11.84 and Non-injured 33.74 SD=12.09). A review of the data suggests a strong tendency toward positive ratings, regardless of injury history. There was a trend toward rating those who had worked at XYZ Company for longer periods in a slightly more positive direction.

As was hypothesized, there were no group differences on the SRA measures (Injured Pictorial M=50.87 SD=14.03, Mechanical M=38.35 SD=10.92; Non-injured Pictorial M=51.49 SD=15.34, Mechanical M=38.82 SD=9.82).

Interpretation

The differences found on the Style Insights Instrument are suggestive of specific behavioral tendencies that may impact safety. The score on the Basic D scale suggests that individuals who are more cautious and undemanding as part of their preferred style of behaving will be less likely to engage in behavior that could increase the probability of injury. Additionally, a basic tendency toward high levels of consistency, patience, and predictability will lend itself to taking adequate time rather than pushing oneself or acting impulsively. This is shown in the Basic S scale score. These behavioral tendencies represent the way the individual sees himself and are likely to be expressed when places under a great deal of pressure.

The style differences found in the response to environment reflect the individual's understanding of the demands of his environment. The individual who is less likely to be injured recognizes that his environment requires an even greater tendency to be cooperative and cautious. This is especially important in a work environment where injuries are frequent and can be very severe. The low Response D reflects an awareness that the potentially threatening environment is best dealt with by exercising deliberation and caution.

The high Response S further emphasizes the perception of the environment as one in which patience and steadiness are highly adaptive. Loyalty and a team orientation are also seen as mechanisms that reduce unpredictability and threats to security in the work environment. These tendencies are further reinforced by a tendency toward compliance and rule following, as shown by the high Response C of the non-injured sample.

RESEARCH

MAINTENANCE WORKER'S SAFETY STUDY

Style picture that describes the individual less likely to be injured is that of a basic core of Low D and High S qualities, with a shift to enhancing these tendencies in the work environment. These individuals in the work environment exhibit High C characteristics, with rule-following behavior and a team orientation.

The team orientation is further strengthened by the high social value score. This score suggests a concern for others and a tendency to define oneself in terms of the group, especially the small work unit which may serve as a primary source of identity.

This identification enhances behaviors which tend to support the group, such as rule following, compliance, and acquiescence. The high social value supports and strengthens the style tendencies of Low D, High S, and High C. The profile of Low D, High S, and High C is descriptive of the sample of maintenance workers who had not experienced serious on-the-job injuries.

The scores of the Safety Analysis exhibit no between-group differences and are within the low average score range that has been found in previous research on industrial and transportation workers. The level of the scores suggests that the educational component of the XYZ Company safety program is having an effect on workers' knowledge of safety-related factors. The response to the individual items on the Safety Analysis provides some insight into the workers' understanding of safety. As a group, the maintenance workers tend to view the presentation of accident statistics, the viewing of the results of "horrible" accidents, and the presence of safety posters as the most effective ways to build safety attitudes. This likely reflects the workers' experience with safety programs at XYZ Company.

It appears that although these techniques are having some impact, they have not affected areas that may be more directly related to injury prevention and an understanding of the determinants of safe behavior. Respondents show a very strong tendency to emphasize experience over training as primary factors in safety. This is shown by the erroneous endorsement of answers stating that experience is more important than company policy or specific company directed training. The fact that this sample of workers have very long work histories with XYZ Company likely accounts for this tendency. However, this belief may make it very difficult to develop new, safer work habits and should be a concern for the safety program.

MAINTENANCE WORKER'S SAFETY STUDY

Further influencing the training of safer work habits is the tendency of the respondents to endorse items that reduce personal responsibility for accidents and do not recognize the relationship between personal attitudes and on-the-job safety behavior. These views need to be considered when developing training programs so that these issues are directly addressed.

The lack of group differences on the supervisor's ratings reinforces previous research which has found that supervisors do not make distinctions based on performance such as knowledge of safety or safe behavior. Rather, they tend to base ratings on factors not usually assessed by behaviorally based ratings such as liking and perceived similarity to the supervisor.

The lack of group differences on the measures was expected in that they are not conceptually tied closely to safety-related issues, especially at the maintenance worker's level. Although these measures have some utility in assessing basic intellectual functioning and flexibility, they are not helpful in differentiating injured from non-injured workers.

Recommendations

Analysis of the data suggests a number of recommendations that may enhance the safety program at XYZ Company.

1. The use of the DISC Style Insights and Personal Interests, Attitudes and Values as components of XYZ Company's applicant screening process. The data presented strongly suggests a profile that is related to increased level of safety. It is recommended that a goodness of fit approach be used in screening applicants so that those who most fit the profile derived in this study would receive a positive weighted score that would be added to previous job history, performance on tests of mechanical flexibility and problem solving, and recommendations. Scores on the DISC Style Insights and Personal Interests, Attitudes and Values scale would serve as positive inclusive rather than exclusionary criteria.

MAINTENANCE WORKER'S SAFETY STUDY

2. The use of the Safety Analysis as a tool to assist in the development of training programs that help train workers in appropriate safety techniques. The Safety Analysis would serve as a useful pre/post-test measure of learning in the Safety Program.

3. The data gathered in this study suggest avenues to explore to further develop the existing safety program. Among the suggested changes are an increase in the use of direct training techniques, such as job-related training where direct modeling of appropriate safe behavior is conducted with immediate feedback and reinforcement. An example would be a lifting module where appropriate lifting techniques are modeled with opportunities for the trainee to engage in the behavior, with corrective feed back and reinforcement. This active approach would be used along with the passive techniques of files, booklets, and posters.

4. The use of reinforcement of safe behavior, based on the performance of both individuals and small work groups. The emphasis on group performance may be used to enhance group identification and concern for other workers of their small work group. The reinforcements need to be relevant, immediate, and tangible. (For example: quarterly, group-based bonuses, if allowed by contract.)

5. The training of supervisors in recognition and evaluation of safety-related behaviors. There is a need to have objective standards of evaluation to provide valid feedback to the workers.

6. The continuation of databased assessment of each functional level at XYZ Company to develop assessment and training strategies that are specific to the nature of the job rather than general and generic.

OBJECTIVES REVISITED

At this time you should feel comfortable that all TTI assessments are not only valid, but have been revalidated in 2004.

BIBLIOGRAPHY

Biema, David V.
Gored, but not Gone
Time Magazine, 1993

Boone, Lewis
Quotable Business
Random House, 1992

Burnet, J.
Greek Philosophy: Thales to Plato
MacMillan, 1964

Hippocrates/Galen
Great Books of the Western World
Encyclopedia Brittanica, 1952

Jung, Carl J.
Psychological Types
Princeton University Press, 1971

Marston, William M.
The Emotions of Normal People
Persona Press, 1979

Stengal, Richard
I'll Fly Away
Time Magazine, 1993

